S023-221
D1642297

Ivory Hammer 3

Ivory Hammer 3

The Year at Sotheby's & Parke-Bernet

The Two Hundred and Twenty First Season

1964–65

Longmans

LONGMANS GREEN & CO. LTD
48 Grosvenor Street, London W1
and associated companies, branches
and representatives throughout the world

© Sotheby and Co 1965

Memories of my first Tycoon © Joan O'Donovan 1965

First Published 1965

Made and Printed in Great Britain by
PERCY LUND, HUMPHRIES & CO. LTD.
London & Bradford

Edited by MICHEL STRAUSS

Designed by CAMERON POULTER, MSIA

Contents

A Penny Farthing Bicycle, wheel diameter 54 in
London £65 ($185)

Memories of my first Tycoon

BY JOAN O'DONOVAN

James was a wide boy in every sense, four feet high, five across and full of original sin. But he didn't, as previous lads had done, snarl my *Guardian* on the letter box, or fling it into a basement puddle, or leave the *Mirror* instead: he delivered the right paper unflawed, and on his first day in office even rang the bell to introduce himself.

'Morning, miss. New piper boy. Nimer James.'

I took in vast raw-meat cheeks, lively damson eyes and a presence like that of a shrewd and portly seal.

'Oh? Really?' I said, somewhat at a loss. 'Well, thank you very much.'

James grinned.

'That's all right', he soothed; 'just thought you'd like to know.' Then he came politely back down the steps to add, 'Here, and I take orders for wood. Delivery after school or weekends. I could fit you in Sat'dy.' Those knowing eyes appraised me. 'I mean good wood, miss,' he hinted.

We live in a smokeless zone, but what the hell. I respect enterprise, and clearly James had plenty of that: so, of course, had the serpent in Eden, but the parallel didn't strike me at the time.

Saturday came, and with it not only good wood but also an impressive after-sales service; for James took it upon himself to stack the logs and sweep my yard, and then, believe it or not, he actually refused a tip. Fair, he told me, was fair.

'I wouldn't mind an apple, though,' he observed, squinting in at the fruit dish. 'For me weight. Clinic says I gotter lose twenny-eight pounds. She'll be lucky! That's two stun innit, miss?''

Oh, indeed, James was a bright boy – like Forster, always connecting. The mother in me had capitulated at once and now the pedagogue, too, was ensnared. Over an apple, I asked how long he'd been in the timber business.

'Only since I was fir'een. Larsmumf. You can't work till you're fir'een,' he reproved; 'you mustn't even have a piper round. It's against the law.'

And he became suddenly so censorious, so full of civic zeal, that I should have guessed then what it took me weeks to worm out of him, that James hadn't, in fact, been fir'een larsmumf but would be twelve next.

But by the time I discovered that I knew James pretty well. Or thought I did. At least I knew him well enough not to have qualms about his welfare, or worry lest he should have lacked the law's protection during his tender years. Frankly, I can't imagine anyone exploiting James and getting away with it; and as for tender years, I doubt if he ever had any, not what you'd call tender. At a guess, he was hard at it in the pram flogging National Health orange juice to more ignorant babies – unless, that is, he'd already flogged his pram.

No, looking back, I realize that I was the one who needed protection. Life hadn't educated me for James, as he saw the moment he clapped eyes on me: and this, perhaps, is why I feel impelled to jot down these recollections while they are still fresh, in the hope that when your turn comes – as it will – it may be remembered in my favour that at least I tried to pass the word around.

But to continue: I soon learnt that James wasn't one of those constipated specialists. The wood and paper round were just by way of no harm: he handled anything and everything that came along; and, in spite of what they say about forewarned being forearmed, I usually found afterwards that I'd bought it from him. For instance, there were some water-repellant towels, and an egg-beater with rigor mortis, and a couple of pillows whose seams oozed fearful droppings like chopped flesh. But head and shoulders above these enormities stands the memory of a certain cuckoo clock which I forced James to sell me against his will and my better judgment – or, if I didn't, that's the impression I was left with.

Out it came one Saturday morning, an object I took, at first glance, to be a slab of chocolate studded with little sugar edelweiss: then reverently, James unveiled the face.

'What about this, then? Lovely job, and dirt-cheap at two quid. *Swiss*,' he breathed, as though 'swiss' were some priceless mineral. 'Genuine Swiss cuckoo. Guaranteed.'

Genuine? Guaranteed? I looked coldly at James, for I knew all about that pair. Some while before I'd let him order me a pen, a genuine fountain-pen, guaranteed; and although it emerged that there was no filling mechanism, and the nib kept falling out, there was a guarantee enclosed, oh dear me yes, and the guarantee was genuine. It said so. *THIS*, ran the gutteral gothic type, *IS A GENUINE GUARANTEE*. But in spite of this appearance of awesome legality, there was no mention of where I should address my complaint or who was going to give me my money back.

I said, with perhaps less tact than usual, 'No thanks, you can fob that off on somebody else for a change.'

James was deeply shocked. He was also hurt. I saw his lip quiver. Clearly, my lack of delicacy had wounded James. The bruise of disillusion dark in his eye, he returned the clock to its cradling tissues.

'I'm afraid you misunderstood, miss,' he said quietly; 'it's not for sale. I brought it to show you because I thought you'd be interested. I could only get two as good as this, see, and I gave the other to Mum. For Muvver's Day.'

So, in point of fact, it was I who remarked that it seemed to be a very handsome clock, and that I'd often thought how well a cuckoo clock would look in an old-fashioned kitchen like mine.

But James resisted that idea. He resisted it vigorously. He did his best to talk me out of such a notion.

'Cor no, miss! Too gloomy. You don't want wood on wood; you want a nice bit of chrome or plastic, something to cheer the place up. Like what about a good bright red, eh? Or a high-gloss blue?'

I told him like what with some distaste; and, having forced him to listen to my views on synthetics, made him peer into the living grain of the wall: then, to illustrate the point, I held out my hand for the clock.

Regretfully, James shook his head.

'Sorry, miss, but I'd better not. I oughtn't really to have opened the box at all, not when I'd promised my Auntie first refusal.'

'But I only want to show you what I mean,' I protested. I meant, of course, that I wanted to show myself. I'd found my arguments powerful persuaders.

'Well, I dunno . . .' James was doubtful. He hesitated, glanced at me, wavered. 'Just a peep, then.' And, whipping off the wrappings, he posed the clock with an authentic *Homes & Gardens* flourish against the far wall. He gaped at it along the length of his arm and the effect appeared to stun him. 'Cor!' he cried, 'You're right! It's just the job!'

I discovered I was forcing pound notes into his grey pneumatic palm; and though James didn't want to take them, he let himself be talked round.

'Oh well, never mind, eh?' he capitulated at last. 'What she hasn't had she won't miss. Besides, she isn't really my Auntie, she's Mum's Bingo mate; I just call her Auntie . . .' He broke off. 'Here!' he said accusingly, 'You've gone and given me ten bob too much: it isn't two quid to *you*, y'know. How many times've I told you you gotter learn to *bargain*?' he scolded. 'No wonder you're always getting done! Stands to reason!'

Still lecturing me on the sin of gullibility, he fixed the clock to the wall and then accepted an apple. By now, the apple had become a ritual. I kept apples in the house especially for James.

'Thanks. Though I dunnarf hate the things,' he told me, biting deep. 'I only do it to please Clinic – you know, stop her nagging. Here, how's your garden? Have any luck with those herbs?'

And out he came to scrutinize and advise, for there was nothing that James didn't know or couldn't cope with. He took one look.

'Ants,' he said, disgusted. 'Trust you!'

He tracked the skein across the lawn and down to some stones at the bottom of the garden.

'The nest's under that lot. Mind you scald it out or you'll have them everywhere. I'll put a drop of water on to boil for you now.'

He went back to fill the kettle and a couple of pans; and when he returned it was with the news that he'd detected blackfly on the beans. He remarked that some people didn't deserve to have gardens.

James left at last, by the side gate, and I went in to find the kitchen an inferno of steam and that I needed a new kettle, for in the blackfly drama the ants had been forgotten. But a burnt-out kettle and saturated walls weren't all I found: on the floor was a huddle of sticky boards and a sort of yellow nut with its beak open. I picked up the bits of disintegrated clock and began to piece them together; and, though I'm not mechanically minded, it did dawn on me after a while that maybe something was missing. Something was. The works.

So all right, I'm a foolish woman; but this time Master James had gone too far, even for me. I was up at dawn next day, and lay in wait for him, patient and vindictive; and at the first thrust of newsprint at letter box, I pounced.

But it wasn't James. The terrified little lad in whose ear I shrieked, 'Cuckoo!' had never heard of James, or so he said, and ran off snivelling to put it about that I was a criminal lunatic and possibly associated with the Great Train Robbery; besides which, he left two papers, both wrong: and when I went to the newsagent to sort it out he asked what I imagined I was playing at, assaulting an innocent child, and that he was a father himself and he wouldn't be surprised if the parents took legal action, and it was no good standing there bleating, '*Observer*!' because he hadn't got one, and no, he didn't know where his old paper boy was, he'd just left; and so had his new one, thanks to me, and what did I propose to do about it?

I looked out for James the following Saturday, but there was no sign of his familiar barrow then nor during the weeks to come. Months went by, and after a while I stopped searching and wrote him off. But I found I couldn't put him out of my mind as easily as that. I even began to mourn him, in an irritated kind of way, vacillating between an irrational dread lest he'd been killed and a sense of grievance because he hadn't written.

Then, nearly a year later, there was a ring at my bell; and when I went to the door, there stood James, wider and blander than ever.

He touched a finger to his plaster of comb-grooved hair.

'I'm afraid I've got nothing for you today, miss,' he murmured. (He never did explain his absence.) 'I just dropped round' he said solicitously, 'to make sure you were all right.'

Twelve months is a long time, long enough to forgive if not to forget. Besides, I'd missed our unequal battle of wits and was, I discovered, delighted to see James again. I invited him in and, matching courtesy with courtesy, kept to safe topics like his father's bad leg.

James grinned. He assured me that his dad was hopping around like a flea.

'We got two tellies and a Consul out of it, though,' he told me. 'Cor, y'ought to have heard him groaning! Got a telly in every room now. Bar one.'

'Oh? From the insurance, you mean?' I asked, mystified.

'You don't change, do you, miss?' James said fondly. 'Look, what's the sense in paying a premium when you can soo? That's what he did, sood. And they settled. Bit of a giggle, really.'

But he found it even more of a giggle when at last he tumbled to the fact that I was a teacher.

'Cor, I bet that's a carve-up!' he announced; and as those shrewd little eyes looked me over I could see he was picturing himself in my class, carving – a situation I, too, had visualised, though without relish. But when he'd got over his hilarity, James became thoughtful; and it was then I realized that he must have been quite fond of me, in a contemptuous fashion. He gave the room a pricing scrutiny, and this appeared to confirm his suspicions.

'Look, miss, can't you do nothing else? Like get yourself a nice rich feller, f'rinstance? I wouldn't be a teacher, not unless I had to. I mean, all them books! Cor,' he said, sorry for me, 'you might as well be in your grive! No offence meant.'

When I told him I was happy and that I happened to like books, James grew embarrassed.

'Oh well, never mind, eh? I dare say it takes all sorts,' he conceded, though without conviction.

I think he was genuinely put out, for he came back later in the day to bring me a present. This consisted of a stuffed white satin kitten mounted on a fold of gilt cardboard edged with lace; and inside, opposite the scrawl of James's love and kisses, was the somewhat foxing caption: *FOR MY SWEET LITTLE NIECE.*

One way and another I had some interesting conversations with James – or perhaps 'alarming' is a more adequate word, especially on the subject of education. James went to a new secondary modern school, an establishment which resembled a latter-day Crystal Palace but probably cost a great deal more than the original; but when I asked him about school he remarked that it was boring but he supposed it helped to pass the time.

I pressed for something more specific. Couldn't he name one subject he liked, just one?

'Oh, I dunno.' James thought about it. 'Yeah,' he said, brightening, 'I like science. Now he's a giggle if you like. We drive him nutty.'

I looked at him with reproach, four feet by five the wrong way round; but James grinned back, unrepentant.

'We treat sir horrible,' he said complacently.

'Even teachers are human, Jim.'

'*Jimes*, please, if you don't mind,' he corrected, suddenly stiff. 'It's the business,' he confided, unbending a little. ''Jimes'' sounds more successful – you know, better for me image.'

Clearly, success was a factor James had given thought to. I asked him what he wanted to be.

'Thin,' he said promptly, 'but without stopping eating.'

'I meant your career.'

'What I'm going to *do*, you mean? That's easy. Make my first million,' he told me, grinning, 'then start on my next.'

I recalled James's antipathy to the printed word and his vestigial efforts to read and grinned back. His cheek always amused me.

'Well, why not?' he challenged. 'It's only a matter of time. The sky's the limit when you got flair, and I got flair.'

'One of these days you'll be making a take-over bid for Sotheby's, I suppose?' I teased.

He was on to it at once. James never joked about business himself or allowed for such frivolity in others.

'Sotheby's? Who's Sotheby? What's his line?'

'It's a place in New Bond Street. They're famous auctioneers.'

'What, like that feller I seen up Petticoat Lane? Marvellous he was,' James said admiringly. 'He did Mum proper. She still can't see how she came to pay a quid for three plastic egg-cups and a doll's brush and comb.'

'Sotheby's' I said coldly, 'is a highly respected and gentlemanly firm – *if* you can grasp such a concept, James. They deal only in rare and beautiful objects, or items of cultural interest. I doubt if they've even heard of plastic egg-cups.'

'Go on!' James said, giving me the indulgent look with which he met each fresh example of my ignorance of the world and its affairs. 'If you mean poor and posh I'm not interested.'

But, providing the instruction was outside the walls of school, James learnt fast. He was round again before the week was out and his tone had changed considerably.

'Here, I've seen about that place you mentioned. It was in the piper, miss. Cor!' He showed me the cutting. 'See? They sold a book yesterday for six farsand. Six farsand! Just for some old book!'

His eyes flickered from me to the shelves and back again, and it struck me that, for the first time, they surveyed me with something approaching respect.

'Yeah,' he added after a thoughtful pause, 'and what slays me is that it *wasn't even printed*!'

This was a brave new world indeed. Like stout Cortez, James stared ahead, seduced by all its possibilities: then he put the cutting carefully away in his post office savings book, and even, in a moment of unwonted trust, let me inspect that sacred document itself. It was my turn to be impressed. The bank book was much thumbed and had an air of having spent the greater part of its life nestling up against a parcel of chips; but it did reveal that James was well on the way to his first thousand.

I saw James only once after that. He appeared one evening in splendid new clothes and explained that he'd come to say goodbye. It seemed to be as great a bombshell to him as it was to me.

'We gotter house,' he told me, depressed. 'Yeah. Up Emelempsteadnootown. Smashing barfroom. Who wants a barfroom?'

He was so upset that he even refused an apple. I tried to comfort him.

'Still, think of the business you'll do. Hundreds of people moving down from London, all wanting things . . .'

I didn't mean to be immoral – heaven knows, I didn't approve of his nefarious exploits – I just wanted to take his mind off his troubles: but, to my astonishment, James shook his head.

'No, business can wait – except for a little fiddle now and then to keep my hand in. You see, I've been thinking. I reckon the best thing I can do when we move is go to classes.'

'*Classes?*' I said, staggered.

He wriggled self-consciously.

'Yeah, well, improve myself, sort of. I know when I'm bested. That feller who sold them scribbled-on old pages, he's got the edge on me all right. Then I remembered what you said, see? So I went up the West End to have a look. Nice little place they got,' James said airily. 'Still . . . I'm on my way.' He grinned suddenly and patted his bank book. 'And thanks for putting me on to it. I won't forget to send you a p.c. to let you know when I've actually took over.'

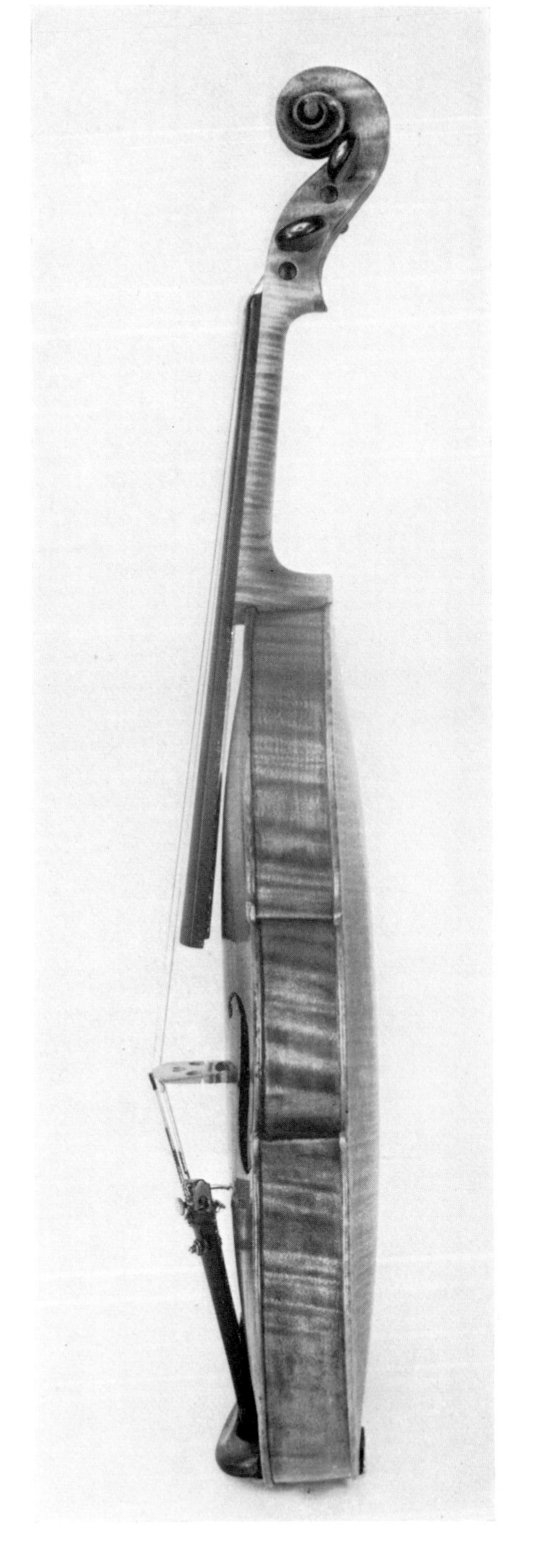

A Violin by Antonio Stradivari, made in 1726.
London £10,500 ($29,400).
From the collection of the late George J. Gould, Esq.

Looking at this Year from Outside

BY FRANK DAVIS

As far as I am concerned the most memorable moment at Sotheby's during the past year had nothing to do with money or records or turnover or the balance of payments or even the benign presence of Mr Dimbleby one evening as, pleasingly cherubic, he hovered high up in a corner by kind permission of the Early Bird Satellite; none of these things impressed me so much as entering the little room on the right of the entrance stairs one morning late in April and finding there as choice an array of small medieval works of art as one could wish to see anywhere in the world. As twenty of them came from the famous, one might almost say legendary, Adolphe Stoclet collection in Brussels, sent over from New York for disposal by his grandson, Philippe Stoclet, one had no genuine excuse for surprise; even so, that small toplighted gallery, glowing as it did that morning with so many jewel-like objects, is not to be forgotten. Apart from the Stoclet pieces, there was a series of 14th-century stained glass windows formerly in the church at Bad St Leonhard, Lavanttal, Austria, which had been originally sold in 1935 to pay for a new church tower, and twenty-one rare enamels, bequeathed to the Birmingham and Midland Institute in 1863 by Sir Francis Scott, a disciple of Ruskin and patron of Gilbert Scott, the architect, and now sold on the instructions of the Trustees amid some local grumbles. Among the Birmingham enamels a little four inch square 12th-century champlevé Pentecost plaque – I wonder how many people in Birmingham knew of its existence? – was sold for £35,000. The windows, originally in the Austrian church, went for £32,000 while, from among the Stoclet pieces, a 14th-century Byzantine mosaic icon of the Virgin and Child surrounded by the twelve Apostles executed in gold, silver, lapis lazuli and other colours was sold for £34,000, a late 12th-century Limoges enamel *chasse* for £32,000 and a remarkable morse ivory chessman, also of the 12th century – a king crowned and robed beneath a semicircular arch, a soldier on each side of him – for £10,000. Paintings from the Stoclet collection had been sold a month previously, the most impressive of them a Crucifixion by the unknown called the St Francis Master, an austere, haunting work now the property of the nation and which no one was surprised to see sold for £100,000. A few days after the dispersal of the enamels, twenty-seven of the Stoclet Chinese works of art realized over £50,000, when the British Museum paid £28,000 for a well-known late Chou dynasty bronze bell, last seen in London in 1935 at the Exhibition of Chinese Art at Burlington House. It bears a date corresponding to 482 B.C. by our reckoning, is superbly cast and decorated with formal dragons, birds and monster masks, and belongs to a chime of five, of which the four others are known, two of them in the Fogg Museum of Art, Cambridge, Mass., one in Amsterdam, the fourth formerly in Berlin but now lost. A small gilt-bronze stele from the same collection dated A.D. 516, Wei dynasty – a standing figure of Avalokitesvara against a tall mandorla – went for £5,200. Altogether Philippe Stoclet's share of his grandfather's superb collection was disposed for a total of £354,093, while during the final weeks of the season other pieces, the portion of another member of the family, Madame Michele Stoclet, were also sold, one of them, a 12th-century gilt-bronze figure of the crucified Christ, acquired on behalf of the British Museum for £21,000, in the opinion of many one of the noblest works of art of its kind seen in the auction rooms for a generation.

A less serious occasion was the evening experiment during which simultaneous bidding in London and New York was seen by a vast audience on both sides of the Atlantic – fascinating to watch, I am assured, in front of a television set, and no less fascinating, if a trifle less comfortable, to see in the round; arc lights, a galaxy of technicians, many complicated yards of cable. A bright thought paid homage to the Early Bird satellite which made the affair possible by making Audubon's famous *Birds of America* the subject of the sale – a series of plates from the first edition which was dispersed to various purchasers on both sides of the Atlantic for a total of £6,955. Proceedings were interrupted for a few moments to include three paintings – a characteristic Degas pastel of dancers which went for £20,000, another pastel by Degas' friend and pupil, the American banker's daughter, Mary Cassatt – a mother and child for £12,500. The third, a painting of Menaggio on Lake Como by Sir Winston Churchill, executed in 1945 when Sir Winston was staying there to recover from the disappointment of that year's election and subsequently given to his bank manager, realized the phenomenal price for a work by an amateur of £14,000. The previous highest price for any Churchill painting was £9,200. This seems an appropriate place to put on record a confidence given to me that evening by an unknown young woman seated beside me: 'Comforting, isn't he?' she whispered, gesturing towards Dimbleby in his corner. 'I don't always listen to what he says, but I always switch on and *look* at him.' Another evening sale a month later was also a simultaneous London–New York occasion but considerably less exhausting for the audience and I imagine far more efficient. This was worked by means of the nice old-fashioned telephone, with coloured slides projected on to a screen in New York as each lot was put up for sale in London. The collection chosen for this experiment was that of Charles Zadok of New York City – modern paintings, drawings and sculpture, thirty of them – total £232,010, with Raoul Dufy's *Regatta at Cowes*, 1929, going for £25,000, an early Derain – a Thames view painted in 1905–06 – for £30,000, while £9,500 was paid for a brilliant Paris street painting of 1944 by Jean Dubuffet, £11,000 for Giacometti's painting of his brother, Diego, and £12,700 for George Rouault's *Femme au Chapeau Fleuri* of 1938. Comment by the owner: 'I am grateful that I am still alive in these exciting times because as a young man I would not have dreamed that an auction could be held simultaneously in London and New York.' The following morning we returned to normal with 132 other Impressionist and Modern works which added £597,510 to the previous evening's score without the intervention of scientific marvels. Among them, a well-known Paul Klee of 1927, the playful, subtle *Departure of the Ships* realized £22,000, and Sisley's *Clover Field*, 1874, for £22,500. After that *La Sorti* by Bonnard went for £18,000, and Berthe Morisot's charming picture of children in a garden, for £14,500. In brief, it was an opulent evening and forenoon, on a par with the £829,200 sale of 232 paintings, drawings and sculptures before Christmas, when £90,000 was paid for the Paul Gauguin *Tahitienne et Garçon*, dated 1899, £20,200 for a Degas drawing with pastel, *Danseuse à la Barre* and £22,000 for a late Matisse still-life with lemons. Towards the end of the season an Old Master sale of the usual entertainingly varied sort – from severe 14th-century saints to gay little Guardi fantasies – accounted for £490,090. The National Portrait Gallery gave £4,000 for a contemporary portrait of Lady Jane Grey. *A Woman and a Boy by Candlelight* (an interesting experiment by Rubens) went for £19,000 and four Venice views by Marieschi realized between them £69,000, while a very small capriccio by Francesco Guardi fetched £19,500, and an opera rehearsal by Marco Ricci, who was painting scenery in London in 1709, for £12,000. This dispersal was followed by another a week later, confined to 18th and 19th-century pictures. On this occasion a famous Turner, painted in 1835 and exhibited in the Royal Academy the same year, Lord Allendale's *Ehrenbreitsein with the Tomb of Marceau*, made the record auction price for a Turner of £88,000. The highest previous sum paid for a Turner at auction was the 29,000 gns given by Agnews for a view of Venice in the Ross sale at Christie's in 1929, a painting which was bought by Governor Fuller, Boston and has been left by him to the National Gallery of Washington. Lord Allendale's painting had been bought in the Bicknell sale in 1863 for Thomas Brocklebank for £1,890, and remained in the Brocklebank family until 1942, when the present Lord Allendale's father acquired it, also from Agnew's. It is scarcely necessary to point out that, in today's currency, the rise in market value is more apparent than real.

In spite of these and many other spectacular happenings, to numerous people Sotheby's means books and manuscripts just as it did in the days of the founder way back in 1744. I sometimes suspect that the book department, with a nice, newly contrived room at its disposal, a trifle remote and immersed in its erudite cogitations, is tempted to look upon its comparatively upstart, less sedate colleagues much as a Trollopian bishop would regard the caperings of a newly-hatched gaggle of curates. None the less, it soldiers on with increasing success, astonishing even its own bland self this season by a total turnover of £1,250,436, or about £200,000 more than the record established during 1960–61, when the outstanding event was the Dyson Perrins disposal. This year it established a record for a single sale of printed books, excluding manuscripts – the £157,172 achieved for the 694 lots of Major J. R. Abbey's library. This celebrated collection included such items as the six volumes of the works of Molière, Paris, 1732, the only copy bound in contemporary blue morocco gilt which had been priced in a 1793 bookseller's catalogue at 7 gns, had made several auction-room appearances since (the most recent at Geneva in 1954 when it made the equivalent of £2,000) and was now sold for £7,000. Another considerable rarity was the first edition of the Aldine Aristotle in Greek, 1495–98, bound in Paris about 1560 in one of the noblest bindings of that or any other century – brownish-red morocco gilt in a superb pattern of floral tracery – which went for £7,600. Among later bindings was one almost certainly designed by Athenian Stuart himself for his *Antiquities of Athens*, 1762, which now fetched £600 after having been sold in the same rooms in 1948 for £70. Other notable book sales were the scientific books, mostly acquired between the wars by Professor E. N. da C. Andrade, which realized £39,000 (£8,290 for thirty-five works by Robert Boyle, £9,052 for forty-six by Sir Isaac Newton), and yet another

The Saleroom in London during the auction relayed by television between London and New York via the Early Bird Satellite. The auctioneer is taking bids from the screen at the back of the room which shows the saleroom in New York.

The Saleroom in New York showing the screen relaying the picture by Mary Cassatt being sold in London.

selection of manuscripts from the vast accumulation made by the half-crazy Sir Thomas Phillipps with which Sotheby's have been dealing for a generation and more. Among them – this selection of lots sold for £84,414 – was a remarkable literary discovery, a hitherto undetected commonplace book in verse and prose, much of it in the handwriting of Robert Herrick, which, after spirited bidding, was bought for America at £34,000, while America and the Bibliothèque Nationale were determined competitors for the great mass of Graffigny papers which were already in Phillipps' possession by 1842 and were now dispersed for £18,815.

It is well-known that there is nothing like a high price to winkle rarities out of their hiding-places. The previous season a very rare Breughel print – Pieter Breughel the Elder's only etching, *The Rabbit Hunters* – had been sold for £10,000. This year another impression, not so fine but fine enough, turned up among forty-eight prints by and after Breughel and was sold for £6,500 (the whole forty-eight realized £15,318), and in a £925,500 sale of Old Masters the following day – the same dispersal in which the Stoclet Master of St Francis Crucifixion appeared – a flower painting dated 1611 by Roelandt Savery, who was one of the Emperor Rudolf II's tame artists at Prague, went for £8,000, another flower painting, by Jan Breughel the Elder, for £16,800, a Boucher landscape for £15,000, while of two Rembrandts, a portrait of Saskia, painted in 1635, made £125,000 – she is dressed as Minerva – and a portrait of an unknown man £140,000.

Among some notable Arms and Armour, the Runes collection of firearms, sent over from New York, was sold in 94 lots for £53,248, when £5,000 was given for a Dresden double-barrelled wheel lock pistol from the early 17th century, and the armour, mostly collected by Sir Edward Barry in the 1890's, realized £44,546. Many of these pieces were acquired for the Tower Armouries. A specially beautiful object was a bascinet of about 1380, said to have come from the Arsenal at Zurich and to have been looted during the Napoleonic wars, which made the formidable sum of £9,000 – I thought it the most elegant tin hat ever provided for a soldier, the sort of subtle geometry aimed at by modern sculptors and so rarely achieved.

Precious stones, though notoriously a girl's best friends, leave me unmoved, so I did not bat an eyelid when I saw a mastodon among emeralds, a stone of 142 carats, sold to New York for £52,000, and a diamond just under 21 carats going to Antwerp at £40,000. More interesting, because of the current fad for *Art Nouveau* objects, was a near neighbour of these two rare and precious geological specimens – a gold and enamel butterfly brooch in the form of a nude sprouting huge wings, by René Lalique, which half a dozen years ago might perhaps have made £60 and was now bought for £300. The following day, in a £46,905 sale of silver, a pair of George II salvers by Edward Vincent, 1728 was sold for £6,500 and a Charles II wall-sconce decorated with foliage and Chinoiserie figures for £3,600, and the following week, in a notable sale which attracted I thought not very much attention, a set of the first four Shakespeare folios went to New York at £23,000, as did a copy of the second, and first illustrated, edition of Chaucer's *Canterbury Tales*, printed by Caxton about 1484, at £30,000.

A collection which caused no stir but which was none the less fascinating was that belonging to the late Professor F. H. Garner whose name must be known to a very wide

Left An Evening Dress in black jacquard brocade with pale blue cornflowers and strawberry leaves, the sleeves in pale blue-green velvet, by D. H. Evans, London. London £24 ($67).
From the collection of J. L. Jervoise, Esq.

Right A Lilac Corded Silk Afternoon Dress, by Mme. M. H. Douglass, New York. London £32 ($89).
From the collection of the Countess of Craven.

An early 19th-century Bone Ship Model.
London £950 ($2,600).

circle as the author of the invaluable Faber monograph *English Delftware*, a book unlikely to be superseded for at least a generation. This was dispersed in three parts for £27,465. The emphasis, naturally, was on Delft, but there were numerous other rarities, such as a late 17th-century redware Elers mug which went for £320 and two Fulham stoneware cups by Dwight of about 1690; one was sold for £370, the other, silver-mounted, for £400. This was one of those sales which provided local museums with the opportunity to acquire things of particular interest to the neighbourhood; Gloucester, for instance, paid £65 for three Lambeth plates no doubt ordered by a local dealer at the time of the Tewkesbury election of 1754 and painted with 'Calvert and Martin forever'. A fine tulip charger, orange, yellow and green made £240, a Lambeth puzzle jug dated 1742 £320, and a barber's bowl dated 1706, amusingly painted in the centre with the barber-surgeon about to lead his horse into its stable and the rim with the tools of his trade, £680. Another well-known collection, the Allman collection, was sold for £12,126, when a salt-glaze crinoline figure wearing a wide bell skirt was bought for £1,650. Nine hundred and forty English drawings belonging to the late Sir Bruce Ingram, whose purchases of both drawings and paintings began early in his career and continued until the day he died last year at the age of eighty-three, came to Sotheby's and were dealt with in five separate sales for £78,369, while £212,793 was obtained for the paintings. Of several marathon furniture sales I remember best an afternoon and then the following morning at the end of April because it began with a Stradivarius of 1726 which was sold for £10,500, included an extremely amusing pair of Louis XV ormolu firedogs in a design of scrolls, monkeys and dragons at £3,000, a pair of Louis XVI ormolu-mounted Japanese pot-pourri vases at £3,400, and ended with two exceptional pieces of furniture. One of them was an early Louis XV library table of kingwood with exceptionably fine ormolu mounts, which was bought for £24,000, the other a painted commode of considerable historic interest. It had been made by Joubert and the brothers Martin for the bedroom of Madame Adélaide, eldest daughter of Louis XVI, and was acquired by the Museum of Versailles and the Trianon for £20,000. Part 2 of the Ionides collection of English enamels added £35,242 to the £27,492 already realized for the first part – an early Staffordshire knife-case painted with river-landscapes and flowers was bought for £2,500 – and the late Mrs Meyer Sassoon's porcelain, eighty-one items including sixty-five Chelsea scent bottles made just over £30,000. One of the scent bottles, modelled as a parrot and a Cochin China hen, made £1,050, a pair of Sèvres blue ground pots of flowers £2,400 and a Vincennes chimney garniture of three *gros-bleu* vases £2,300. The previous day witnessed a European auction record for a Japanese print from the Stoclet collection, the £2,000 given for an early work by Kiyomasu – the poet Teika on a horse led by a girl and accompanied by a samurai – and the set of seven Marriage prints by Harunobu were dispersed for £2,420.

Every two or three months someone pays a record price for a painting by Munnings – the latest was registered at Sotheby's in July – £10,200 for an admirable composition of wide skies and gypsies – *On the Downs*. Among the sales which are classified under the somewhat vague term, *Antiquities*, the one which made the greatest impression was the collection of the well-known Paris and New York dealer Ernest Brummer, a magnificent array of Egyptian and Near Eastern works, which were sold just before Christmas for

£58,062. A bronze foundation figure from Lagash *circa* 2125 B.C. – a deity with a tiered headdress holding a foundation post – sold for £4,600, and an Assyrian relief of the 7th century B.C., two female captives and a boy, for £4,000.

To a London, and so a necessarily remote, observer the Sotheby – Parke-Bernet matrimonial experiment, the two partners sharing one another's resources, has all the appearance of a great success.

A total of $13,471,833 has been achieved during the season – the second highest in the history of the New York firm and an increase over the previous season of almost $3,000,000. The collection of jewels and silver formed by Mrs. A. Hamilton-Rice was sold in New York for $1,341,560 and $360,800 respectively, the former a world record total for a sale of jewels, and the latter a record in America for a sale of silver.

The long term effect of this Anglo-American treaty on the New York market will perhaps not be seen for some time. Meanwhile the success of the specialised sales noted above, the high prices secured for 19th and 20th century paintings from the Ross, Haupt and Dotrement collections and a record total for a sale of Impressionist and Modern pictures on April 14th have made this a notable transatlantic honeymoon.

Illustrations

THE MASTER OF THE MAGDALEN
The Madonna and Child Enthroned.
On panel. 36½ in. by 20½ in.
London £16,000 ($44,800).
From the collections of the late Adolphe Stoclet and Mr Philippe R. Stoclet.

Part of the collection of Old Master paintings and European and Oriental works of art formed by the late Adolphe Stoclet was sold by Mr Philippe R. Stoclet during the spring and the summer of 1965 for £354,093 ($991,460).

THE MASTER OF ST FRANCIS

A Crucifix.

The Master of St Francis worked in the Lower Church of Assisi during the second half of the 13th century. On panel. 36 in. by $27\frac{3}{4}$ in.

London £100,000 ($280,000).

From the collections of the late Adolph Stoclet and Mr Philippe R. Stoclet.

Now in the National Gallery, London.

FOLLOWER OF GIOTTO, *circa* 1320
The Deposition.
On panel. $14\frac{1}{2}$ in. by $9\frac{7}{8}$ in.
London £17,000 ($47,600).

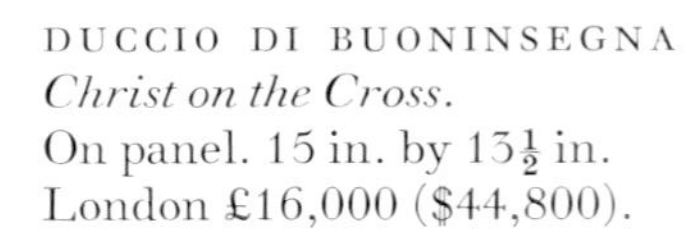

DUCCIO DI BUONINSEGNA
Christ on the Cross.
On panel. 15 in. by $13\frac{1}{2}$ in.
London £16,000 ($44,800).

From the collections of the late Adolphe Stoclet and Mr Philippe R. Stoclet.

BERLINGHIERO BERLINGHIERI
The Madonna and Child.
On panel, triptych $16\frac{1}{2}$ in. by 20 in.
London £18,000 ($50,400).
From the collection of the late Adolphe Stoclet and Madame Michele Stoclet.

LORENZO MONACO
The Madonna and Child.
On panel. $40\frac{1}{2}$ in. by 24 in.
London £32,000 ($89,600).
From the collection of Captain P. J. Drury-Lowe, Locko Park, Derbyshire.
Now in the National Gallery of Scotland.

BERNARDO DADDI
The Arrival of St Ursula with the Virgin Martyrs at Basel.
On panel. 23¼ in. by 25 in.
London £14,000 ($39,200).
From the collection of the late Adolphe Stoclet and Madame Michele Stoclet.

Part of the collection of Old Master paintings and Byzantine and Medieval works of art formed by the late Adolphe Stoclet was sold by Madame Michele Stoclet in June and July 1965 for £79,000 ($221,200).

FILIPPINO LIPPI
Saint Apollonia and a Sainted Bishop.
On panel. $61\frac{1}{2}$ in. by 23 in.
Sold with its pair (facing page).
London £84,000 ($235,200).

FILIPPINO LIPPI
Saint Paul and Saint Zenobius.
On panel. 61½ in. by 23 in.

FRANCESCO UBERTINI called BACCHIACCA
The Baptism of Christ.
On panel. $22\frac{3}{4}$ in. by 16 in.
London £16,000 ($44,800).
From the collection of Gwen, Lady Melchett.

GIOVANNI DI PIETRO, called LO SPAGNA
St Louis, St Mary Magdalene and the Blessed Giacomo della Marca
On panel. Each 15½ in. by 5½ in.
London £7,500 ($21,000).
From the collection of Gwen, Lady Melchett.

GIUSEPPE ARCIMBOLDO
A Fantastic Head of a Woman.
On panel. 31¾ in. by 24 in.
London £8,500 ($23,800).
From the collections of Emperor Rudolph II, Prague, Queen Christina of Sweden and the late Dr Axel Wenner-Gren.

GIUSEPPE ARCIMBOLDO
Flora.
On panel. 29½ in. by 22½ in.
London £5,000 ($14,000).

GIUSEPPE ARCIMBOLDO
Spring.
29¾ in. by 22 in. (one of a pair)
London £4,200 ($11,760).

GIUSEPPE ARCIMBOLDO
Air.
29½ in. by 22 in.
Sold with its pair, *Fire.* London £4,000 ($11,200).
All from the collection of the late Dr Axel Wenner-Gren.

GIUSEPPE ARCIMBOLDO
Fire.
29½ in. by 22 in.

FRANCESCO GUARDI
The Piazza San Marco, Venice.
Signed. 19 in. by 33 in.
London £34,000 ($95,200).
From the collection of Mrs. L. Bootle-Wilbraham.

BERNARDO BELLOTTO
A View of Dresden.
$36\frac{3}{4}$ in. by 64 in.
London £27,000 ($75,600).
From the Royal Gallery in Dresden and the collection of Mr G. Huntington Hartford, New York.

MARCO RICCI, *The Rehearsal of an Opera.*
It is probable that the man in the red cloak on the extreme right is Dr Pepusch, the man seated beside him, holding an open book, Heidegger, the impresario of the Italian opera, and the woman singing beside the harpsichord, Margherita Lepine, a famous opera singer. One of the other women may be Katherine Tofts, a singer and rival of Margherita Lepine, who retired to Venice in 1709. Marco Ricci is known to have been connected with the Italian opera in London, for whom he was painting scenery in 1709. 18½ in. by 22 in.
London £12,000 ($33,600).
From the collection of Lt.-Col. Sir Watkin Williams-Wynn, Bt.

FRANCESCO GUARDI
A Caprice with a Ruined Arch and a Pyramid.
$9\frac{1}{4}$ in. by $11\frac{3}{4}$ in.
London £19,500 ($54,600).

MICHELE MARIESCHI
Venice: Palazzo Pesaro.
22 in. by 32 in.
London £18,500 ($51,800).

MICHELE MARIESCHI
Venice: San Geremia and the Cannaregio.
$21\frac{1}{4}$ in. by $32\frac{1}{2}$ in.
London £15,000 ($42,000).

MICHELE MARIESCHI
Venice: The Grand Canal from the Pescheria.
21½ in. by 32½ in.
London £17,500 ($49,000).

MICHELE MARIESCHI
Venice: The Grand Canal and Palazzo Rezzonico.
21½ in. by 32½ in.
London £18,000 ($50,400).
All from the collection of Miss C. M. Smith.

ALBERT BOUTS
The Nativity.
On panel. $27\frac{1}{4}$ in. by $21\frac{1}{2}$ in.
London £12,500 ($35,000).
From the collection of the Convent of the Assumption, Kensington.

LUCAS CRANACH THE ELDER
Venus and Cupid.
On panel, signed with the winged serpent. Diameter $4\frac{1}{2}$ in.
London £16,000 ($44,800).

SIR PETER PAUL RUBENS
A Woman and a Boy by Candlelight.
Painted *circa* 1616. On panel. 29¼ in. by 23¾ in.
This is one of the first examples of the candlelight scenes which later became so popular in the Netherlands. It was engraved a number of times, at least twice in Rubens' lifetime. At the Bibliothèque Nationale in Paris there is a proof of one of these prints inscribed by Rubens himself with two lines concerning the subject of the picture:

'Quis vetet apposito, lumen de lumine tolli
Mille licet capiant, deperit inde nihil'

[Light can be taken a thousand times from another light without diminishing it.]
London £19,000 ($53,200).
From the collection of Francis Francis, Esq., Bahamas.

REMBRANDT HARMENSZ VAN RIJN
Portrait of a Man.
On panel. Signed and dated 1635. $26\frac{1}{4}$ in. by $20\frac{3}{4}$ in.
London £140,000 ($392,000).
From the collection of Mr William B. Leeds, New York.

JAN BREUGHEL THE ELDER
Flowers in a Glass.
On panel. 16½ in. by 13 in.
London £15,800 ($44,240).

PIETER BREUGHEL THE YOUNGER
A Village Fête.
On panel, signed. 20 in. by 31½ in.
London £9,000 ($25,200).

PIETER BREUGHEL THE YOUNGER
Peasants Dancing at a Wedding.
On panel. 16½ in. by 22¼ in.
London £7,000 ($19,600).

HENDRICK TERBRUGGHEN
A Boy Musician Singing
Signed with the monogram. $28\frac{1}{4}$ in. by $25\frac{3}{4}$. in.
London £5,800 ($16,240)
From the collection of the late Dr. Axel Wenner-Gren.

BALTHASAR VAN DER AST
Flowers in a Vase.
On panel, signed. 19 in. by $14\frac{1}{4}$ in.
London £5,200 ($14,560).

Spring.
8¼ in by 12 in.
London £1,400 ($3,920).

DAVID TENIERS THE YOUNGER, after FRANCESCO BASSANO
Spring, Autumn, Winter.
Teniers was keeper of the collection assembled in Brussels by the Spanish Regent, Archduke Leopold Wilhelm of Austria, which forms an important part of the Austrian Imperial collection now in the Vienna Gallery. Teniers painted small copies of many of the Italian pictures in the collection and published a volume of engravings made from his copies. Teniers painted these pictures from originals by Francesco Bassano in the Archduke's collection that have since been lost.
From the collection of Henry A. Rudkin, Esq., Southport, Connecticut.

Autumn.
8¼ in. by 12 in.
London £1,300 ($3,640).

Winter.
8¼ in. by 12 in.
London £1,400 ($3,920).

JAN DAVIDSZ DE HEEM
A Still Life with a Dish of Crabs.
On panel. Signed and dated 1651.
24½ in. by 35 in.
London £5,000 ($14,000).

MELCHIOR D'HONDECOETER
An Assembly of Birds.
Signed. 83½ in. by 66½ in.
London £3,900 ($10,920).

LUIS EUGENIO MELENDEZ
A Still Life.
Signed. 15½ in. by 24 in.
London £6,000 ($16,800).

JACOB ROOTIUS
Flowers in a Vase.
Signed and dated 1674. 35 in. by $28\frac{1}{4}$ in.
London £3,000 ($8,400).
From the collection of Guy Argles, Esq.

WILLEM VAN AELST
A Flower Piece.
Signed and dated 1666. $31\frac{1}{4}$ in. by $25\frac{3}{4}$ in.
London £6,500 ($18,500).
From the collection of Guy Argles, Esq.

JAN VAN GOYEN
A River Landscape with a Château.
On panel. Signed and dated 1645. $25\frac{3}{4}$ in. by 38 in.
London £8,000 ($22,400).
From the collection of R. Neville, Esq.

GERRIT VAN HONTHORST
King Charles I.
It has been suggested that the likeness of Charles I as Apollo in *The Seven Liberal Arts presented to Apollo and Diana* by Honthorst at Hampton Court was based on the present portrait.
30¼ in. by 25¼ in.
London £4,000 ($11,200).
From the collection of Monsieur Ulysse Moussali.
Now in the National Portrait Gallery, London.

Lady Jane Grey.
On panel. 72 in by 37 in.
London £4,000 ($11,200).
From the collection of the
late J. F. Minken.
Now in the National
Portrait Gallery, London.

ALLAN RAMSAY
Portrait of Lord Auchinleck.
49½ in. by 39½ in.
London £4,500 ($12,600).
From the collection of Sir Arthur Boswell Eliott, Bt.

SIR JOSHUA REYNOLDS
Portrait of James Boswell.
The portrait was painted in 1787 in pursuance of a bargain proposed by Boswell, who undertook to pay for it from his first fees from the English bar. 29¼ in. by 24¼ in.
London £25,000 ($70,000).
From the collection of Sir Arthur Boswell Eliott, Bt.
Now in the National Portrait Gallery, London.

GEORGE STUBBS
Bulls Fighting.
Signed and dated 1786, on panel. 24¼ in. by 32½ in.
London £10,500 ($29,400).
From the collection of Mrs M. A. Hope Barton de Ross.

WILLIAM MARLOW
A View on the Arno, Florence.
Signed. 34 in. by 46 in.
London £4,800 ($13,440).
From the collection of Ellen, Countess of Hardwicke, C.B.E.

THOMAS GAINSBOROUGH,
A Wooded Landscape with Hagar and Ishmael.
29¾ in. by 36½ in.
London £10,000 ($38,000).
From the collection of Lt-Colonel Sir Watkin Williams-Wynn, Bt.

WILLIAM MARLOW
A View of Whitehall looking North East.
Signed. 27½ in. by 35½ in.
London £3,900 ($10,920).

JAMES BARRY
Portrait of James Gandon.
He was the architect of the Four Courts, the Kings Inns, the East Portico of Parliament House and the Custom House in Dublin. $48\frac{1}{4}$ in. by $38\frac{1}{4}$ in.
London £650 ($1,820).

Below JAMES STARK
The Beach at Low Tide, near Cromer.
Signed and dated 1834. $29\frac{3}{4}$ in. by $39\frac{3}{4}$ in.
London £3,000 ($8,400).
From the collection of the 1st Earl of Balfour.

ARTHUR DEVIS
Portrait of Mr Munday of Osbaston.
Signed and dated 1749. 29 in. by 23¼ in.
London £5,200 ($14,560).
From the collection of Desmond O'Brien, Esq.

Below J. ZOFFANY
The Reverend Wilson and his Family.
The Reverend Wilson was tutor to William Pitt the Younger and a memorial to the statesman is seen in the picture.
27½ in. by 36 in.
London £3,000 ($8,400).

HENRY FUSELI
Mrs Siddons as Lady Macbeth seizing the Daggers.
$39\frac{1}{4}$ in. by $48\frac{3}{4}$ in.
London £3,800 ($10,640).
From the collections of T. E. Lowinsky and Mrs John Stanley-Clarke.
Now in the Tate Gallery, London.

JACQUES LAURENT AGASSE
Acinonyx Jubatus.
13½ in. by 11¾ in.
London £1,100 ($3,080).

JACQUES LAURENT AGASSE
Lama Vicugna.
13½ in. by 11½ in.
London £680 ($1,704).

JACQUES LAURENT AGASSE
Neofelis Nebulosa.
13¾ in. by 11¾ in.
London £1,200 ($3,360).

JACQUES LAURENT AGASSE
Lycaon Pictus.
13½ in. by 11¾ in.
London £320 ($896).

These animals were brought from Sumatra to the Royal Menagerie at Windsor, where they were painted. In 1830 the animals at the Royal Menagerie were divided between the Zoological Gardens in Dublin and Regents Park.

JOSEPH MALLORD WILLIAM TURNER
Ehrenbreitsein, with the Tomb of Marceau.
$35\frac{1}{4}$ in. by $47\frac{1}{2}$ in.
Painted in 1835 and used as an illustration to Byron's *Childe Harold:*
'By Coblentz, on a rise of gentle ground,
There is a small and simple pyramid.'
London £88,000 ($246,400).
From the collections of Thomas Brocklebank and the Rt Hon. the Viscount Allendale, D.L.

SAMUEL SCOTT
The Thames and the Tower of London on the King's Birthday.
Signed and dated 1771. $38\frac{3}{4}$ in. by $75\frac{1}{4}$ in.
London £20,000 ($56,000).
From the collections of Walter S. M. Burns and Harold Peake, Esq.

JOHN SELL COTMAN
Landscape with a White Cloud.
Watercolour, signed. Drawn *circa* 1832. 12½ in. by 18½ in.
London £5,600 ($15,680).

JOSEPH MALLORD WILLIAM TURNER
The Interior of St Peter's.
Watercolour, signed. Executed in 1821. $11\frac{1}{4}$ in. by 16 in.
London £2,900 ($8,120).

JOHN ROBERT COZENS
Isola Bella.
Pencil and blue and grey washes.
Signed and dated 1790. 12 in. by 18 in.
London £3,200 ($8,960).
From the collection of Mrs L. Gray.

Above THOMAS GAINSBOROUGH
A Peasant and Cattle approaching a Wooded Stream.
Black chalk and watercolour.
$11\frac{3}{4}$ in. by $14\frac{1}{4}$ in.
London £1,400 ($3,920).
From the collection of the late
Sir Bruce Ingram, O.B.E., M.C., F.S.A.

THOMAS ROWLANDSON
The Canterbury-Dover Coach.
Signed. 11$\frac{1}{2}$ in. by 17$\frac{1}{2}$ in.
London £800 ($2,240).
From the collection of Mrs Gilbert Miller.

Above JAMES WARD
A Study of a Poodle.
Pencil and coloured chalks on grey paper, signed with the initials. 11$\frac{1}{4}$ in. by 10$\frac{3}{4}$ in.
London £360 ($1,008).
From the collection of the late
Sir Bruce Ingram, O.B.E., M.C., F.S.A.

JOSEPH FARINGTON
The Mons Gate, Valenciennes, after the Siege of 1793.
Watercolour, signed. $15\frac{3}{4}$ in. by $23\frac{3}{4}$ in.
London £460 ($1,288).
Now in the Musée de Valenciennes.

EDWARD LEAR
Florence, a View from the Villa San Firenze.
Pen and ink and wash, dated June 15–19, 1861.
$21\frac{1}{4}$ in. by $14\frac{1}{2}$ in.
London £600 ($1,680).
From the collection of Lt-Colonel A. Malcolm-Scott.

Facing page EDWARD DAYES
The Governor's House at Besupstad.
Pen and ink and coloured washes, signed and dated 1791. 14 in. by $19\frac{1}{2}$ in.
London £720 ($2,016).
From the collection of the Rt Hon. Lord Stanley of Alderley.

DAVID ROBERTS
The Front Elevation of the Great Temple of Abu Simbel.
Watercolour, heightened with white, inscribed and dated Nov 11, 1838. $12\frac{3}{4}$ in. by $19\frac{1}{4}$ in.
London £400 ($1,120).
From the collection of the late Sir Bruce Ingram, O.B.E., M.C., F.S.A.

EDGAR DEGAS
La Répétition de Ballet
Gouache and pastel, signed. Painted in 1875. $21\frac{3}{4}$ in. by $26\frac{3}{4}$ in.
New York $410,000 (£146,370).
From the collections of Mrs H. O. Havemeyer
and Mr George C. Frelinghuysen, Beverly Hills.

CAMILLE PISSARRO
Jeune Femme, les Mains jointes derrière le Dos.
Charcoal and coloured chalks. Signed.
Executed *circa* 1888. 20 in. by 14 in.
New York $17,500 (£6,250).

EDGAR DEGAS
Femme se Grattant.
Charcoal and pastel, signed. Executed *circa* 1885. $12\frac{1}{2}$ in. by $9\frac{1}{2}$ in.
London £6,500 ($18,200).
From the collection of Harvard University.

CLAUDE MONET
Les Peupliers.
Signed and dated '91. 36 in. by 32 in.
New York $95,000 (£33,925).
From the collection of Mr and Mrs Robert E. Ricksen, New York.

PIERRE BONNARD
Ma Maison à Vernon (Le Jardin Inculte).
Signed. $19\frac{1}{4}$ in. by $23\frac{3}{4}$ in.
New York $60,000 (£21,425).

PAUL GAUGUIN
Tahitienne et Garçon.
Signed and dated '99. 36½ in. by 23 in.
This painting was included in Gauguin's last shipment of paintings from Tahiti to Paris in 1901.
London £90,000 ($252,000).

PIERRE BONNARD
La Glace Haute.
Signed. Painted *circa* 1914. 49 in. by $32\frac{1}{2}$ in.
New York $155,000 (£55,350).
From the collections of Mr and Mrs Adolphe A. Juviler, sold at Parke-Bernet in October, 1961 for $101,000 (£36,060), and Mr Nicholas Reisini, New York.

VINCENT VAN GOGH
Les Déchargeurs.
Painted at Arles in August 1888.
Van Gogh wrote in letter 516 to his brother Theo 'I saw a magnificent and strange effect this evening. A very big boat loaded with coal on the Rhône, moored to the quay. Seen from above it was all shining and wet with a shower; the water was yellowish-white and clouded pearl grey; the sky lilac, with an orange streak in the west, the town violet. On the boat some poor workmen, dirty blue and white, came and went carrying the cargo on the shore. It was pure Hokusai'. 21¼ in. by 25½ in.
New York $240,000 (£85,705).

ANDRÉ DERAIN
La Tamise.
Signed. Painted *circa* 1905–6. 25½ in. by 29½ in.
London £30,000 ($84,000).
From the collection of Mr and Mrs Charles Zadok, New York.

GIOVANNI BOLDINI
L'Homme au Plastron.
On panel. $10\frac{3}{4}$ in. by $8\frac{3}{4}$ in.
London £2,300 ($6,440).

Below,
CHARLES-FRANÇOIS DAUBIGNY
La Lavandière au Bord de l'Oise.
On panel, signed and dated 1871.
15 in. by 26 in.
London £3,900 ($10,920).
From the collection of
Harvard University.

JEAN-BAPTISTE-CAMILLE COROT
Saules et Chaumières.
Signed. 14 in. by 10½ in.
Painted *circa* 1860.
London £9,000 ($25,200).

Below,
ANTOINE-LOUIS BARYE
Tigre Couché
Signed. 10¼ in. by 13½ in.
London £1,950 ($5,460).

BERTHE MORISOT
Fillettes au Jardin, La Hotte.
Painted in 1885 in the garden at the Rue de Villejust. 23½ in. by 28¾ in.
London £14,500 ($40,600).
From the collection of Mr David Daniels, New York.

MARY CASSATT
Maternité
Pastel, signed. 18 in. by $23\frac{3}{4}$ in.
London £12,500 ($35,000).

ANDRÉ DERAIN
Le Port de Douarnenez.
Signed. Painted in 1936. $17\frac{1}{2}$ in. by 21 in.
London £6,000 ($16,800).
From the collection of The Rt Hon. The Lord Harvey of Tasburgh, G.C.M.G., G.C.V.O., C.B.

MAURICE PRENDERGAST
The Beach at St Malo.
Signed. Painted in 1907. $17\frac{1}{2}$ in. by 21 in.
New York $21,000 (£7,490).
From the collection of Mr and Mrs Walter Ross, New York.

EDOUARD VUILLARD
Portrait de la Comtesse de Noailles.
Signed, Painted *circa* 1930. $43\frac{3}{4}$ in. by $50\frac{1}{2}$ in.
New York $74,000 (£26,425).
From the collection of Mr and Mrs William Weintraub, Long Island.

JOAN MIRÓ
Le Porrides, *Prades*.
Signed and dated 1917. 20 in. by 24¼ in.
London £10,000 ($28,000).
From the collection of Mr and Mrs Charles Zadok, New York.

HENRI MATISSE
Gorges du Loup.
Signed. Painted *circa* 1922–3. $18\frac{1}{4}$ in. by 22 in.
New York $62,000 (£22,140).
From the collection of Mr Gustave Berne, Long Island.

HENRI MATISSE
Citrons et Mimosas.
Signed and dated '44. $21\frac{1}{4}$ in. by $28\frac{3}{4}$ in.
London £22,000 ($61,600).

NICOLAS DE STAËL
Fleurs.
Signed. Painted *circa* 1951–2. 58 in. by 38½ in.
New York $68,000 (£24,280).
From the collection of the late Ira Haupt, New York.

GEORGES ROUAULT
Fleurs Décoratives.
Painted *circa* 1930–40. 28 in. by 23 in.
New York $46,000 (£16,425)
From the collection of Mr and Mrs Walter Ross, New York.

The collection of 60 paintings and sculpture formed by Mr and Mrs Walter Ross was sold in October 1964 for $675,900 (£241,360).

AMEDEO MODIGLIANI
Portrait de Morgan Russell.
Painted in 1918. Morgan Russell was the American painter who, with Stanton Macdonald-Wright, founded Synchromism in Paris in 1913. This was a movement that was a rival to Delaunay's Orphism, and though their theories were more advanced, their paintings were not so very different from Delaunay's. Signed. 39 in. by 25 in.
London £31,500 ($88,200).
From the collection of Dr and Mrs H. V. Evatt, Sydney.

PABLO PICASSO
Verre, Bouquet, Guitare, Bouteille.
Signed and dated '19. 39½ in. by 32 in.
New York $117,500 (£41,960).
From the collection of Mr and Mrs Walter Ross, New York

DIEGO RIVERA
Portrait of Ilya Ehrenburg
Signed and dated 1915. $43\frac{3}{4}$ in. by $35\frac{1}{4}$ in.
In his diary Ehrenburg recalls, 'I also posed for Rivera. He told me to read or write, but asked me to sit on a mat. The portrait is cubistic, but, in spite of this, has a great likeness.'
New York $21,000 (£7,490).

ALBERTO GIACOMETTI
Diego Assis.
Signed and dated '49. 32 in. by $21\frac{3}{4}$ in.
London £11,000 ($30,800).
From the collection of Mr and Mrs Charles Zadok, New York.

30 twentieth-century paintings, watercolours and sculptures from the collection of Mr and Mrs Charles Zadok, of New York, were sold in London in June 1965 for £232,010 ($649,628)

EDGAR DEGAS
Cheval Gallopant sur son Pied Droit.
Bronze, signed. Length 18½ in, height 12¼ in.
London £8,750 ($24,500).

MARINO MARINI
Cavallo e Cavaliere.
Bronze, stamped with the initials and numbered 1/5.
Executed *circa* 1946–7. Height 35 in.
London £7,200 ($20,160).
From the collection of Mr and Mrs Charles Zadok, New York.

GASTON LACHAISE
Jumping Dolphins.
Bronze. Signed and dated 1924. Height 18 in., length 42 in.
New York $14,000 (£5,000).

AUGUSTE RODIN
Mouvement de Danse A.
Bronze, signed. Height 12½ in.
London £2,200 ($6,160).
From the collection of Lt.-Col. R. B. Gardner.

HENRI MATISSE
Le Serf.
Bronze. Signed and numbered 9.
Executed *circa* 1900–3. Height 36 in.
New York $29,000 (£10,355).

JEAN ARP
Evocation d'une Forme Humaine, Lunaire Spectrale.
White marble. Executed in 1950. Height 33 in.
New York $26,000 (£9,285).
From the Dotremont Collection.

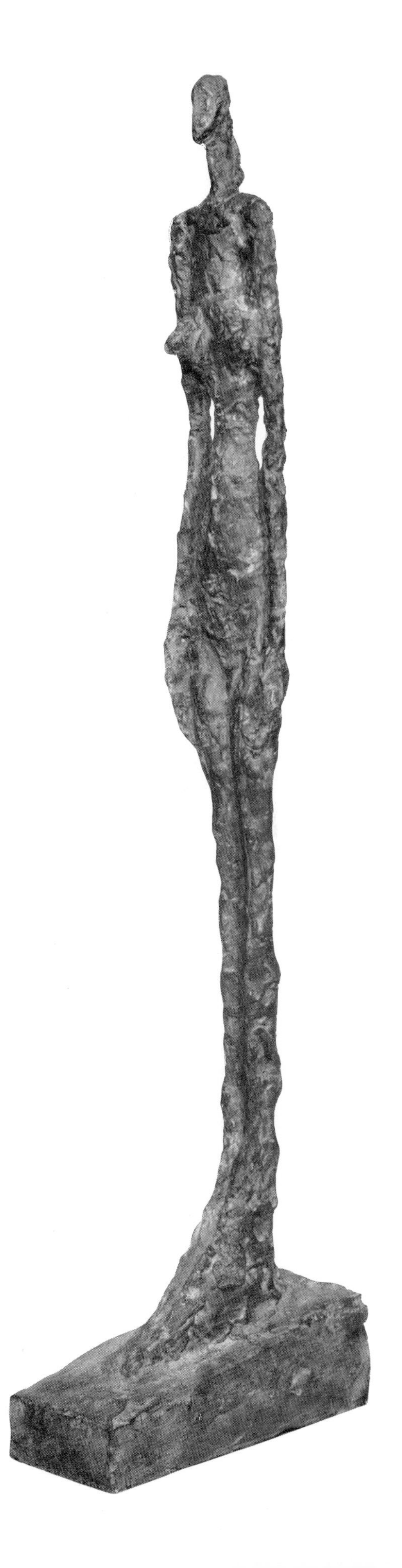

JULIO GONZALES
Tête de Montserrat II.
Bronze, signed, stamped with the founder's mark and numbered 2/6. Executed in 1942. Height 13 in.
London £4,800 ($13,440).
From the collection of Mr and Mrs Charles Zadok, New York.

ALBERTO GIACOMETTI
La Demoiselle de Venise V.
Bronze, signed and numbered 4/6. Executed in 1956. Height 44 in.
London £8,500 ($23,800).

KEES VAN DONGEN
Le Coquelicot.
Signed. Painted *circa* 1925. 21½ in. by 18 in.
London £14,000 ($39,200).

MARC CHAGALL
La Madone du Village.
Signed and dated 1938–42. 40 in. by 39 in.
New York $82,500 (£29,460).

RAOUL DUFY
Régatte à Cowes.
Signed and dated, Cowes 1929. 52 in. by 64 in.
London £25,000 ($70,000).
From the collection of Mr and Mrs Charles Zadok, New York.

MAURICE DE VLAMINCK
Nature Morte.
Signed. Painted *circa* 1908–9. 28 in. by $35\frac{1}{2}$ in.
London £10,500 ($29,400).
From the collection of Mr and Mrs Stefan Osusky, Washington D.C.

PAUL KLEE
Abfahrt der Schiffe (*Departure of the Ships*).
Signed and dated 1927. 20 in. by $25\frac{3}{4}$ in.
London £22,000 ($61,600).
From the collection of Mr and Mrs Edward M. M. Warburg, New York.

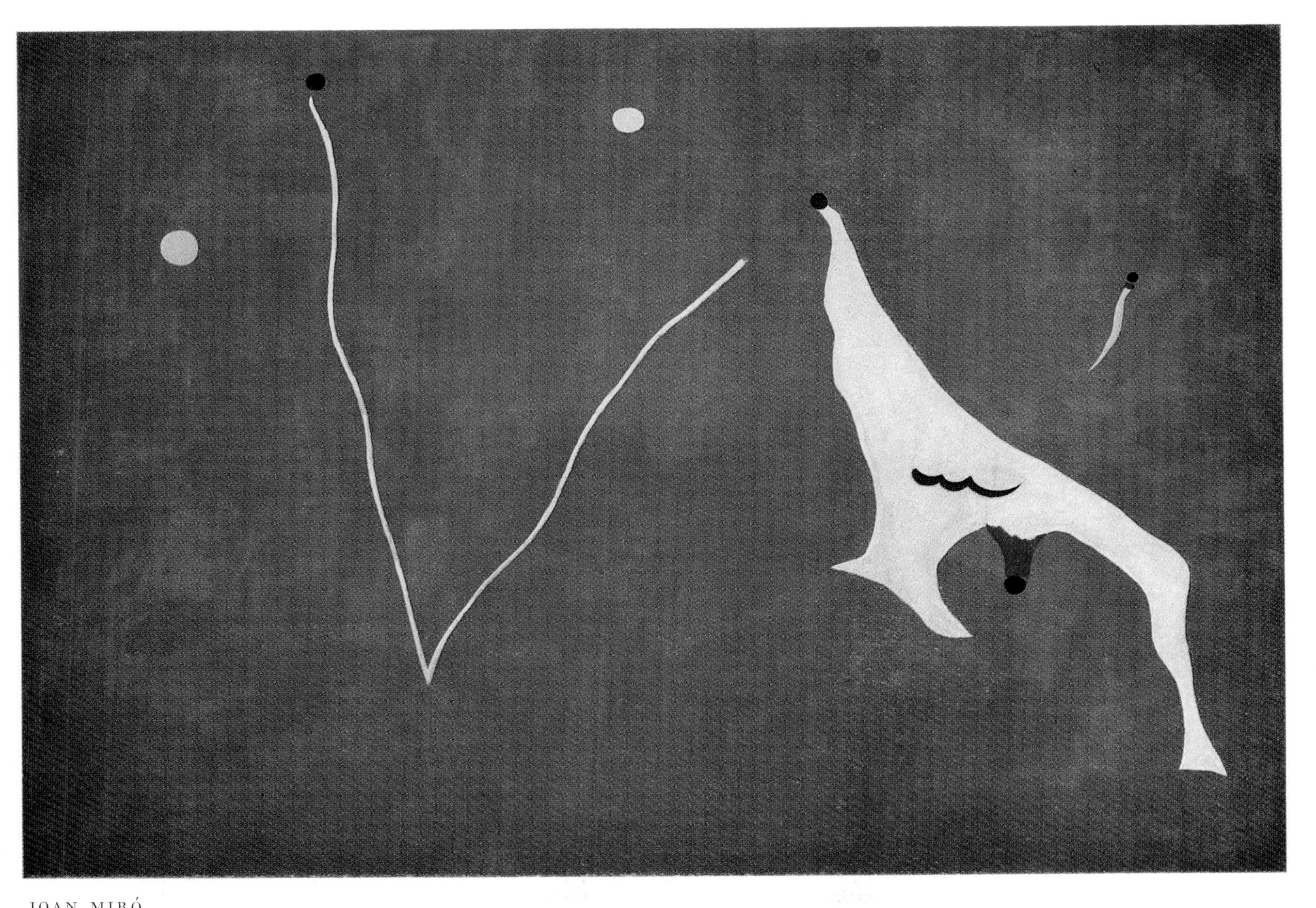

JOAN MIRÓ
Cheval du Cirque.
Signed and dated 1927. 76½ in. by 110¼ in.
New York $57,500 (£20,530).
From the Dotremont Collection.

JACKSON POLLOCK
Blue Unconscious.
Signed and dated '46. 86 in. by 56 in.
New York $44,000 (£15,710).
From the Dotremont Collection.

43 contemporary paintings and sculptures, mobiles and collages, from the Dotremont Collection, were sold in New York in April 1965 for $510,000 (£182,120).

PIET MONDRIAN
Composition with Great Blue Plane, and Red and Yellow.
Signed and dated '21. 23½ in. by 19¼ in.
New York $42,000 (£15,000).
From the collections of S. B. Slijper and the late Ira Haupt, New York.

The collection of 40 twentieth-century paintings formed by the late Ira Haupt, of New York, was sold in January 1965 for $437,750 (£156,320).

JACQUES VILLON
Chantilly, Promenade des Chevaux.
Signed and dated '50. 20 in. by 58 in.
London £11,500 ($32,200).
From the collection of Mr and Mrs Charles Zadok, New York.

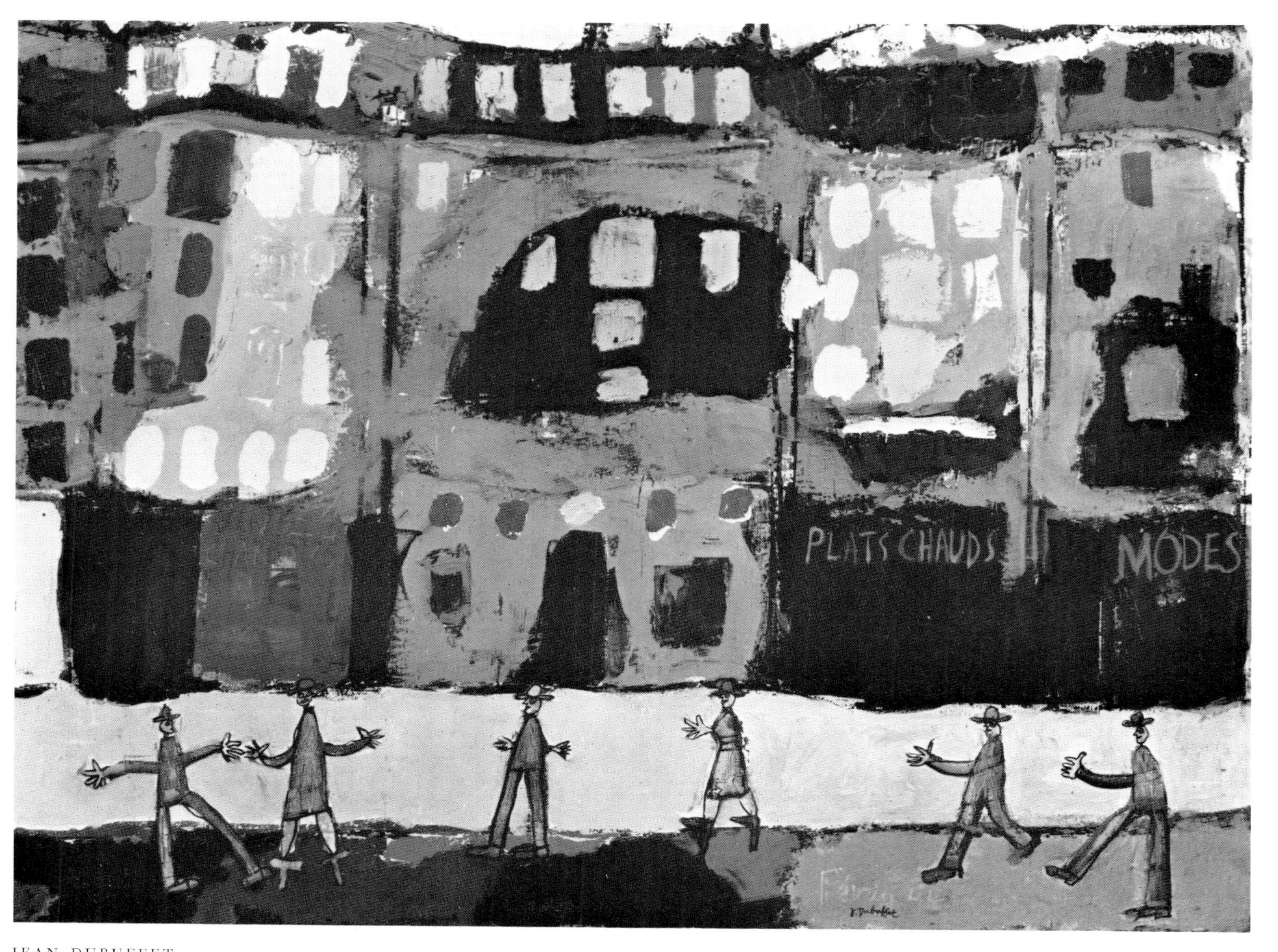

JEAN DUBUFFET
Vue de Paris aux Piétons Furtifs.
Signed and dated Février '44. 35 in. by 44½ in.
London £9,500 ($26,000).
From the collection of Mr and Mrs Charles Zadok, New York.

WILLEM DE KOONING
Merritt Parkway.
Signed. Painted in 1959. 80 in. by 70½ in.
New York $40,000 (£14,280).
From the collection of the late Ira Haupt, New York.

ROBERT RAUSCHENBERG
Summer Storm.
Combine-painting. Signed and dated 1959. $78\frac{1}{2}$ in. by $62\frac{3}{4}$ in.
New York $13,000 (£4,630).
From the collection of the late Ira Haupt, New York.

ADOLPH GOTTLIEB
Crimson Spinning No. 1.
Signed and dated 1959. 88 in. by 71 in.
New York \$12,000 (£4,285).
From the Dotremont Collection.

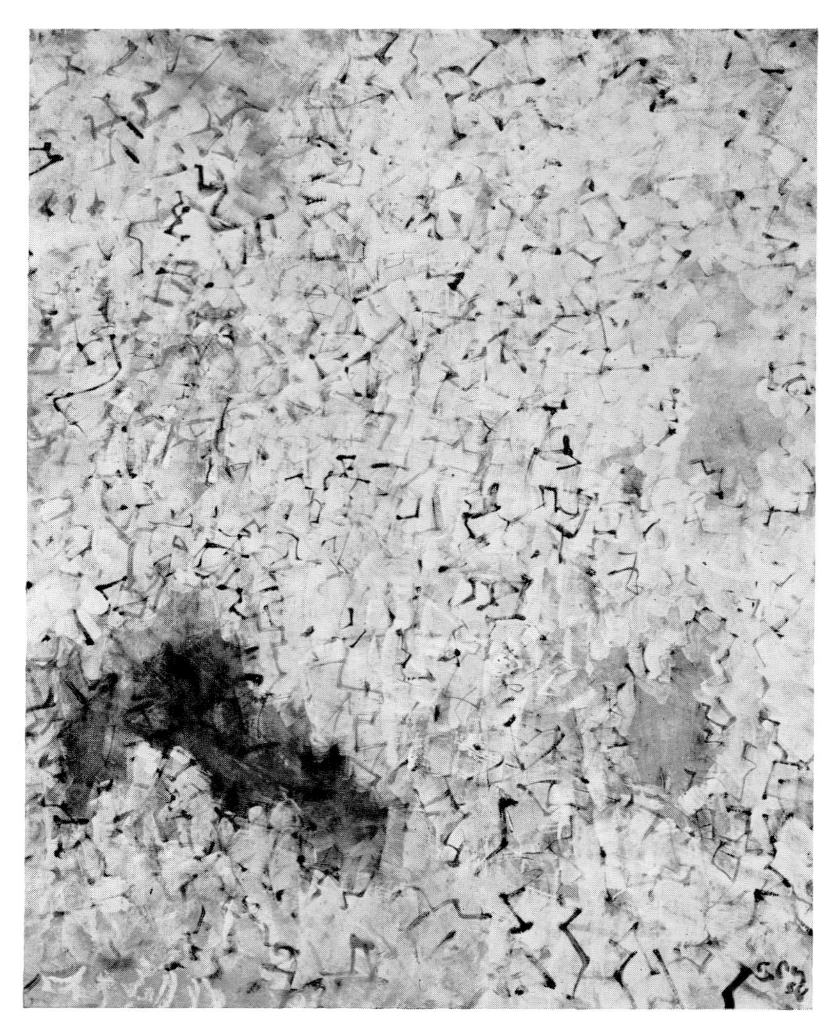

MARK TOBEY
Above the Earth VI.
Tempera on paper. Signed and dated '58. $44\frac{1}{4}$ in. by $34\frac{3}{4}$ in.
New York \$10,500 (£3,750).
From the collection of the late Ira Haupt, New York.

PHILIP GUSTON
Urn.
Signed, and dated 1957. 68 in. by $60\frac{1}{2}$ in.
New York \$10,000 (£3,570).
From the Dotremont Collection.

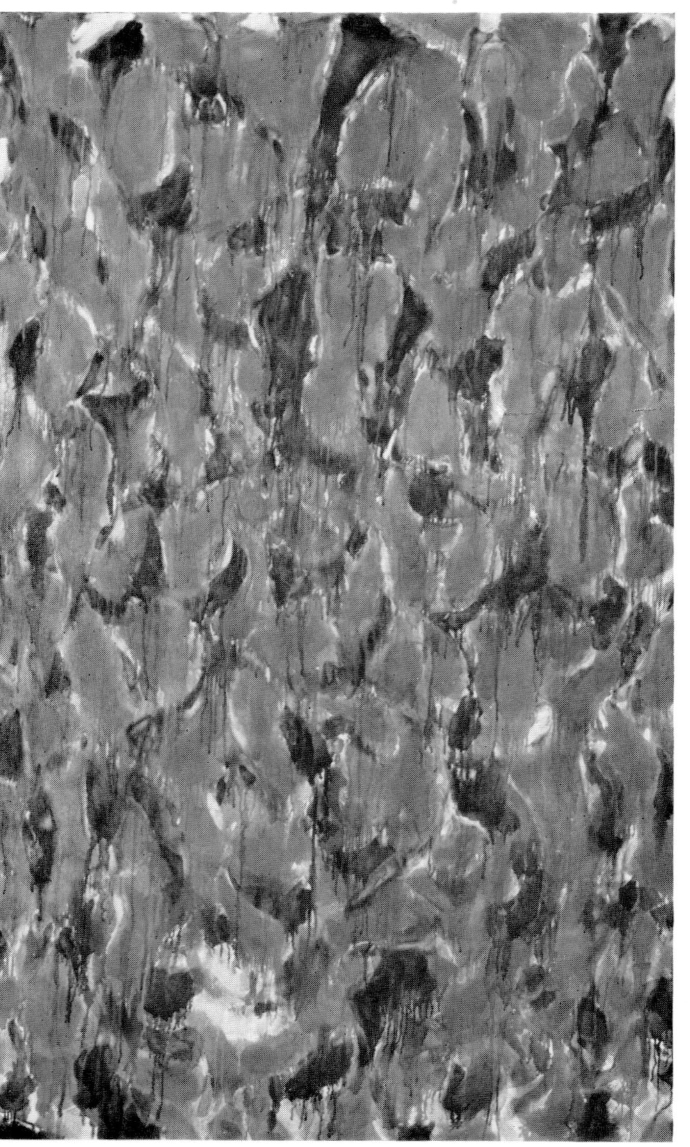

SAM FRANCIS
Red No. 2.
Signed. Painted in 1954. 76 in. by 45 in.
New York \$16,500 (£5,890).
From the collection of Mr and Mrs Walter Ross, New York.

SIR WINSTON CHURCHILL
Menaggio, Lake Como.
This was painted in Italy after the General Election of 1945 and given to the previous owner by Sir Winston in March 1946.
Signed with his initials. 19½ in. by 29 in.
London £14,000 ($39,200).
From the collection of Mr G. C. Mason.

SIR ALFRED MUNNINGS
On the Downs at Epsom.
Signed 29½ in. by 35½ in.
London £10,200 ($28,560).
From the collection of the late Hubert Moss, Esq.

JAMES ABBOTT McNEILL WHISTLER
Design for a Mosaic.
This drawing, sometimes known as the Gold Girl, was the preliminary study for a scheme of decoration for the Central Gallery in the South Kensington Museum which Sir Henry Cole had asked Whistler to do in 1873. A cartoon was prepared but the commission never completed.
Pastel, signed with the butterfly device. $10\frac{1}{2}$ in. by $6\frac{1}{2}$ in.
London £2,600 ($7,280).
From the collection of the late the Hon. Mrs David Fellowes.

SIR WILLIAM COLDSTREAM
Portrait of W. H. Auden.
Painted in 1937. 36 in. by 28 in.
London £650 ($1,820).
From the collection of the late
Mrs Evelyn Besterman.

WALTER RICHARD SICKERT
The Piazzetta and St. Mark's, Venice.
Pencil, black chalk and
watercolour.
Signed and inscribed.
Executed *circa* 1903.
12 in. by 15¼ in.
London £520 ($1,456).
From the collection of
Barry Sainsbury, Esq.

HENRY MOORE
Draped Figure against a Wall.
Bronze. Executed in 1957. Width $15\frac{3}{4}$ in.
New York $11,000 (£3,930).
From the collection of Mr and Mrs Walter Ross, New York.

WILLIAM DOBELL
The Guitar Player, 1944.
Signed, on board. 12 in. by $8\frac{1}{2}$ in.
London £1,000 ($2,800).
From the collections of Dr Eugene Ormandy and Mrs R. Coleman, New York.

HENRY MOORE
Madonna and Child.
Bronze. Height $5\frac{1}{2}$ in.
Executed in 1943 and one of an edition of seven.
London £1,900 ($5,320).
From the collection of J. M. Richards, Esq.

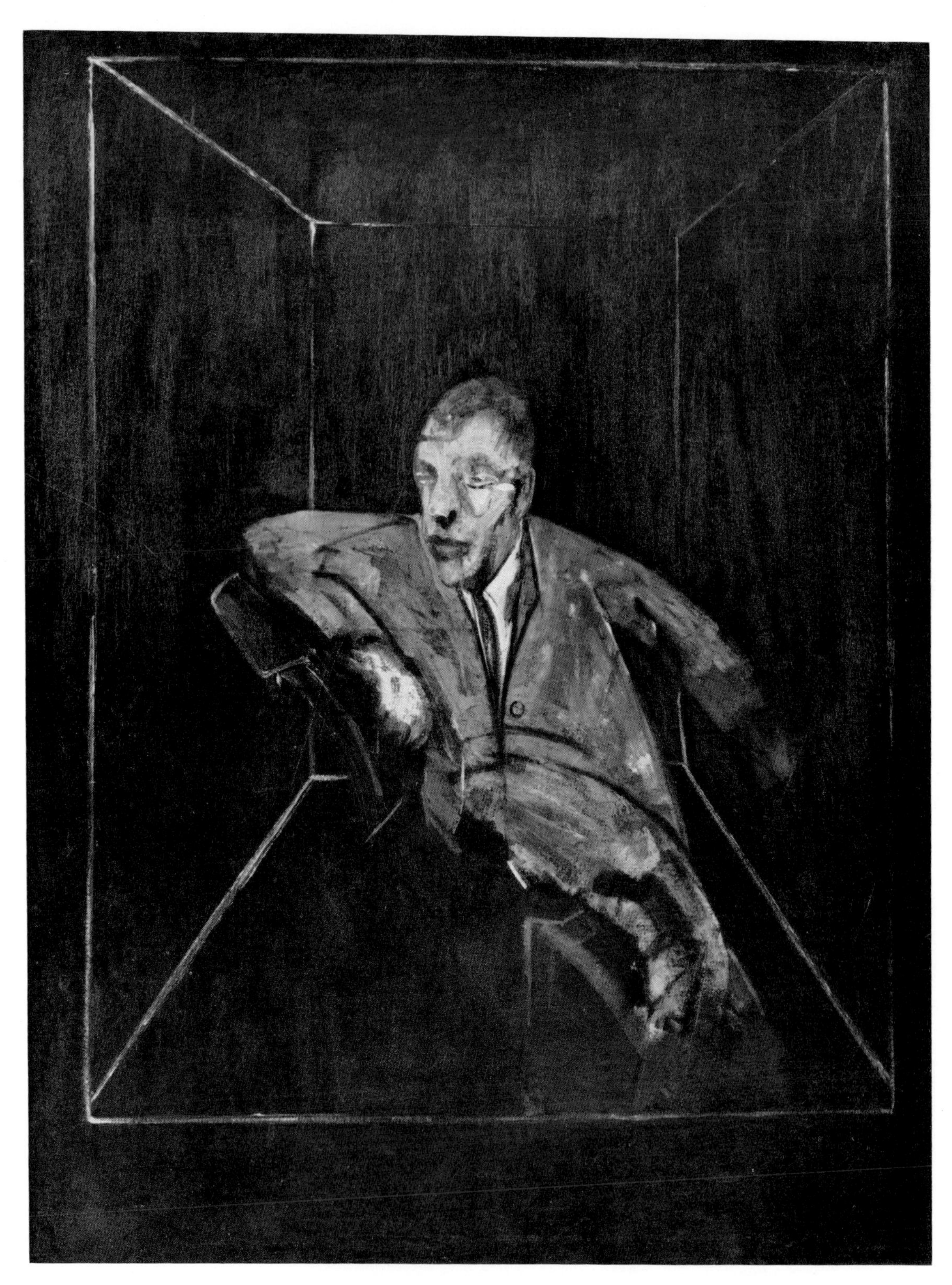

FRANCIS BACON
Study for Figure V.
Painted in 1956–7. $59\frac{1}{2}$ in. by $46\frac{1}{2}$ in.
London £4,200 ($11,760).

BEN NICHOLSON
April 1957.
Mixed media on masonite. 48 in. by 41½ in.
New York $14,000 (£5,000).
From the collection of Mr and Mrs Walter Ross, New York.

MICHELANGELO BUONAROTTI
Ascanius Pulling Aeneas away from Dido's Bed.
Black chalk. $3\frac{3}{4}$ in. by $2\frac{7}{8}$ in.
London £12,500 ($35,000).
From the collection of Dr and Mrs Victor Bloch.

GIOVANNI DE'VECCHI DA BORGO S. SEPOL
St John the Evangelist.
Pen and ink and grey washes, heightened with white, over black chalk. $10\frac{1}{2}$ in. by 10 in.
London £480 ($1,344).
Formerly in the collections of Thomas Hudson, Sir Joshua Reynolds, and Samuel Rogers.

The collection of Old Master drawings formed by Dr and Mrs Victor Bloch was sold in 1964–5 for £68,850 ($192,780).

CORREGGIO
Study of Christ.
Red chalk. 6¼ in. by 5¼ in.
London £3,500 ($9,800).
From the collections of
Jonathan Richardson, senr., and
Lord David Cecil.

CIRCLE OF ANDREA MANTEGNA
Sheet of Studies.
Pen and ink. 7½ in. by 9½ in.
London £2,400 ($6,720).
From the collection of E. A. Wrangham, Esq.

GIAN LORENZO BERNINI
Two Angels Holding a Globe.
Pen and ink and wash over black chalk.
$9\frac{1}{2}$ in. by $5\frac{3}{4}$ in.
London £740 ($2,070)

Below AGOSTINO CARRACCI
Sheet of Studies.
Pen and ink, on buff paper. $8\frac{3}{4}$ in. by $15\frac{3}{4}$ in.
London £700 ($1,960).
From the collections of Richard Cosway and
E. A. Wrangham, Esq.

GIOVANNI BATTISTA TIEPOLO
The Annunciation.
Pen and ink and brown wash.
$10\frac{1}{4}$ in. by $6\frac{3}{4}$ in.
London £3,800 ($10,640).
From the collection of the late
Tomas Harris, Esq.

Below DUTCH SCHOOL, 18th Century
Design for a State Gondola.
Pen and ink and brown wash,
over black chalk.
$11\frac{1}{4}$ in. by $20\frac{3}{4}$ in.
London £280 ($740).

PETER PAUL RUBENS
Samson.
This is one of the earliest known drawings by Rubens and is after the woodcut by Tobias Stimmer.
Pen and ink. $6\frac{1}{4}$ in. by 5 in.
London £1,100 ($3,080).

REMBRANDT VAN RIJN
A Cottage Beside a Canal.
Black chalk. $4\frac{3}{4}$ in. by $7\frac{7}{8}$ in.
London £1,250 ($3,500)

Above JACQUES DE GHEYN II
A Horse.
Pen and ink, on buff paper. 8 in. by 9¼in.
London £1,500 ($4,200).
From the collection of F. A. Driver, Esq.

Below NICOLAES MAES
A View of Dordrecht.
Pen and ink and grey and brown washes. 7⅜ in. by 10½ in.
London £1,850 ($5,180).

CLAUDE MELLAN
Portrait of the Cardinal de Richelieu.
Black chalk. 6 in. by $4\frac{3}{4}$ in.
London £1,500 ($4,200).
From the collections of Captain E. G. Spencer Churchill, Jules Strauss and Mr Claude Sorbac.

Below CHARLES-JOSEPH NATOIRE
The Villa D'Este at Tivoli.
Pen and ink and watercolour, over red and black chalk. $12\frac{1}{4}$ in. by $18\frac{3}{4}$ in.
One of a series of landscape drawings made by Natoire between 1756 and 1776 while he was Director of the Académie de France, Rome.
London £900 ($2,520).

ROSALBA CARRIERA
Portrait of George,
First Marquess Townshend.
Pastel. 22½ in. by 17½ in.
London £1,300 ($3,640).

Below MARCO RICCI
Landscape.
Gouache (one of a pair). 12 in. by 18 in.
London £1,300 ($3,640).

FLORENTINE SCHOOL *circa* 1470
The Bear-Hunt.
Engraving. 11½ in. by 8 in.
London £1,900 ($5,320).
From the collections of Sir Mark Masterman Sykes, sold at Sotheby's in May 1824 for £21 ($59), and Miss Olive Lloyd-Baker, C.B.E., J.P.

Barwick Baker

A Glimpse of Victorian Enthusiasm

BY ADRIAN EELES

On 29 June Sotheby's sold a collection of old master engravings formed in the first part of the 19th century by Thomas Barwick Lloyd Baker. A collection of such unusual quality, intelligently formed by a remarkable man, deserves some comment.

Barwick Baker (as he was always called) was born in 1807 and died in 1886. He was a man of great energy and enthusiasm. His activities, so diversely directed and so diligently pursued, were those of a typical Victorian in the best sense. He was a gentleman of leisure, certainly, but there was hardly a moment of his day, or a day of his life, that was not devoted to those suffering misfortune or to the edification of his own mind. He would probably like to be remembered for his work in connection with social reform. Juvenile crime – as it was then called – occupied much of his time, and the first successful boys' reformatory was set up on a farm on his estate. He took his magistrate's duties seriously, published papers on the penal system (later collected into one volume entitled *War with Crime*), did much work for vagrancy and originated the Poor Law Conferences. He even toured Europe with the specific intention of observing the progress of social reform in other countries. It was said of him that, having worked for and secured a particular reform, he was quite content to retire from the scene and let others take the credit. It was also said that when his colleagues were faced with some particularly difficult problem they would turn confidently to Barwick Baker and declare: 'This requires the application of so-many Baker-power'. Such were his priorities that, even when out hunting, he would happily give up the chase in order to interrogate tramps that he met on the way-side.

Private interests included collecting fossils and shells, stuffing birds (an art which he had learnt from Gould, the well-known ornithological artist), and the founding of the Cotteswold [*sic*] Naturalist Field Club. He was also connected with Henry Elwes in a study of trees and planted a small arboretum in the grounds of his house.

In addition he formed a very distinguished collection of engravings. The object was to illustrate the development of the art from its first beginnings until his own day, and thus the collection ranged from 15th-century metal-cuts to 19th-century engravings by Raphael Morghen. There were about two hundred items in the collection. It started with very rare German and Italian works dating from 1470 to 1500, when the technique of engraving was still in its infancy; then followed excellent examples by Israhel van Meckenem, Martin Schongauer, The Master M.Z. and Albrecht Dürer, showing an ever improving technique and a widening range of subject-matter. After Dürer's enormous achievement one cannot help regarding other 16th-century engravers' efforts as somewhat falling away, but Barwick Baker obtained creditable examples with his *Adoration of the Magi* by Lucas van Leyden, and a very unusual, almost baroque *Cupid on a Snail-shell* by Hans Leinberger. France was represented by an illustration to the Apocalypse by

Jean Duvet, the goldsmith, and by two strange prints from the School of Fontainebleau. The Italians, less expert and imaginative engravers than their northern counterparts, despite (or because of) prolific output, were represented by Marcantonio and his pupils, in particular a delightful *Rhinocerus* by Aenea Vico. Coming into the 17th century, there were good examples of engraving technique by Hendrik Goltzius, Jan Müller and Count Goudt, to name only a few.

Meanwhile there was the associated art of etching. So far the only notable example in this medium had been a fine *Annunciation* by Federico Barocci (see page 114 above). The advantage of etching was that it allowed for greater linear freedom, but this was not exploited to the full by any artist before Rembrandt. With Rembrandt the art of etching reached its greatest heights, never since attained. Barwick Baker had eleven examples of his work, all good ones and some excellent. The particular mastery of Rembrandt's work was well demonstrated in the portraits, such as of *Ephraim Bonus, the Jewish physician*, landscapes like *The Windmill* and *The Three Trees* (see page 114 below), or New Testament scenes like *The Death of the Virgin* and *Christ preaching* (see page 113 below).

After Rembrandt, as after Dürer, there is the inevitable falling-off. Nevertheless the collection had interesting examples by Jan Lievens, Ferdinand Bol and Van Dyck (his self-portrait). The Italians, now with more originality but still rather indifferent craftsmen, were represented by Pietro Testa, G. B. Castiglione and a few others. The exceptions to this stricture on the Italians are the Tiepolos (not represented in the collection) and Canaletto, of which Barwick Baker had two very good etched views of the Venetian district. The rest of the collection consisted of Dutch genre scenes, some French portrait engravings and one of the first essays in mezzotint, *The Standard-bearer* by Prince Rupert (see page 113 above). Finally there were the early 19th-century works by artists like Raphael Morghen, no doubt competent engravings but, for our taste, sentimental and uninspired.

In some cases the previous owners were known. The Italian prints were mostly from the collections of Sir Mark Masterman Sykes (his sale took place at Sotheby's in 1824), or Giuseppe Storck, a Milanese collector, while the early German prints came from Christian Josi, obviously a friend of Barwick Baker's, who had a sale at Christie's in 1829. Two of the finest 17th-century items had passed through the hands of Pierre Mariette (the great French print dealer of that time) and several were from the collection of a certain Monsieur de Ceteveau. According to one of Barwick Baker's notes, M. de Ceteveau was paymaster-general to the forces of Napoleon, but there is no record of his having had a sale at any time.

Nearly all the prints were collected between 1830 and 1840 and Messrs Molteno & Graves, printsellers in Pall Mall, were his chief source of supply. Most of the bills are still preserved and they now make fascinating reading. To take a few instances: a German dotted print of *St George and the Dragon* (see page 109 centre), purchased in 1837 for 10*s* 6*d*, fetched £320 at auction in 1965. *A Grotesque Letter E*, formed by a seated man, two dogs, a cat and a bird, by the Master E.S. (see page 109 right), purchased in 1834 for £2 12*s* 6*d*, made £1,000. *The Bear Hunt* (Florentine, *circa* 1470) (see page 108), described on the invoice as 'Baldini – Boar Hunt – Very Curious' and priced at 5 gns, fetched £1,900. Rembrandt's *Three Trees*, purchased for 6 gns in 1831, realised £3,000. On the other hand, Marcantonio's *Massacre of the Innocents*, bought for 15 gns, the most that was paid for any print in the collection, was sold for exactly the same sum in 1965. Such are the changes in taste.

All the engravings were mounted on sheets of thin card and Barwick Baker, in his careful hand, added titles, catalogue references and comments. The whole collection was kept in three specially made portfolios. There was a charming manuscript note pasted inside the cover of the first portfolio which read: 'Gentlemen are requested (I need not add Ladies, they are always careful), not to touch the Engravings, but merely to slide the Cardboards to the open leaf of the portfolio, without turning them over – or should they wish to take up a sheet to examine it, *to take it with both hands*.'

This was the collection which, carefully assembled with an eye for the quality of each item, whether important or secondary, is said to have cost Barwick Baker about £600. From 1840 onwards it remained in the library of his house, Hardwicke Court near Gloucester, much cared for by the family, but otherwise virtually unknown. One hundred and twenty-five years later it emerged in the saleroom and realized £33,120.

MARTIN SCHONGAUER
St John the Baptist.
Engraving. $6\frac{1}{4}$ in. by $4\frac{1}{2}$ in.
London £1,100 ($3,080).

From the collection of Miss Olive Lloyd-Baker, C.B.E., J.P.

Above THE MASTER E.S.
The Grotesque Letter E.
Engraving. $5\frac{1}{2}$ in by $3\frac{1}{4}$ in.
London £1,000 ($2,800).

Centre GERMAN SCHOOL, 1470–1500
St George Slaying the Dragon.
Metal-cut in the '*manière criblée*'. $1\frac{3}{4}$ in. by $1\frac{1}{3}$ in.
This print is the only recorded impression.
London £320 ($896).

ITALIAN SCHOOL, 15TH CENTURY
Chavalier VI
Engraving. $7\frac{1}{4}$ in. by 4 in.
London £600 ($1,680).
From the collection of the late Tomàs Harris, Esq.

After PIETER BRUEGHEL THE ELDER
A Man-of-War in Full Sail with the Fall of Icarus.
Engraving, by Frans Huys, first state. $8\frac{1}{2}$ in. by $11\frac{1}{2}$ i
London £220 ($616).

JACOPO DE' BARBARI
Mars and Venus
Engraving. 10½ in. by 6¾ in.
London £1,300 ($3,640).

FRANZ CRABBE
The Adoration of the Shepherds.
Engraving. $9\frac{1}{2}$ in. by 7 in.
London £1,400 ($3,920).

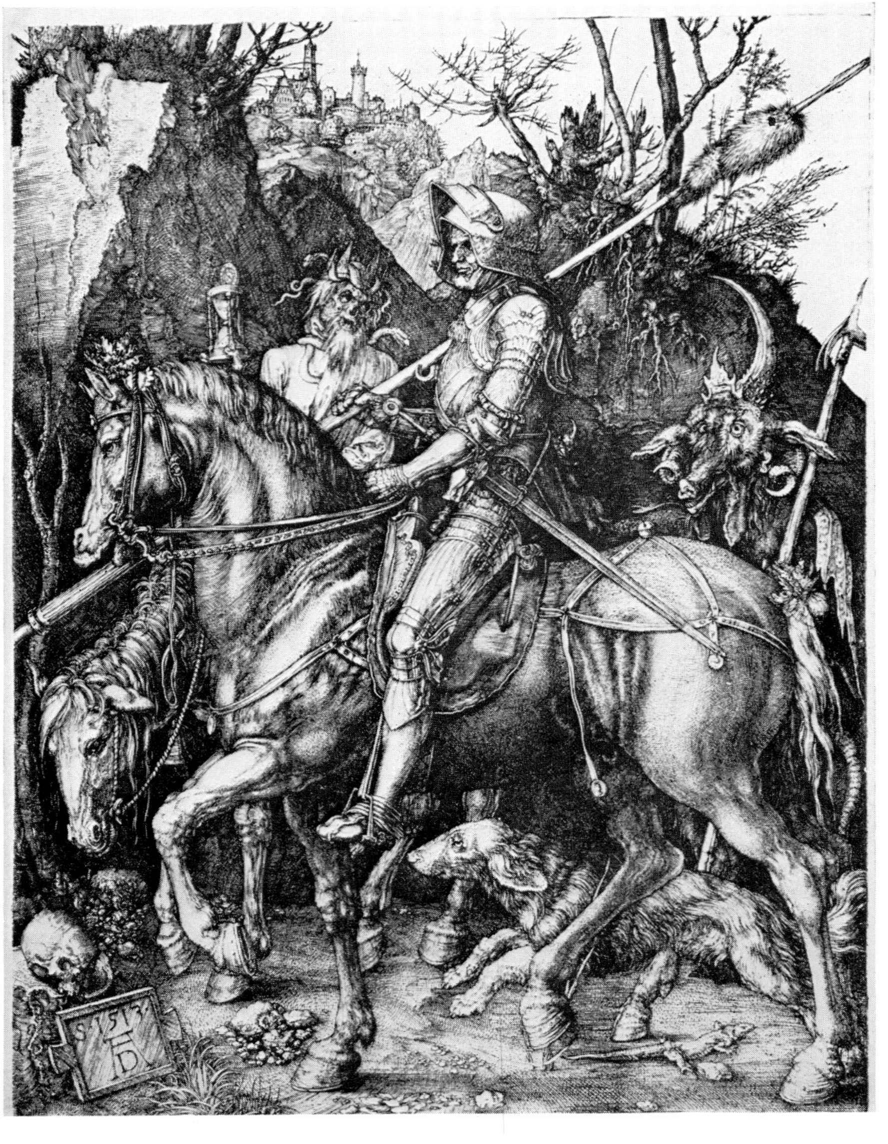

ALBRECHT DÜRER
The Knight, Death and the Devil.
Engraving. $9\frac{2}{3}$ in. by $7\frac{1}{2}$ in.
London £2,600 ($7,280).
From the collection of the late Louis H. Silver, Chicago.

ALBRECHT DÜRER
Adam and Eve.
Engraving. $9\frac{3}{4}$ in. by $7\frac{1}{2}$ in.
London £3,500 ($9,800).
From the collections of Baron Edmond de Rothschild
and the late Louis H. Silver, Chicago.

ALBRECHT DÜRER
The Coat-of-Arms with a Skull.
Engraving. $8\frac{2}{3}$ in. by $6\frac{1}{4}$ in.
London £1,200 ($3,360)
From the collection of Miss Olive Lloyd-Baker, C.B.E., J.P.

PRINCE RUPERT
The Standard-Bearer, after Giorgione.
Mezzotint, first state. 11 in. by 8 in.
London £900 ($2,520).
From the collection of
Miss Olive Lloyd-Baker, C.B.E., J.P.

Below REMBRANDT HARMENSZ VAN RIJN
Christ Preaching, or La Petite Tombe.
Etching, only state. $15\frac{1}{8}$ in. by $8\frac{1}{8}$ in.
London £2,500 ($7,000).
From the collection of
Miss Olive Lloyd-Baker, C.B.E., J.P.

FEDERIGO BAROCCI
The Annunciation.
Etching. $17\frac{1}{4}$ in. by $12\frac{1}{2}$ in.
London £650 ($1,820).
From the collection of
Miss Olive Lloyd-Baker, C.B.E., J.P.

Below REMBRANDT HARMENSZ VAN RIJN
The Three Trees.
Etching, only state, $8\frac{1}{2}$ in. by 11 in.
London £3,000 ($8,400).
From the collection of
Miss Olive Lloyd-Baker, C.B.E., J.P.

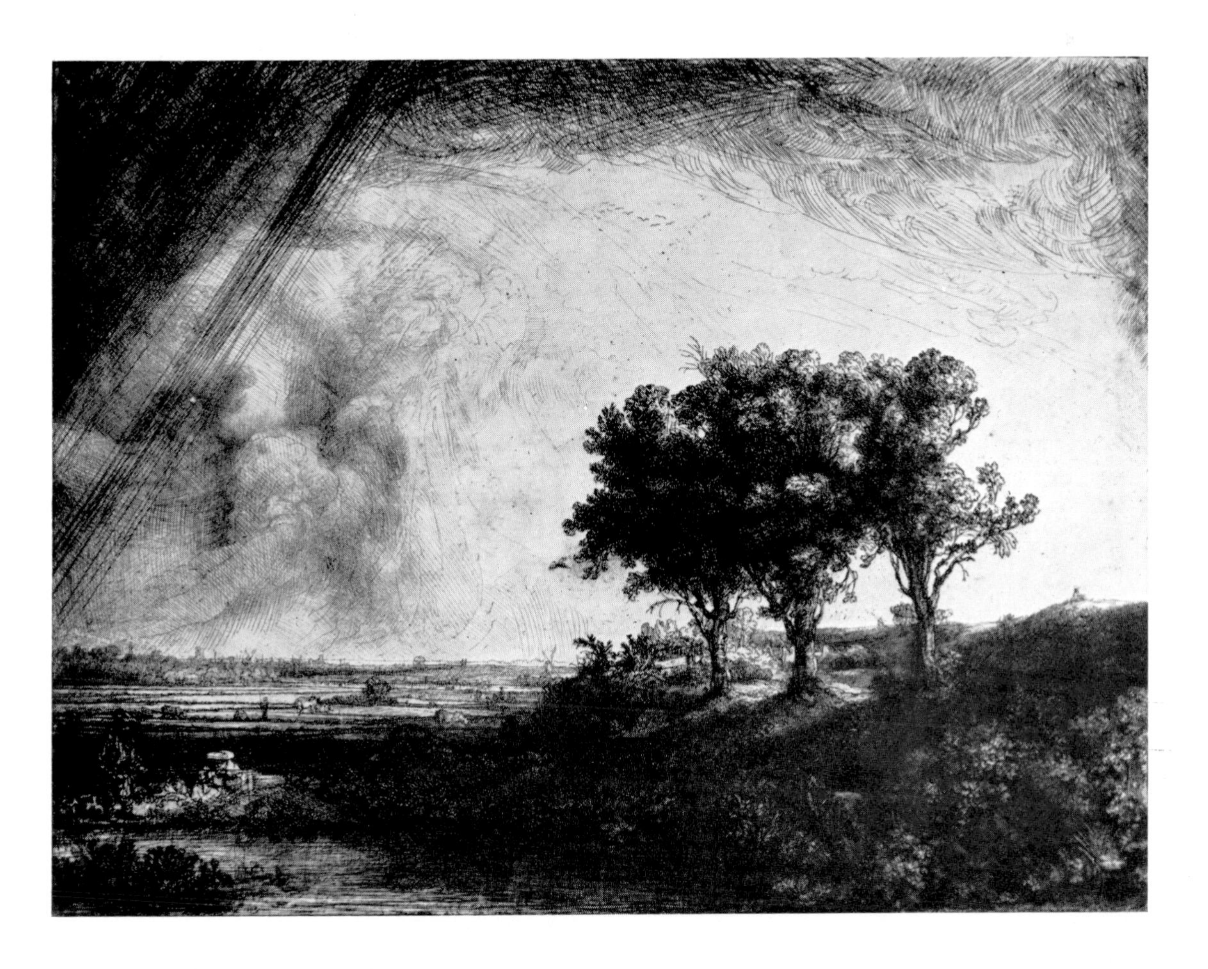

A View of St Dunstans, Fleet Street, one of twenty-six coloured lithographs, by Thomas Shotter Boys, from *London As It Is*, published by Boys in 1842.
London £1,600 ($4,480).
From the collection of G. C. Wyndham, Esq.

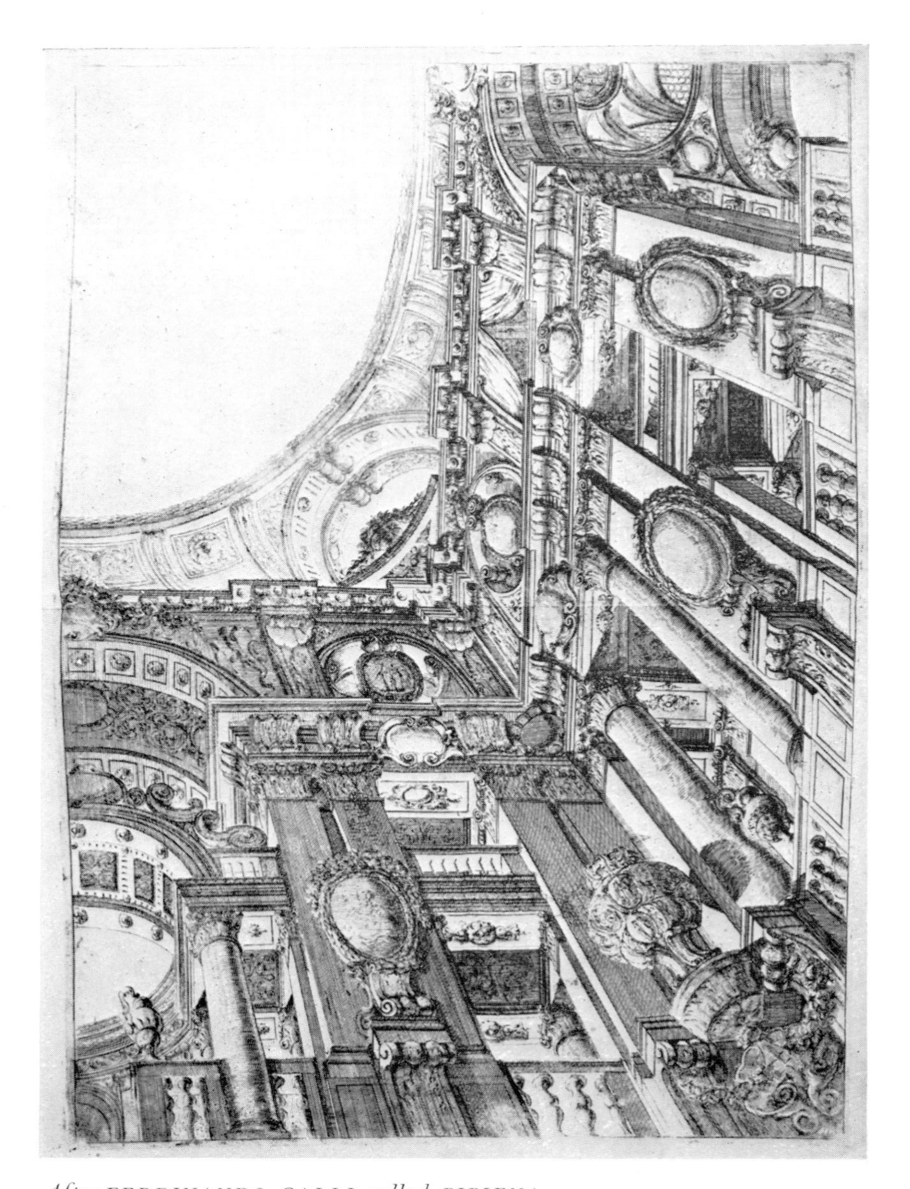

After FERDINANDO GALLI *called* BIBIENA
One of the plates from *Varie Opere di Prospettiva Inventate de Ferdinando Galli.*
Etching, folio.
London £650 (($1,540).

G. B. PIRANESI
One of the plates from the *Carceri*. First state.
London £3,400 ($9,520).

JOHN JAMES LAFOREST AUDUBON
Snowy Owl.
Coloured aquatint, by R. Havell, published 1831.
35 in. by $22\frac{2}{3}$ in.
London £360 ($1,008).
From the collection of Mrs E. D. Strover.

ODILON REDON
Arbre.
Lithograph, one of twenty-five examples on Chine appliqué. 19 in. by $12\frac{1}{2}$ in.
London £660 ($1,840).

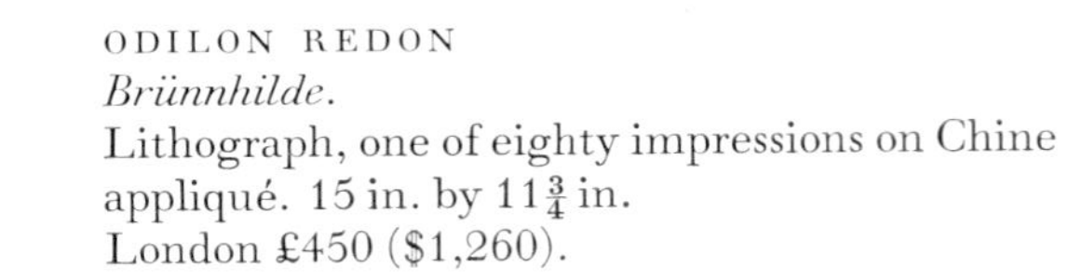

ODILON REDON
Brünnhilde.
Lithograph, one of eighty impressions on Chine appliqué. 15 in. by $11\frac{3}{4}$ in.
London £450 ($1,260).

PAUL GAUGUIN
Idole Tahitienne.
Coloured woodcut, one of four copies. 6 in. by $4\frac{1}{2}$ in.
New York $1,900 (£680)

PIERRE-AUGUSTE RENOIR
Le Chapeau Epinglé.
Lithograph, rare proof of the coloured edition, before the published edition. 24 in. by $19\frac{3}{4}$ in.
New York $3,200 (£1,140)

A collection of first editions of Newton's work.
London £1,848 ($5,175).
From the collection of Professor E. N. da C. Andrade, F.R.S.

The Libraries of Newton, Hooke and Boyle

BY H. A. FEISENBERGER

The collecting of early scientific books has assumed almost frenzied proportions to-day, as recent sale-room prices have proved: see, for instance, the sale of the fine library collected by Professor E. N. da C. Andrade, FRS, sold at Sotheby's on July 19–20, 1965. Most of the books presumably find their final resting place in public institutions, though there are a few keen and shrewd scientists, particularly in America, who form collections, either iu general terms or on their particular subjects. How did their predecessors fare in this respect? They, of course, formed their libraries at a time when books were easy to find – and cheap. But what did they select for their particular reading? For example, what did the libraries of the three greatest scientists of the 17th century, Sir Isaac Newton, Robert Hooke and Robert Boyle, look like?

Fortunately in the case of Newton, the history of his books is now fairly clear, thanks to the devoted labours of Colonel R. de Villamil,[1] but it is a sad reflection on our attitude to our great intellectual leaders that this library of the greatest English scientist, whose work changed the world for hundreds of years, was not taken care of, was, in fact, forgotten and at times entirely neglected.

Newton died intestate in 1727, but an inventory of his possessions was unearthed by Colonel de Villamil at Somerset House. It mentions the library: '362 books in folio, 477 in quarto, 1,057 in octavo, 12mo and 24mo, together with above one hundredweight of pamphlets and waste books'; a total of 1,896 volumes, valued at £270, to which must be added personal manuscripts valued at £250. We are concerned here only with the books.

A neighbour of Newton's, John Huggins, Warden of the Fleet Prison, came round immediately and bought books to the value of £300; but we now know that he did not obtain all Newton's books. His receipt and a list of those he bought, dated 20 July, 1727, are in the British Museum.[2] He sent the books to his son Charles, Rector of Chinnor, near Oxford. Charles Huggins placed his bookplate in all of them (see fig i); they show his arms and his name, 'Revd. Carol Huggins, Rector of Chinner (sic) in Com. Oxon.' When he died in 1750 the living was presented by his brother William (who had inherited the patronage from his father) to his friend and, later, son-in-law, The Rev. Dr James Musgrave, LL.D., who purchased the Newton library from the estate of Charles Huggins for the sum of £400. He in his turn placed his own bookplate over that of Huggins. It is composed of the Musgrave arms, dexter, and the Huggins arms, sinister, surmounted by the Musgrave crest and the motto 'Philosophemur', and it was engraved by B. Green (1736–1800) (see fig. ii). All the books were now catalogued and pressmarks written in ink on the bookplate; the catalogue is still in existence and has been printed by Colonel de Villamil. After Musgrave's death in 1778, his son, who became the eighth Baron Musgrave, inherited the library which he moved to his seat at Barnsley Park,

Fig. i.

Fig. ii.

Gloucestershire; some of the books have the pencil-marks 'Barnsley' and a pressmark. Eventually, in 1875 the estate of Barnsley Park descended to Mrs Georgina Wykeham-Musgrave, of Thame Park, and by this time all connection with Newton had been completely forgotten. In 1920 a sale took place at Thame Park, and among the books – sold in lots and bundles by an ignorant auctioneer – there were evidently some of Newton's that had been removed from Barnsley Park. Later their significance was recognised by Mr Zeitlinger of the firm of Sotheran and Co. in London. But in 1927 Colonel de Villamil discovered that there was still a substantial part of Newton's library at Barnsley Park, together with the Musgrave catalogue, 858 volumes, in fact, and it is this collection which, through the generosity of the Pilgrim Trust, was presented to Trinity College, Cambridge, in 1943.

But John Huggins evidently did not get all Newton's books in 1727. Others, with his notes, have turned up, notably annotated copies of the *Principia*, now in Sydney, and the *Opticks*. Of the history of these and some other books we so far know nothing. On 22nd March, 1813, Sotheby's held a sale of 'The Library of the late Mrs Anne Newton, containing the Collection of the Great Sir Isaac Newton, etc.' (1,261 lots, which realised £462 17s). Mrs Newton was evidently the wife of a collateral descendant of Sir Isaac, and the collection contained eleven books described as having Newton's autograph: four on science, three on history, a dictionary, and one each on mythology, theology and geography. The majority of the other books in this sale were published after Newton's death, and it is impossible to know which of the other earlier ones really belonged to him and which had been purchased by other members of the family. Their character is certainly somewhat different from what we would expect after studying the Huggins list. There are three incunables, including a 1491 *Hortus Sanitatis* and Vincent de Beauvais' *Speculum Naturale*, described as *circa* 1470; also one of the philological tracts published by Wynkyn de Worde in 1516. There is little science, but one notices a copy of Hooke's *Micrographia*, 1665 (which sold for £1 13*s*). There is some travel and literature: Dante, Rabelais, Boccaccio, Montaigne, but not many English writers except a second folio Shakespeare, Donne, Burton, Cowley, Otway and Waller. But there are quite a number of novels; and can one see Newton purchasing *The Mysteries of Love and Eloquence, or the Arts of Wooing and Complementing*, 1658 (lot 559), or books on falconry and horsemanship? By what we know of Newton's character and the clear evidence of the Huggins list, many of the books here do not strike one as likely to have belonged to him, and as we have no real evidence as to their ownership it has been thought justifiable to disregard this collection for the purposes of this short article.

In order, therefore, to judge the contents of Newton's library, the only reliable evidence we have – apart from a few books with his notes which have turned up – is the Huggins list and, to a much lesser extent, the Musgrave catalogue. Villamil has printed both of these, but they should be used with some caution for there are a number of misprints in the dates, and the Musgrave list really describes Dr Musgrave's library and contains many books published after Newton's death. Villamil has starred the books in the Musgrave catalogue which, according to him, are also on the Huggins list of 1727, but unfortunately even this is not reliable, as he included among them a number of books published after 1727; but we can, nevertheless, obtain a general idea of Newton's tastes from this material.

Based on an examination of the whole of the books in the 1727 list only – and the picture does not materially change if we include the whole of Dr Musgrave's catalogue – we get the following result (the figures here are approximate): science and medicine, 270; theology, ecclesiastical history, philosophy, 190; classics and post-classics, 95; general literature and chronology, 85; history, 80; voyages, geography, navigation and trade, 70; archaeology, numismatics, etc., 58; philology, 28; topography, 5; literature and poetry, 4; music, 1; cookery, 1. Eighty-one of the books are in French, but there are none in any other living language so this was evidently the only modern foreign language known to Newton.

In considering this situation, the most remarkable feature appears to be the almost complete absence of all works of the imagination; there are few poets represented, Milton, Pope and Prior, Butler's *Hudibras* and Cowley. No Shakespeare or Chaucer or any other of the great poets and dramatists. And only one book on music! An austere mind indeed! This lack of imaginative literature is perhaps not surprising because, when asked his opinion on poetry, Newton replied: 'I'll tell you that of Barrow; he said that poetry was a kind of ingenious nonsense'.

There is a considerable interest in theological matters, socinianism and deism; many books on numismatics – Newton was, of course, Master of the Mint – and chronology, a subject on which he himself wrote. Turning to the most important section, science and medicine, the picture is most surprising. There are over 100 books on alchemy (if one includes the whole Musgrave catalogue) – Newton himself was an experimenter – but very little on pure chemistry, except Boyle. The books by Boyle were probably mostly presented to Newton by the author; Boyle's *Essay on Effluviums*, 1673, inscribed to Newton, was in the Duveen collection, now in the University of Wisconsin (Duveen catalogue, p. 94). No Helmont, Glauber or Mayow, although there is a copy of the 1621 edition of Agricola. But the collection of books on the exact and medical sciences lacks nearly all the great names. There is very little on astronomy, only Flamsteed of the classical writers, and Galilei (a Latin translation of the *Dialogo*, 1699, twelve years after the publication of the *Principia*!) no other Galilei, no Regiomontanus, Ptolemy's *Almagest*, Copernicus, Tycho Brahe, Hevelius, or Kepler. In mathematics and physics there is no Cardanus, Tartaglia, Stevin, Vieta, Pascal, Gilbert or Guericke, and practically nothing on optics. It is also noteworthy that there is none of Hooke's important works, except the two relatively minor posthumous books, but then Newton and Hooke had quarrelled so this is perhaps the reason for their omission. The only great contemporary fairly well represented is Boyle, presumably presentation copies. In medicine, there are really only some minor works, none of the important, epoch-making books, and, curiously enough, in all fields very little by Newton's colleagues in the Royal Society. It should also be said, though it is perhaps less surprising at that period, that practically all the books are contemporary, there is hardly any early book, nothing at all printed in the 15th century and very little in the 16th.

The impression left by this library is that it is certainly the collection of an earnest and dedicated scientific thinker, creating his own mathematical and cosmological system without perhaps wishing to admit his indebtedness to the other great figures of his own or earlier times. There is no concession to pleasure, relaxation or to the pure imagination; it was a man of severe austerity of mind who surrounded himself with these books.

When we turn to Robert Hooke, his contemporary and one of the greatest geniuses the world has ever known, we get a very different picture. Fortunately, we are fairly well informed about his activities as a book-collector. In his Diary, of which the sections covering August 1672 to December 1680 and November 1688 to August 1693 have been published, there are very many references to his purchases of books; and also, after Hooke's death – he died intestate – his library was sold by auction and the catalogue survives (see fig. iii). It has a preface by Richard Smith, the publisher to the Royal Society and a bookseller often mentioned in the Diary, in which he draws attention to the large collection of scientific and travel books and to the fact that many of the books have notes by Hooke.

Hooke was a great book collector. Hardly a day went by without his recording a purchase either at auction or from booksellers, and we continually come across one of his abbreviations – of which the Diary is full – 'MF', which stands for Moorfields, where in those days there were many bookstalls and bookshops. The first entry in the published Diary recording a purchase is of Tradescant's *Collection of Rareties*, 1656, on 5 August, 1672, for sixpence (sold in his auction in 1707 for 2*s*), and the last is on 15 July, 1693: 'pd. 8d. for 12 tracts of music'. He collated the books he purchased, sometimes he returned them for imperfections, and he read them. He inscribed many of them, and two characteristic examples of his signature are shown (figs. A and B).

In his sale there were over 3,000 volumes (some doubtless containing several titles), a

Bibliotheca Hookiana.

SIVE

CATALOGUS

Diversorum Librorum:

VIZ.

MATHEMATIC. PHILOSOPHIC. MEDICORUM, } { PHILOLOGICOR. HIST. NATURAL. NAVIGAT. &c.

Plurimis Facultatibus Linguisque

INSIGNIUM

Quos Doct. R. HOOKE,

Mathem. Professor, & Regal. Societ. Londin. Socius, Magno Sumptu, & Summa Curâ, sibi congessit.

Quorum Auctio habenda est Londini, in Edibus vulgo dictis *Inner Lower-Walk* in *Exeter-Exchange* in the *Strand*, the 29th of *April*, 1703.

Per Edoardum Millington, *Bibliop. Londin.*

Catalogues may be had at *6 d.* each of *R. Smith* at the Angel and Bible without *Temple-Bar*, of Mr. *Yeo* at the General Post-Office at *Charing-Cross*, of Mr. *Hartley* near *Middle-Row, Holbourn*, and of Mr. *Strahan* over-against the *Royal-Exchange*.

Fig. iii.

Ex Lib: R:H:

A

Lib: Rob: Hook

B

very large library for that period. Approximately half were in Latin, about 1,000 in English, 200 in French, 200 in Italian and 20 in Spanish.

As is to be expected, the large majority of his books was scientific and medical. They were a superb collection on those subjects and even in his own time they must have been remarkable. None of the great names is missing and Hooke by no means confined himself to books by his contemporaries; he had many books of the 16th century. There is one incunable only: Albumasar's *Introductio in Astronomiam*, Venice, 1489 (which sold for 1*s*). The two earliest books in the 16th century are: Euclid, *Elements*, 1518(?) – followed by many other editions of this author including both the first Greek, 1533, and the first English, 1570 – and Bartholomaeus Anglicus, Nuremberg, 1519 (sold for 1*s* 9*d*). The first edition of Agricola, *De re metallica*, 1556, is present (bought by Hooke on 2nd January, 1673 for 8*s* from Pitt, the map publisher and bookseller). On 6 February, 1673 he reports: 'saw Copernicus at booksellers', and on 18 February: 'bought Copernicus tower hill 2sh.' The following year, on July 6 he notes: 'received from Mr Aubery [John Aubrey, FRS., the antiquary, 1626–97] Copernicus.' Did Hooke therefore possess two editions of this great book? At any rate, in his sale only the second edition, Basle, 1566, was offered and sold for 1*s*.

His other 16th-century books are, of course, practically all in Latin; only some books by Digges and a *Regimen of Health*, 1575, are in English. But everybody of note in the 16th century is represented: Aristarchus, Ptolemy's *Almagest*, 1528, Regiomontanus, Porta, Cardanus, Oronce Finé, Bassantin, Palissy, Dürer, Bruno, Dee, Agrippa, Fernelius, Paracelsus, Paré, etc., etc.

When we come to the 17th century the collection is as complete as one could possibly wish, beginning with both the works of Gilbert (the *De Magnete*, 1600, sold for 3*s*; its last price at Sotheby's was £1,500 in July 1965). There is a long series of the works of Boyle[3] (but only the second edition of the *Sceptical Chemist*, 1680, not the first), Kepler, Huygens, Galilei (with a copy of the English translation: Salisbury's *Mathematical Collections*, 1661), and Hevelius – including the latter's *Machina Coelestis*, complete in three volumes, which sold for £3 15*s* and was one of the most expensive books in the whole sale (Sotheby's sold a presentation copy in the Signet sale in 1960 for £2,100). Hooke had a copy of Newton's *Principia*, 1687, also highly priced at £2 3*s* 6*d*, but apparently nothing else by Newton. There was a copy of that optical classic – today extremely rare – Grimaldi, *Physico-Mathesis de lumine*, Bologna, 1665, even then rather expensive at £1 5*s*, while Napier's *Logarithms*, 1614, sold for 2*s* (the last copy at Sotheby's for £1,300). He had a copy of Cavalieri with its important contribution to the invention of the calculus, which apparently Newton did not possess. Curiously enough, there is Harvey's *De generatione homini*, 1651 and *De circulatione sanguinis*, 1649, but no *De motu cordis*. There are no less than four different books on the new world in the moon, probably all that had been published on the subject. Of his own publications there was a copy of the *Micrographia*, the

Philosophical Collections, 1674, and his first scientific book, *An Attempt for the Explication of the Phenomena* . . . 1661. He also owned books on stenography and a universal language. But it would be wearisome in this article to go on enumerating titles; all the scientific classics and many minor ones are present, as are, of course, the scientific journals.

Another fine section of the library was devoted to herbals and books on plants, from Brunfels to Hernandez, Ray, Clusius and many others. Hooke was also interested in maps and map-making and he had a splendid series of atlases including an 11 volume Blaeu, a Dutch edition of Waghenaer, 1584, a coloured Saxton (sold for 7*s* 6*d*), Speed, etc. His Jansson's *Atlas*, 1675, at £4 2*s* 6*d* appears to have been the highest priced book in the sale. There are many books on navigation, voyages and rare Americana such as Thevet's *France Antarctique*, 1558 (sold for 1*s*), Sir F. Gorge's *America painted to life*, 1659 (bought in 1673 for 8*d* and sold for 1*s* 6*d*), Hakluyt, Wright, Bond, Moxon, Dampier and several of the Jesuit Relations on Canada. There are quite a number of the classics and a good many books published by the Elzevir Press; also copies of the works of Sir Thomas More and Spinoza.

There is comparatively little theology – usually the largest section in a 17th century library – although there were, of course, a number of Bibles. These included a New Testament in Dutch, a Bible in Irish, and Eliot's Indian New Testament, Cambridge, Mass., 1661 (sold for 3*s*); Hooke also possessed his Indian Grammar, 1666. He was well supplied with dictionaries and grammars in French, Spanish, Portuguese, German, Italian and Arabic. And, of course, the great architect Hooke had a fine collection of architectural books by Palladio, Vitruvius, Serlio, Alberti, Barozzi and others. He had Vasari, Lomazzo and Bellori on the history and theory of art, Leonardo on painting and Gauricus on sculpture. There were several books on music, by Descartes, Butler, etc., and a *Solace on the Citharet*, 1659; also a 1665 *Dancing Master*.

In English literature, unlike the case of Newton's library, the dramatists were well represented, and, on the whole, the poets, and, though there is no copy of Chaucer, there is a Piers Plowman, 1550. There are some novels, and a number of works with intriguing titles such as *Merry Drollery or jovial Poems* and *The Practical part of Love*, 1660. In the French section Hooke had Molière, Corneille, Du Bellay, Rabelais, Marot and the famous *Princesse de Clèves*, 1674, the first of all novels. In Italian, there were Boccaccio, Dante, Petrarch, Aretino, Ariosto, Machiavelli; in Spanish, Cervantes, Lope de Vega, Boscan and Montemayor.

And to help him in his search for books he had some good bibliography: works by Gesner, Beugen, Naudé, the Bodleian catalogues and others. When we come to what I will call, for want of a better phrase, pure collectors' items, there is nothing much to report, though Hooke did possess the French edition of the *Hypnerotomachia*, Paris, 1554, and there is an intriguing entry: 'Caxton (Will.) Collections, 1490', which sold for 1*s* 6*d*.

Hooke's health was bad and he could not indulge much in the pleasures of the table. Nevertheless, he took a great deal of interest in food. He was particularly fond of chocolate which he drank almost daily, so it is not surprising to find Dufour's *Treatise on Coffee, Tea and Chocolate*, as well as the anonymous book, *The Virtue of Chocolate*. He drank little alcohol, again chiefly for medical reasons, but Preafectus's treatise on wine, 1559, and also a cookery book, Hannah Woolley's *Gentlewoman's Companion*, 1675, had places on his shelves.

When in 1891 the Corporation of London acquired the manuscript of the Diary from Moor Hall, Harlow, Essex, they also purchased some printed books. The librarian of the Guildhall Library has very kindly shown me their accession book for this purchase and also a number of the books. There are 74 which fall into Hooke's period: 32 on politics, 16 on theology, 12 on various subjects and four only on medicine and science. With the evidence of the sale catalogue before us, it seems rather unlikely from the emphasis on politics and religion that these were really from Hooke's library. Admittedly, I have only examined a few of the books, but none of them had any inscription or evidence that they belonged to Hooke. Some of the books have the book-plate of George Scott, Woolston Hall, Essex (whose books were sold by auction on 12 March 1781). Of the four medical books, Grew's *Anatomy of Vegetables*, 1672 belonged to Scott, Collins's *Anatomy*, 1687 is the author's presentation copy to Bishop Gilbert Burnet; so neither of these were Hooke's; Mather's *Life of Eliot*, 1691 was Ralph Thoresby's copy.

The possession of such a library illustrates one of Hooke's chief characteristics, i.e. his extreme sociability. Every day of his life he met some of his many friends among whom were numbered Boyle, Wren, Wilkins and John Aubrey. The latter said of him: 'As he is of prodigious inventive head, so is a person of great vertue and goodness'. The theory, for some unknown reason later prevalent, possibly because of his quarrel with Newton, that Hooke was a jealous, mistrustful and cynical recluse could not have been further from the truth. Not only his Diary proves this, but the fact that anyone who collected this remarkable library round him from which he constantly lent books – as we know from the Diary he did – must have been a man of particularly brilliant and open mind. It covers most fields of human thought and gives due place to the poets and great literature and to many of the pleasures and frivolities of life. Hooke was perhaps the most brilliant representative of the passionate desire for the new knowledge and ideas of his century. There was then a daily social exchange of information on all kinds of subjects, not only those of scientific interest, and Hooke was at the centre of it, his splendid library enabling him to take part in discussions of every kind. His collection has an extraordinarily modern look and could well have been assembled – if the books were available – by a twentieth century man of the widest culture and interests. 'He is certainly the greatest mechanick this day in the world . . . . he is a person of great suavity and goodnesse' were John Aubrey's words about him.

Of Robert Boyle's library we know, unfortunately, practically nothing. In his Will of 18 July, 1691, he left his manuscripts and 'collection of receipts' to his favourite sister, Lady Ranelagh, and his cabinet of minerals and stones to the Royal Society. His printed books are only casually mentioned together with his other chattels, and he instructs his three executors to dispose of them by sale. His executors were Lady Ranelagh – she predeceased him by a week on 23 December, 1691, and in a codicil he replaced her by Sir Henry Ashurst, the Treasurer of the Corporation for the Propagation of the Gospel in New England, Richard, Earl of Burlington and John Warre, his secretary.

At first there was a plan to sell the library from Lady Ranelagh's house, as we know from advertisements in the *London Gazette* (no. 2782, 7–11 July, 1692, and again, in a modified form in no. 2783, 11–14 July, 1692).[4] Hooke refers to this in his Diary: 'with J. War [i.e. John Warre] to Boyles house Pall Mall . . . conditions for selling house for Martin' (12 December, 1692, *see* Gunther, *Early Science in Oxford*, X, p. 196), and again: 'Mr Boyles house lett' (5 January, 1693, *ib.*, X, p. 203). But the attempt to sell the books in or with the house seems to have failed, and they were moved to the bookstalls in Moorfields where some were certainly sold. Again Robert Hooke provides evidence for us: 'In MF I saw neer 100 of Mr Boyles high Dutch Chymicall books ly exposed in Moorfields on the railes: also Raung or Dr Pells Algebra [Rahn's *Introduction to Algebra*, 1668] in high Dutch' (21 March, 1693; *ib.* X, p. 223), and 'in MF paid for Rahn Algebra 1s. for 2 other Dutch chymick books 6d.' (22 March, 1693, *ib.* p. 224), and 'in MF saw many of Mr Boyles German chemicall books, also Bechers word-book [J. J. Becher, *Novum organum philologicum*] (23 March, 1693, *ib.* p. 224).[5] But this was not the end of the story, because on 28 March, 1693, Hooke writes: 'Read a catal. of Morgans and Boyles books at Toms.' (*ib.* p. 225/6). Here Hooke refers to an auction sale at Tom's Coffee House on 5 April, 1693. It was the sale of the library of Sylvanus Morgan (1620–93), an arms-painter and author, who had died on 28 March. His library was being disposed of very quickly, and evidently Boyle's executors, perhaps getting rather tired of the long drawn out method of selling Boyle's books, took the opportunity of including the remainder in this sale. Incidentally, Hooke attended the auction but bought nothing, which was rather surprising in view of his close association with Boyle; but perhaps he had already bought what he wanted at Lady Ranelagh's house and in Moorfields. The Catalogue exists (see fig. iv). But the sale catalogue, consisting of 16 pages with 1,087 lots, does not give us any reliable information about Boyle's Library, as no distinction is made between the books of Morgan and those of Boyle. At the end there are two pages headed 'Libri omissi', i.e. books added to the catalogue after the main part was completed, and Dr John Fulton[6] has suggested that these are Boyle's books. While it is true that there are a number of scientific and medical titles on these two pages (Willis, Glisson, Bartholinus, Pecquet, Steno, Sydenham, Newton, Tulpius, Bruno, Ray, Ashmole, Celsus, Schola Salernitana) there are far more in the catalogue as a whole (Harvey, Malpighi, Aldrovandus, Hippocrates. Euclid, Pliny, Briggs, Fludd, Gilbert, Porta, Mersenne, Borelli, Falloppius, Fernelius, Cardanus, Recorde, Culpepper, Wallis, Bacon, Geminus, Galilei, Grew, Digges, Evelyn, Gellibrand, etc., and many more by Willis); therefore Dr Fulton's argument that the majority of the science titles are on these last two pages is not tenable. Of Boyle's own publications there are three entries: *Boyle on Colours*, *The sceptical Chemist*, and *Esquire Boyles Pieces*, all occurring in the main part of the catalogue. Furthermore the title very definitely states – in italics – that it includes the LATIN part of what is Boyle's library, but many of the books on the last two pages are in English.

The library offered in this auction as a whole is a fairly ordinary one and not particularly distinguished except for the presence of the rather large number of medical and scientific titles. The books were mostly history, a few classics, a little theology and law, and, of course, a good deal of heraldry. But Boyle would surely have owned a large collection of theology? He was an influential figure in the Anglican movement of the 17th

Bibliotheca Morganiana:

OR A d. 399.

CATALOGUE

Of the Library of

Mr. Silvanus Morgan.

Containing all the Valuable and Scarce *English* Historians, with a Curious Collection of Books of Heraldry, Genealogies, Antiquities, Medals, Coins, Inscriptions, *&c.* in

GREEK, LATIN and ENGLISH.

To which is added the *Latin* Part of the Library of an Honorable Gentleman, lately deceased, consisting of Divinity, History, Geography, *&c.*

The whole are generally gilt on the back many of them of the Large Paper curiously adorned.

To be sold by Auction at *Tom's* Coffee-house adjoyning to *Ludgate*, on *Wednesday* the 5th. of *April*, 1693.

Conditions of SALE.

1 THE *highest Bidder is the Buyer.*

2 *The Books for ought we know are perfect, if any appear otherwise, the Buyer may take or leave them.*

3 *That every Person be obliged to give in his Name and Place of Abode, paying also 5s. in the Pound for what he buys; and be obliged to take his Books away within 3 days after the Sale is ended.*

Catalogues are distributed at Mr. *Partridges* at *Charing-Cross*; the Coffee houses about the Inns of Court; *Batsons* Coffee-house against the *Exchange*, and at the Place of Sale.

Fig. iv.

century, and as Governor of the Corporation for the Propagation of the Gospel in New England he corresponded much with that devoted missionary to the Indians, John Eliot. Surely, therefore, he would have owned a copy of Eliot's Indian Bible, 1661? Boyle was also responsible for the publication of a Bible in Irish to which he contributed £700. Neither Bible appears in this catalogue. It is obvious that he would have owned many medical and scientific books, but we need to know what other books he had in order to get further insight into the character of this great man, and this catalogue cannot provide us with reliable evidence.

As already mentioned, one of Boyle's executors was his secretary, John Warre. He had been accused by his co-executor the Earl of Burlington of not properly carrying out Boyle's intentions and also, more seriously, of omitting to account for certain moneys he held on behalf of the estate. If there was any truth in these accusations perhaps some of Boyle's books might have found their way into Warre's library. This was sold at Exeter Exchange, Strand, on 15 May, 1717, but again the catalogue gives us no clue. There are a few minor books by Boyle and two of his collected editions, but no evidence that they had belonged to Boyle himself.

Very few books which by way of inscriptions can be directly connected with Boyle are known. According to Dr Fulton only five such books are known, three of them with Boyle's signature: Franciscus de Ripa, *Tractatus de Peste*, Lyons, 1538 (Wellcome Historical Medical Library); Thomas Horne ΧΕΙΡΑΤΩΓΙ'Α *sive Manductio in aedem palladis*, London, 1641, Wing H.2811 (Yale Medical Library); and Cicero, *Epistolae familiares*, Paris, Estienne, 1550 (Eton College); the two others are inscribed only by the later owners: Dalancé, *Traité des Baromètres*, Amsterdam, 1668 (collection of Dr R. E. W. Maddison); and Louis de Montpersant, *La politique des Jesuites*, London, 1688, an anti-Jesuit tract.

It seems that, even if in the course of time a few more books inscribed by Boyle should appear, we can have little hope of ever knowing now, even approximately, of what the main library consisted.

[1]Villamil (R.-de) Newton the Man [1931].
[2]B.M. Add. MS. 25,424.
[3]A modern collector would give much to find Hooke's own copy of Boyle's *Experiments Touching the Air*, with its continuation and defence, 1662–69, which contains the account of the air-pump which Hooke constructed for Boyle; or his own copy of the rare first issue of the *Mechanical Origin of Qualities* 1675.
[4]Hindle, Oxford Bib. Soc., 3, 340 (1933).
[5]This information is based on the notes in *Nature*, vol. 163, p. 627 (1949) and vol. 165, p. 981 (1950), by Drs Douglas McKie and R. E. W. Maddison.
[6]A Bibliography of the Honourable Robert Boyle, Oxford, 1961, p. V.

An
ATTEMPT
FOR THE
EXPLICATION
Of the
PHÆNOMENA,
Obſervable in an Experiment Publiſhed
by the Honourable
ROBERT BOYLE, Eſq;
In the XXXV. Experiment of his Epiſtolical
Diſcourſe touching the *AIRE.*

In Confirmation of a former Conjecture
made by *R. H.*

Nos cum non ſemper magna referre poſſimus, vera tamen ſed rara recitamus; neq; enim minori miraculo in parvis Natura ludit quam in magnis, Cardan de Vari. *L.8. Cap.* 3.
Tum vero de Scientiarum progreſſu ſpes bene fundabitur, quum in hiſtoriam naturalem recipientur & aggregabuntur complura experimenta, quæ in ſe nullius ſunt uſus, ſed ad inventionem cauſarum & axiomatum tantum faciunt, Verulamii Nov. Org. Aph. 99.

LONDON,
Printed by *J. H.* for *Sam. Thomſon* at
the Biſhops Head in St. *Pauls*
Church-yard, *1661.*

Robert Hooke, *An Attempt for the Explication of the Phenomena Observable in an Experiment published by the Hon. Robert Boyle.* First edition, 1661. 8vo.
London £400 ($1,120).

From the collection of Professor E. N. da C. Andrade, F.R.S.

THE
SCEPTICAL CHYMIST:
OR
CHYMICO-PHYSICAL
Doubts & Paradoxes,
Touching the
SPAGYRIST'S PRINCIPLES
Commonly call'd
HYPOSTATICAL,
As they are wont to be Propos'd and
Defended by the Generality of
ALCHYMISTS.
Whereunto is præmis'd Part of another Diſcourſe
relating to the ſame Subject.

BY
The Honourable *ROBERT BOYLE*, Eſq;

LONDON,
Printed by *J. Cadwell* for *J. Crooke*, and are to be
Sold at the *Ship* in St. *Paul's* Church-Yard.
MDCLXI.

Robert Boyle, *The Sceptical Chymist or Chymico-Physical Doubts and Paradoxes Touching the Spagyrist's Principles Commonly call'd Hypostatical.* First edition, J. Cadwell for J. Crooke, 1661. 8vo.
London £4,800 ($13,440).

An 18th-century French Inlaid Binding, by Jacques-Antoine Derome l'Aîné, on a copy of *Heures Presentées à Madame La Dauphine*, Théodore de Hansy, Paris 1745–6. 8vo. London £2,200 ($6,160).
From the collection of R. J. R. Arundell, Esq.

A Parisian Binding, by Claude de Picques of *circa* 1560,
on a copy of the Bible in Latin, R. Stephanus, Paris 1545. 2 vols., 8vo.
London £1,300 ($3,640).
From the collection of Major J. R. Abbey.

Printed Books and Fine Bindings from the collection of Major J. R. Abbey were sold in June 1965 for £157,172 ($440,081).

The first edition in Greek of the Works of Aristotle, printed by Aldus Manutius and A. Bondinus, 1495–8, bound in Paris *circa* 1560 by Grolier's last binder. 5 vols., folio. London £7,600 ($21,280).
From the collection of Major J. R. Abbey.

Oudry's Edition of *Les Fables de la Fontaine*, Paris 1755–9, in a contemporary Parisian Red Morocco binding with the arms of Louis Phélypeaux, Duc de la Vrillière, 1705–77.
4 vols., folio.
London £3,000 ($8,400).
From the collection of Major J. R. Abbey.

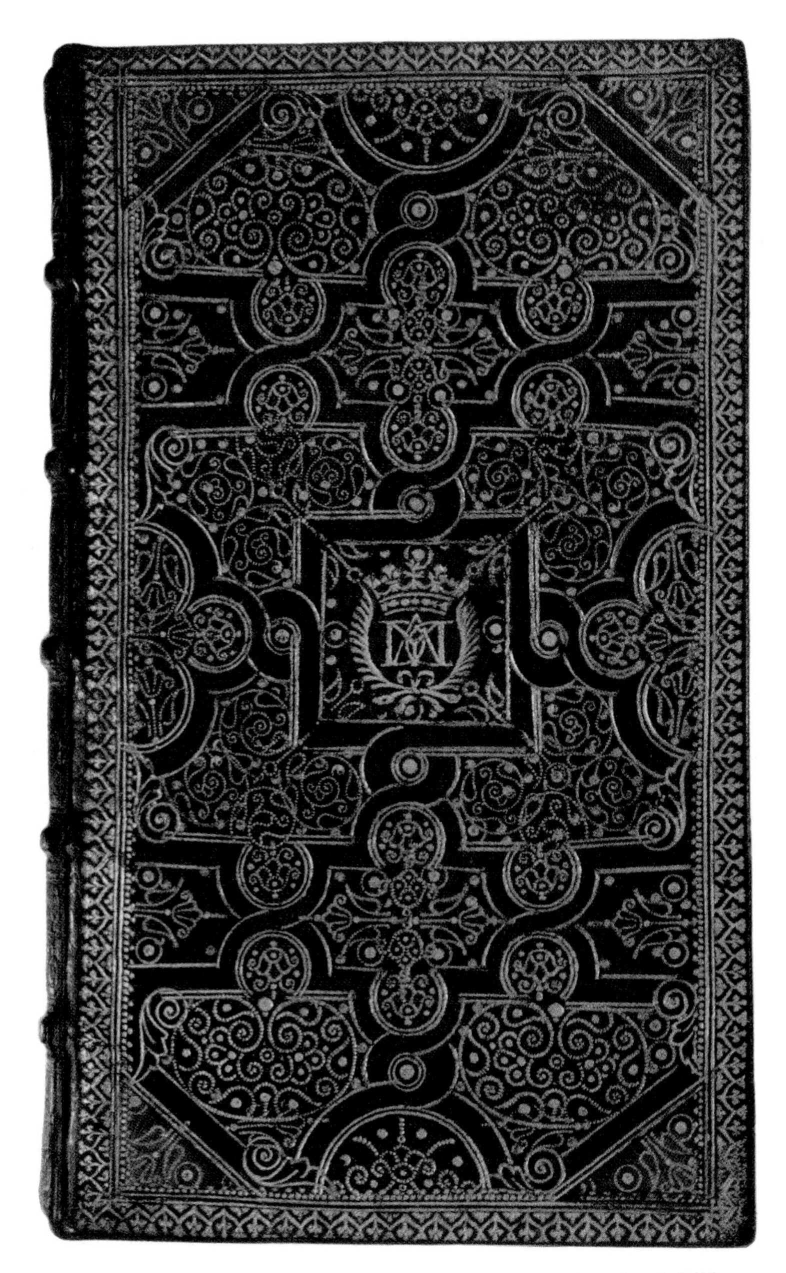

LA PRATIQUE DES VERTUS CHRETIENNES, *ou tous les Devoirs de l'Homme, traduit de l'anglais, dedié à son Altesse royale Madame la Duchesse d'York* (Anne Hyde, Duchess of York, 1637–71), in a contemporary Parisian red morocco binding by Antoine Ruette, 1669. sm. 8vo.
London £850 ($2,380).
From the collection of Major J. R. Abbey.

Facing page Charles Nicolas Cochin, *Voyage Pittoresque d'Italie*,
C. A. Jombert, Paris 1750, bound for Madame de Pompadour. 2 vols., 4to.
London £2,600 ($7,280).
From the collection of Major J. R. Abbey.

Theodore de Beza, *Icones*, Jean de Laon, Geneva 1580, in a contemporary Genevan 'sunk panel' binding. 4to. London £1,100 ($3,080). From the collection of Major J. R. Abbey.

Edward VI's Copy of *The Forme and Maner of Makyng and Consecratyng of Archebishoppes*, first edition, Richard Grafton, March 1549, bound by the 'King Edward and Queen Mary Binder'. 4to. London £2,500 ($7,000). From the collection of Major J. R. Abbey.

Horace Walpole, *Anecdotes of Painting in England*, first edition, Strawberry Hill, 1762–80, bound by the Edwards of Halifax Bindery. The portraits on the covers reproduced are Isaac Oliver (left) and John Evelyn (right). 5 vols. small 4to. London £1,700 ($4,760). From the collection of Major J. R. Abbey.

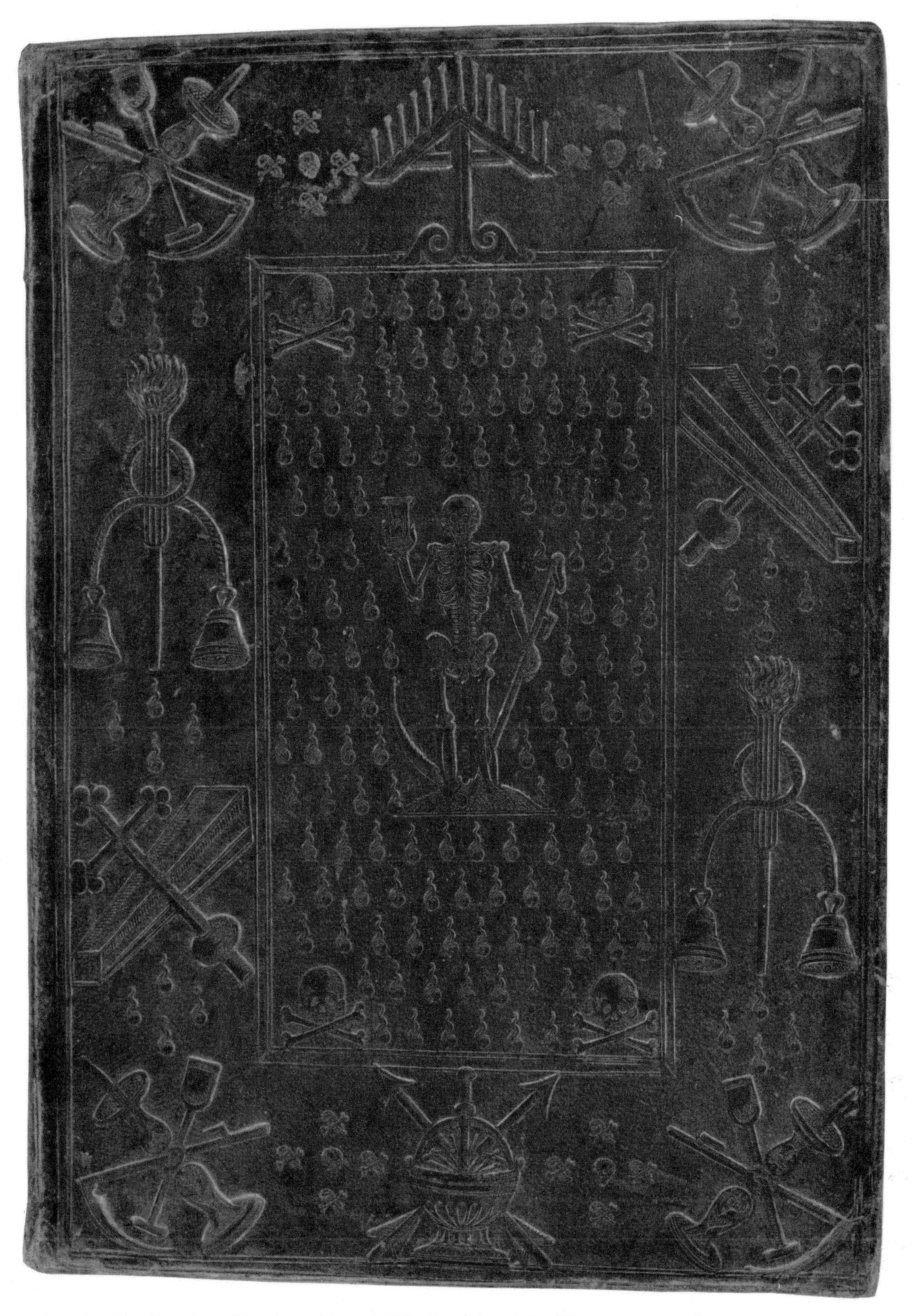

A Macabre Binding for a Member of Henri III's *Confrérie de la Mort*, on a copy of *Le Pseaultier de David*, Jamet Mettayer, Paris 1586. Henri III founded the Confrérie de la Mort in 1585 as a small penitent community among his courtiers and these Psalters were evidently bound by his order and to his specifications as gifts to members of the Confrérie. 4to.
London £1,850 ($5,180).
From the collection of Major J. R. Abbey.

The Boucher Molière, Paris 1734.
This is the Lamoignon copy in a contemporary French blue morocco gilt binding. 6 vols., 4to.
London £7,000 ($19,600).
From the collection of Major J. R. Abbey.

A Roman Binding executed *circa* 1545 for Pier-Luigi Farnese with the celebrated Medallion of Apollo and Pegasus, on a copy of Andreas Naugerius, *Orationes Duae*, Venice 1530. Folio.
London £2,400 ($6,720).
From the collection of Major J. R. Abbey.

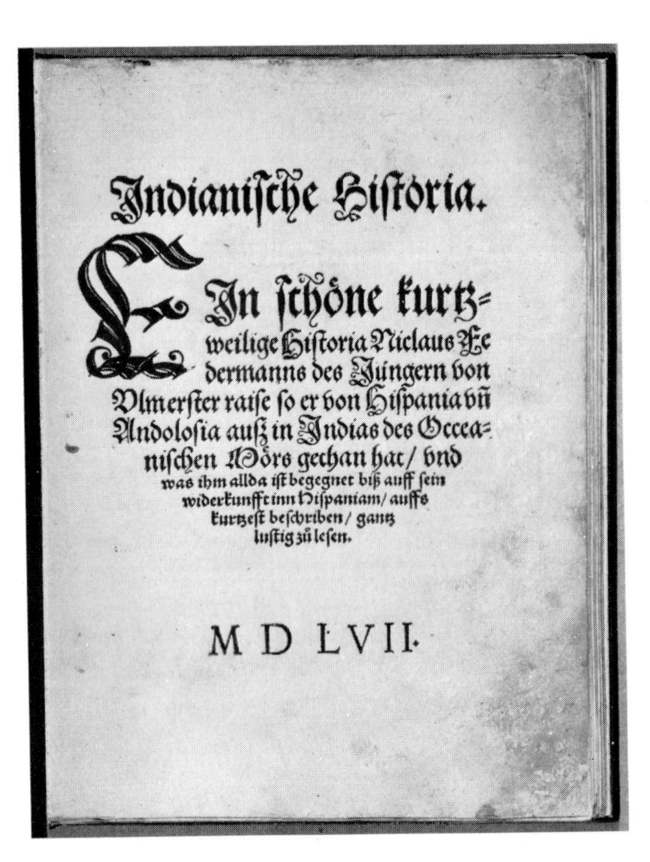

Indianiſche Hiſtoria.

Ein ſchöne kurtz-
weilige Hiſtoria Niclaus Fe-
dermanns des Jüngern von
Vlm erſter raiſe ſo er von Hiſpania vñ
Andoloſia außz in Indias des Occea-
niſchen Mörs gethan hat / vnd
was ihm allda iſt begegnet biß auff ſein
widerkunfft inn Hiſpaniam / auffs
kurtzeſt beſchriben / gantz
luſtig zů leſen.

M D LVII.

Nicolaus Federman, *Indianische Historia*, Hagenau, 1557.
This is an account by the German conquistador
of his expedition to Venezuela. 4to.
New York $2,700 (£965).
From the collection of Mr Arne Pettersen, New York.

The collection of Martin Luther material,
manuscripts, incunabula and Reformation
tracts formed by Mr Arne Pettersen was sold in
November 1964 for $142,530 (£50,893).

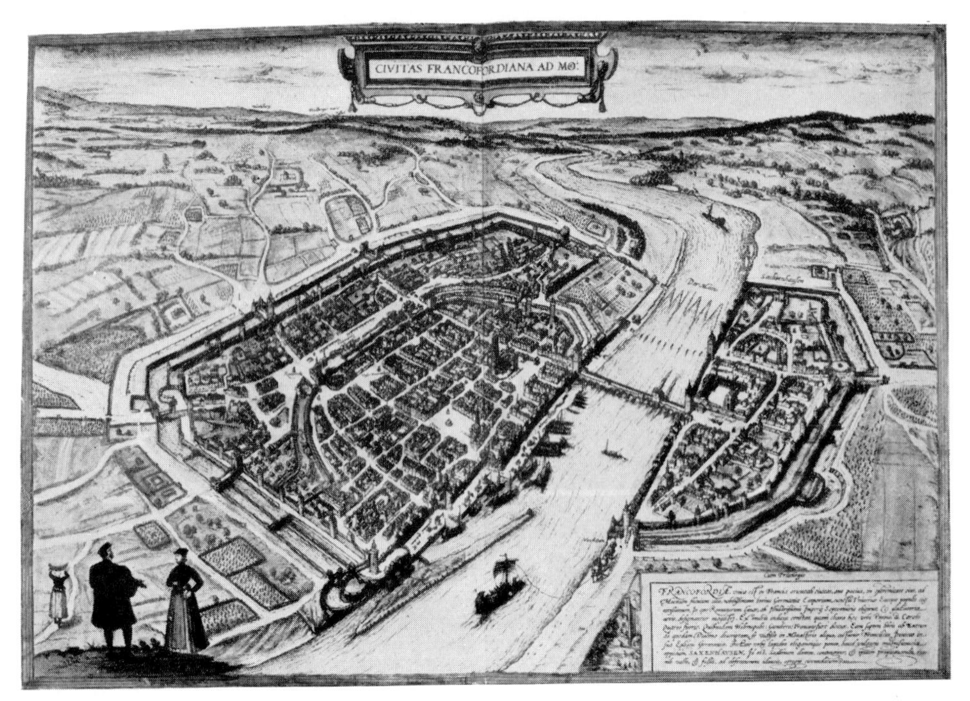

Georg Braun and Franz Hogenberg, *Contrafactur und Beschreibung von den Vornembsten Stetten der Welt*, Cologne 1582–1617. 6 vols., folio.
London £4,400 ($12,320).
From the collection of C. E. Kenney, Esq., F.S.A., F.R.I.C.S.

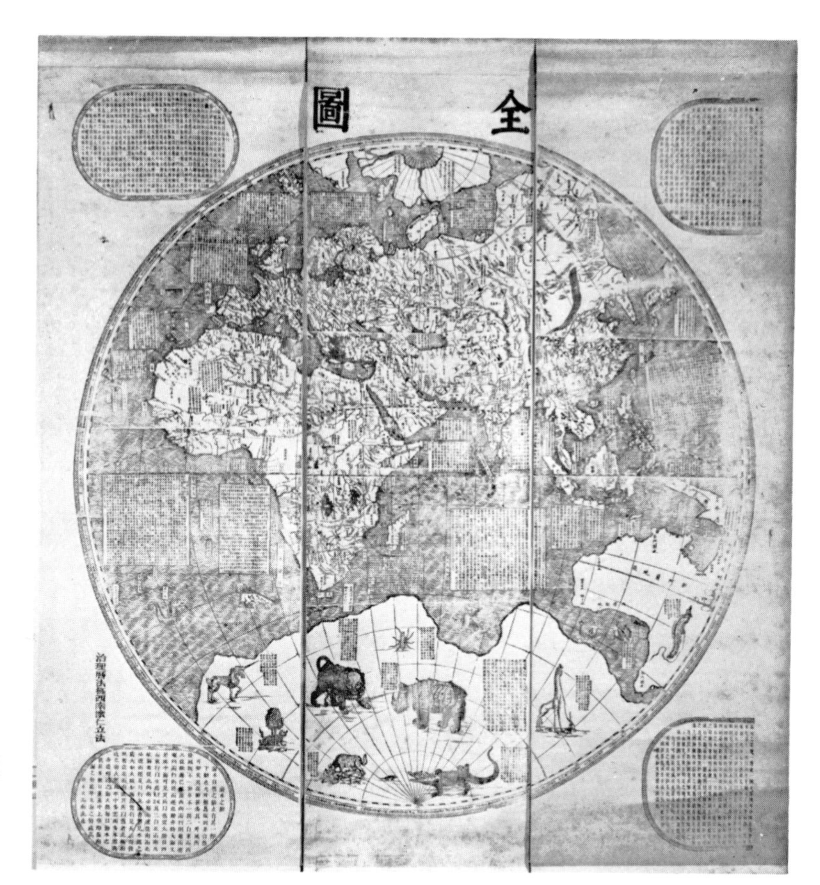

ıer Ferdinand Verbiest, produced for the
ɔeror K'ang-hsi, printed from woodblocks, in
ıese characters, in the cyclical year Chia-yîn
ıe K'ang-hsi dynasty (1674), showing the world
vo hemispheres in stereographic projection.
don £1,600 ($4,480).
n the collection of Sir Michael Gillett, K.C.M.G.

L. Janscha and J. Ziegler, *Collection de Cinquante Vues du Rhin*,
Vienna 1798. Oblong folio.
London £2,500 ($7,000).
From the collections of the late J. W. Harrison, Esq., and Lt-Col. C. J. Nixon.

Redouté, *Les Roses*. First edition, the large paper copy, with an inscription by Redouté, Paris 1817–24. 3 vols., folio. London £7,200 ($20,160).
From the collection of the late J. N. Hart, Esq.

Laurent Berlèse, *Iconographie du Genre Camellia*, Paris 1839–43. 3 vols., 4to. London £3,400 ($9,520).
From the collections of the late J. W. Harrison, Esq., and Lt-Col. C. J. Nixon.

Redouté, *Les Liliacées*, Paris 1802–16. 8 vols., folio.
London £6,200 ($17,360).
From the collections of the late J. W. Harrison, Esq., and Lt-Col. C. J. Nixon.

John Gould, a collection of 237 drawings for *The Birds of Australia*, *circa* 1840–48. 2 vols., folio.
London £3,400 ($9,520).
From the collection of Lt-Col. Sir William Jardine of Appelgirth, Bart.

The Frankeleyns tale

Thou art a squyer and he is a knyght
But god forbede for hys blisful myght
But a clerk coude do as gentyl a dede
As wel as ony of you it is no drede
Syre I relece the thy thousand pound
As now thou were cropen out of the ground
Ne neuer or now ne haddist knowen me
For sire I wol not take a peny of the
For al my craft ne for al my trauaylle
Thou hast wel payd for my vytaylle
It is ynow farwel and haue good day
And took hys hors & forth he goth hys way
Lordynges thys question than axe I yow
Whyche was the most fre as thynkyth yow
Now telyth me er that ye further wende
I can n more my tale is at an ende

Here endyth the frankeleyns tale
And foloweth the prologe of the wif of Bathe

Chaucer, *The Canterbury Tales.*
Second (first illustrated) edition printed at Westminster by William Caxton, *circa* 1484. One of only 13 copies recorded. Folio.
London £30,000 ($84,000).
From the collection of David E. Barnes, Esq.

MR. WILLIAM
SHAKESPEARES
COMEDIES,
HISTORIES, &
TRAGEDIES.

Publifhed according to the True Originall Copies.

Martin Droeshout sculpsit London.

LONDON
Printed by Ifaac Iaggard, and Ed. Blount. 1623.

William Shakespeare, *Comedies, Histories and Tragedies.*
A set of the four folio editions, 1623, 1632, 1664 and 1685.
An engraved portrait of Shakespeare by Martin Droeshout on the title page.
London £23,000 ($64,400).
From the collection of the late John M. Robertson, Esq.

A prophesy found in the
Abbey of St Benedict
in Norfolk.

If 88 bee past then thrive
Thou maist till 44 or 5.
After the maide is dead a Scott
shall governe thee & if a plott
prevent him not: sure then his sway
continue shall full many a day.
the 9th shall dye & then the first
perhaps shal raigne: but o accurst
shall bee the time when as you see
to 16 joined 23.
for then the eagle shall have helpe
by craft to catch the lyon's whelpe,
& hurt them sore, except the same
bee curde by one of the maides name.
In July moneth of yt same yeere
saturne conioines with Jupiter.
perhaps false prophets will arise
& Mahomet shall play his prise.
but sure much alteration
will happen in religion
beleeve this true if then you see
A Spaniard Protestant to bee.

ROBERT HERRICK'S POETICAL COMMONPLACE BOOK.
London £34,000 ($95,200)
From the collection formed by Sir Thomas Phillipps, Bt. (1792–1872).

The Herrick Commonplace Book

This small quarto volume of 352 pages, compiled – as the sequence of topical allusions in its verse indicates – between the years 1612 and 1624, belongs to a class of manuscript which was popular in the 17th century, when a great deal of verse circulated 'by transcription', as Michael Drayton expressed it, without finding its way into print. These Commonplace Books – privately-compiled miscellanies of verse and prose – though an important source for 17th-century poetry, are in almost every case the work of obscure or anonymous compilers, and their texts are notoriously unreliable. In the present manuscript, however, among a variety of scribal hands occurs one hand of outstanding individuality, and it is the identification of this hand as that of Robert Herrick – one of the best-loved of all English lyric poets – which raises the volume to the rank of a major discovery. The volume contains the only poetry in Herrick's own hand so far discovered, and – perhaps even more significant – it is the only miscellany of its kind which can be shown to have belonged to a major poet of the period. *Hesperides*, Herrick's only published collection of verse, did not appear until 1648, after he had spent nearly twenty years as vicar of a remote country parish, while the Commonplace Book belongs to the period of Herrick's life when he must have been in London forming those friendships in literary and court circles which are nostalgically commemorated in *Hesperides*. The volume contains the only authoritative texts of a body of verse – most of it unpublished hitherto – which was circulating in the leading London literary circle during the reign of James I, and provides much new and highly significant material for the consideration of any future editor of Herrick.

In its drab binding of Victorian half calf, the volume remained unregarded for more than a century among the vast collection of manuscripts accumulated by Sir Thomas Phillipps. It was acquired by Phillipps for £2 18*s*, through the booksellers Payne and Foss, at a sale at Puttick and Simpson on 30 May 1849 (lot 158). At this, its only previous appearance in the saleroom, the volume was described as the Commonplace Book of George Abbot, Archbishop of Canterbury, the cataloguer being hopefully misled by the occurrence of 'George Archbishop of Canterbury his grace' among a variety of names and jottings written by a contemporary scribbler on the flyleaf. Phillipps' entry in his own privately printed catalogue (no. 12341*) makes no mention of Herrick, specifies only a few of the numerous contents, and describes the first poem – an elegy on Mary, Queen of Scots – as 'Verses on the Murder of Chas. 1st', thus implying that the volume must have been written at least a generation later than in fact it was.

The volume contains two of Herrick's acknowledged poems (later printed in revised versions in *Hesperides*) written in the elegant hand of a professional scribe, who deliberately left one line blank, evidently because he could not at this point read the manuscript from which he was copying. This fortunate accident provided the clue which led to the identification of Herrick's hand in the book, for the omitted line had been supplied in another hand, which had also made several small revisions elsewhere in the two poems known to be by Herrick, had corrected the volume from beginning to end, and had written several entire poems on various pages occurring throughout. The nature of the revisions – coupled with the highly individual character of the hand – suggested that here we were in direct contact with Herrick himself, and this exciting possibility was confirmed by a comparison with the series of letters which Herrick wrote as an undergraduate at Cambridge to his wealthy uncle applying for advances of money, and which had hitherto been the only known examples of his handwriting.

P. J. CROFT

The Graffigny Papers

Françoise du Buisson d'Happoncourt, Marquise de Graffigny (1694–1758), was left a widow in 1725 by the death of her violent and disagreeable husband in prison. The remainder of her life she devoted to the pleasures of friendship, love and literature, first at the court of Lorraine at Lunéville and after 1739 in Paris. The vast and hitherto virtually unknown accumulation of papers which she left at her death to her friend François Antoine Devaux shows how assiduously she cultivated these three occupations. The largest part of the collection is the series of not less than 4,000 letters exchanged between the two friends, which offers to the student of eighteenth-century France a huge quarry of fresh and first-hand information of a literary, sociological and psychological kind. Mme de Graffigny herself achieved a certain renown as an author by her *Lettres péruviennes* (1741), in which she made use of two favourite literary artifices of the day: the letter-novel and the view of sophisticated society through the eyes of a savage. Of her subsequent attempts to write for the stage the papers have many interesting autograph examples, most of them unpublished. Devaux (1712–1796), known as 'Panpan' to his friends, who spent much time and ink discussing whether nature had intended him for a woman or a man ('une épingle qui se trouva par hasard dans la balance détermina son sexe'), was another Lorrainer, qualified by his varied but somewhat amateurish talents to fill a place in the best literary society of his day. Between them, he and Mme de Graffigny knew everybody and everything of interest that was happening in Lorraine, Paris and Versailles. Their world was dominated by the genius and personality of Voltaire, and several apparently unpublished poems by him are found in the collection. Mme de Graffigny spent some time at Cirey itself in the house of Mme du Chatelet and her letters from this vantage point are the only part of the collection which has been published (*Vie privée de Voltaire et de Mme du Chatelet*, Paris, 1820). An exhaustive study of the whole collection will certainly provide further new insights into the life of Voltaire and into the whole movement of thought which revolved around the production of the *Encyclopédie*. But above all the letters reveal with vivid intimacy the zest and talent and humour and serious feeling which the 18th century devoted to the cult of friendship.

The papers were bought by Sir Thomas Phillipps before 1842, for on 25 April of that year he found 'a white grub with a black head $\frac{1}{4}$ of an inch long' devouring some of them. For the purposes of the sale they were divided into nineteen lots (113–132), of which six (including the Graffigny/Devaux correspondence) were bought for America for a total of £15,700 and twelve by the Bibliothèque Nationale for a total of £3,945.

ANDREAS MAYOR

le jeudi 29 janvier 1739

57
1

113

ie reçu hier deux de vos lettres mon cher panpan
l'une du lundi 19 [illegible] et l'autre du [illegible]
ieudi 22 qui ne l'a pas eté. vous voiés quelles
ont encore l'agrement d'etre de vieille datte.
et partant quelles me deplaisent. ie n'y voyois
que de l'inquietude sur mon compte. et encore
pas un mot des lettres que i'avois ecrites une heure apres que
moins du depart de [illegible] ... a part moi
ie les eu [illegible] et que ie regnognois
md du chatelet m'envoya dire quelle en avoit
reçu une de mr. son mari. qui lui mandoit
que demarest seroit ici aujourdhuy ou demain
quil passeroit a cirey pour prendre mon
argent et quil m'aporteroit un paquet quil
lui avoit renvoyé parce quil seroit ici plutot
que lui. voila la reponce a toutes mes lettres
et me voila bien aise. mais le croiriez vous
mon ami les vapeurs m'ont rendue l'ame si
noire que ie ne sans pas le plaisir. ie ne
fais que le penser. a souper md du chatelet
me confirma encore tout cela et me dit
que mr. du chatelet vous avois fait prier de
l'aller voir et quil etoit surpris que vous n'y
eussiez pas eté. i'espere mon cher ami que
vous reparerai cela et que votre [illegible]
nira pas jusqu'a manquer a ce devoir.
venons apresent a vos lettres. ie commence
par l'article qui me paroit le plus
interessant pour vous. vous etes etonné que
le professeur ne vous ai pas marqué de
ressentiment de la peine que vous lui avez
faites eh qui a t il dextraordinaire a quoi

THE CORRESPONDANCE OF MADAME DE GRAFFIGNY AND FRANÇOIS-ANTOINE DEVAUX, 1733–58
London £11,800 ($33,040).
From the collection formed by Sir Thomas Phillipps, Bt. (1792–1872).

into this artful dress, to give it the
readier currency. — I fancy, I read
in the countenances of some people
on this occasion, more than the dis-
interested zeal of allies — I hope I am
mistaken, & that my fears of mis-
chief, make me refine too much,
and awaken jealousies that have
no suffic[illegible] dation. —
But upon the whole Sir, to
wave every other consideration; I
do not like to add to the number of
our national obligations — I would
wish as much as possible to avoid
giving a foreign power new claims
of merit for services performed to
the United States, and would ask
no assistance that is not indispen-
sable. —
I am with the truest attach-
ment, & most perfect
confidence, — D Sir
Yr most Obedt &
Obliged
Go: Washington
To
His Excelly
Henry Laurens

An Autograph Letter from George Washington to Henry Laurens, President of the American Congress, dated 14 Nov. 1778, in which Washington gives his principal reasons against an invasion of Canada by French and American Forces, and the subsequent possibility of French domination of America.
New York $15,000 (£5,360).
From the collection of the Heritage Foundation, Deerfield, Massachusetts.

Der dreie
Ecolampad macht den text also. Nemet
und esset. Das ist mein LEIB [illegible]
[illegible] DAS und IST
[illegible]
[illegible] Aber das wort LEIB [illegible]
[illegible]
[illegible]

Der [illegible]
[illegible]
[illegible]
[illegible]
[illegible]
[illegible] Theologia [illegible]
[illegible]

[illegible]
[illegible] (Das ist mein leib)
[illegible]
[illegible]
[illegible]
[illegible]

[illegible] Christlichen [illegible]
[illegible]
[illegible] Zwingel, Ecolampad und Schwenckfeld [illegible]
[illegible]
[illegible] Christi [illegible]
[illegible]

[illegible]
[illegible] Christus [illegible]
[illegible]

A Four-page Manuscript Fragment by Martin Luther on the Text '*Das Ist Mein Leib*', from his work *Kurzem Bekenntnis vom heiligen Sakrament*, published in 1544.
New York $11,000 (£3,930).
From the collection of Mr Arne Pettersen, New York.

G^o Washington

A C T S

PASSED AT A

C O N G R E S S

OF THE

UNITED STATES

O F

A M E R I C A,

BEGUN AND HELD AT THE CITY OF NEW-YORK,
ON *WEDNESDAY* THE *FOURTH* OF *MARCH*,
IN THE YEAR *M,DCC,LXXXIX.*

AND OF THE
INDEPENDENCE of the UNITED STATES,
THE THIRTEENTH.

BEING THE ACTS PASSED AT THE FIRST SESSION OF THE FIRST CONGRESS OF THE UNITED STATES, TO WIT, NEW-HAMPSHIRE, MASSACHUSETTS, CONNECTICUT, NEW-YORK, NEW-JERSEY, PENNSYLVANIA, DELAWARE, MARYLAND, VIRGINIA, SOUTH-CAROLINA, AND GEORGIA; WHICH ELEVEN STATES RESPECTIVELY RATIFIED THE CONSTITUTION OF GOVERNMENT FOR THE UNITED STATES, PROPOSED BY THE FEDERAL CONVENTION, HELD IN PHILADELPHIA, ON THE SEVENTEENTH OF SEPTEMBER, ONE THOUSAND SEVEN HUNDRED AND EIGHTY-SEVEN.

NEW-YORK:
PRINTED BY FRANCIS CHILDS AND JOHN SWAINE,
PRINTERS TO THE UNITED STATES.

George Washington's Copy of the Acts of Congress of 1789,
with his signature on the title-page. Folio.
New York $27,000 (£9,640).
From the collection of the Heritage Foundation, Deerfield, Massachusetts.

William Hamilton's watercolour design for the frontispiece of James Thompson's *The Seasons*, 1797, in one of about 10 copies, with the plates printed in colour. Folio.
London £1,100 ($3,080).
From the collections of the late J. W. Harrison, Esq., and Lt-Col. C. J. Nixon.

A mid 14th-century Mamluk Design for an Automaton, from a manuscript of mechanical devices by Ab'ul 'Izz ibn Isma'il ibn a Razzaz al-Jazari, executed for Salih Salah ed Dunia ved Din, Mamluk Sultan from 1351 to 1354.
London £1,800 ($5,040).
From the collections of the late Adolphe Stoclet and Mr Philippe R. Stoclet.

An Assyrian Relief, early 7th century B.C.
London £4,000 ($11,200).
From the collection of the late Ernest Brummer.

Egyptian and Near Eastern Antiquities from the collection of the late Ernest Brummer were sold in November 1964, for £58,062 ($162,575).

An Akkadian Bronze Foundation Figure, *circa* 2125 B.C.
Height $7\frac{3}{4}$ in.
London £4,600 ($12,880).
From the collection of the late Ernest Brummer.

Right A Pre-Dynastic Mesopotamian Cylinder Seal, from Warka. Uruk period, 3400–3100 B.C. Height $3\frac{1}{2}$ in.
London £1,100 ($3,080).
Now in the Ashmolean Museum, Oxford.

Below An Egyptian Black and White Marble, Amuletic Figure of a Frog. Upper Egypt, 1st or 2nd Dynasty, 3200–2780 B.C. Length $1\frac{1}{2}$ in.
London £520 ($1,456).

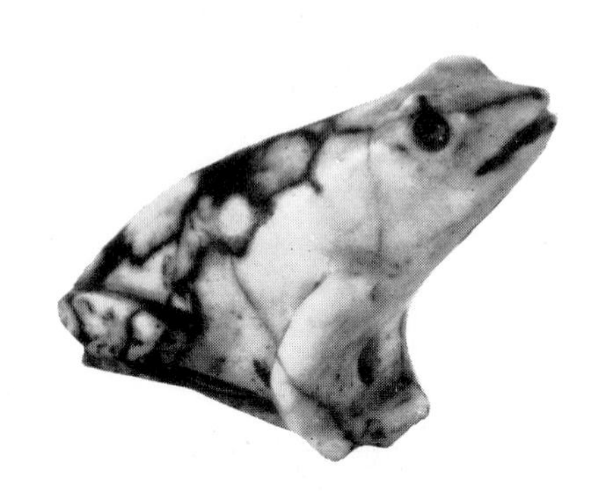

Above An Egyptian Silver Statuette of Nefer-Tum. Saite Period, 664–525 B.C. Height $4\frac{1}{2}$ in.
London £720 ($2,016).

Above right An Egyptian Gold and Enamel Winged Pectoral Scarab, 5th/3rd century B.C. Length $5\frac{1}{2}$ in.
London £1,000 ($2,800).

Right An Egyptian Electrum Amuletic Hawk Amulet.
Saite Period, 664–525 B.C.
Height $2\frac{1}{2}$ in.
London £480 ($1,344).
Formerly in the collection of J. Pierpont-Morgan, New York.

Far right An Egyptian Blue Glazed Composition Figure of a Lion. XXVIIth Dynasty, 525–404 B.C. Height $1\frac{1}{4}$ in.
London £600 ($1,680).

From the collection of the late Ernest Brummer.

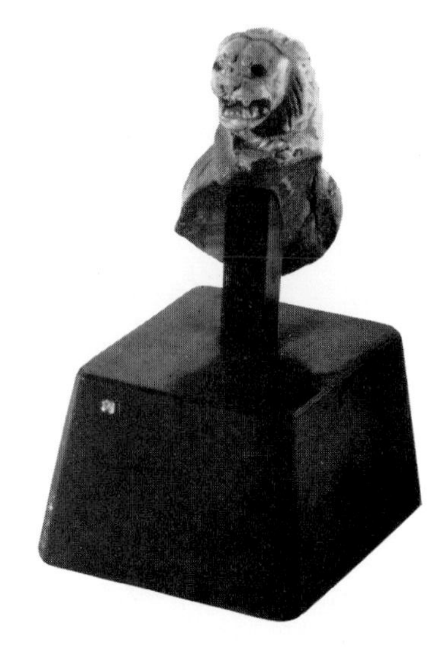

An Achaemenid Silver Phiale, 6th–5th century B.C., found in Mazanderan.
Diameter 12 in.
London £3,000 ($8,400).
From the collection of the late Ernest Brummer.

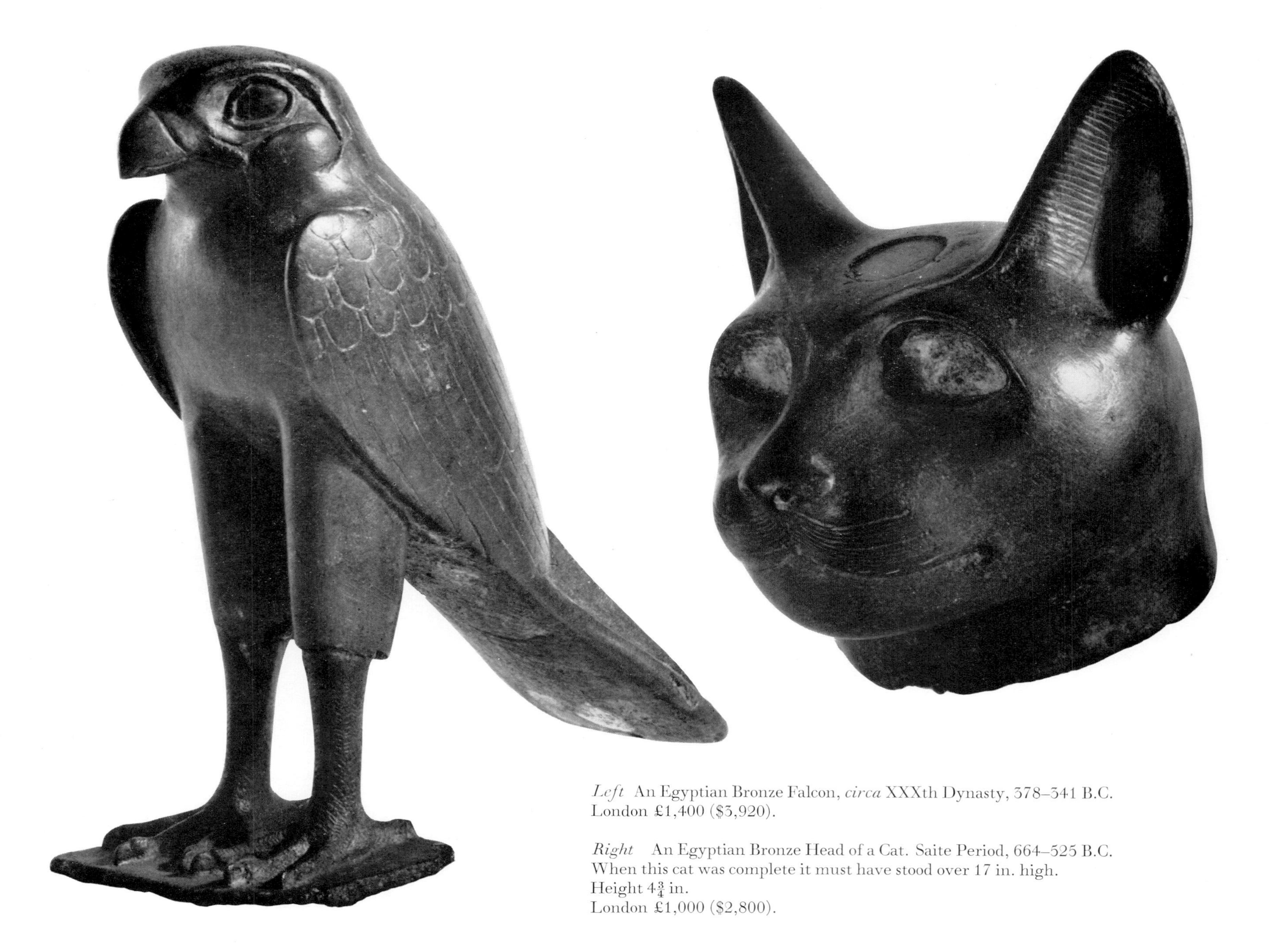

Left An Egyptian Bronze Falcon, *circa* XXXth Dynasty, 378–341 B.C.
London £1,400 ($3,920).

Right An Egyptian Bronze Head of a Cat. Saite Period, 664–525 B.C.
When this cat was complete it must have stood over 17 in. high.
Height $4\frac{3}{4}$ in.
London £1,000 ($2,800).

From the collection of the late Ernest Brummer.

An Egyptian Glass Paste Figure of Maat.
Saite period, 664–525 B.C. Height 6½ in.
London £1,000 ($2,800).

An Egyptian Wooden Salve Holder in the form of a
Trussed Duck, *circa* 1250 B.C. Length 4¼ in.
London £420 ($1,176).

A Scythian or Sarmatian Gold Plaque in the form of
a charging boar, *circa* 2nd/1st century B.C.
Length 3 in.
London £800 ($2,240).

A Roman Marble Portrait Bust of a Man.
Trajanic Period, *circa* A.D. 100
London £2,900 ($8,120).
From the collection of Mr James Osgood, Wayne, Maine.
Now in the Staatliches Museum, Berlin.

An Egyptian Red Quartzite Block Statue of an Important Official.
XIXth Dynasty, 1320–1200 B.C. Height 22 in.
London £1,600 ($4,480).
From the collection of the late Ernest Brummer.

Above A Coptic Glazed Faience Vase and Cover.
Circa 5th century A.D.
London £800 ($2,240).
From the collection of the late Ernest Brummer.

Below A Mycenaean Open Bowl, late Helladic IIIB, 13th century B.C.
London £500 ($1,400).
Now in the Ulster Museum

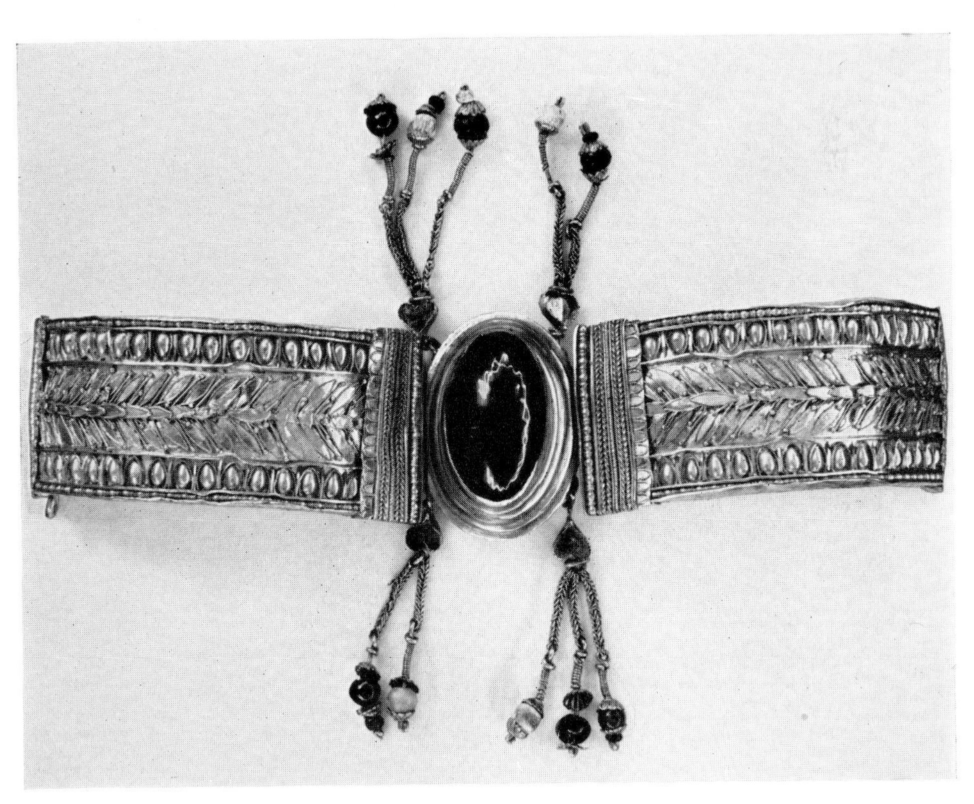

Above A Romano-Egyptian Gold Bracelet, 2nd century A.D.
London £650 ($1820).

Below A Hellenistic Gold Bracelet, 3rd–2nd century B.C.
Found on the Island of Mykonos in the Cyclades.
London £1,100 ($3,080).
Formerly in the collection of Lord Melchett.

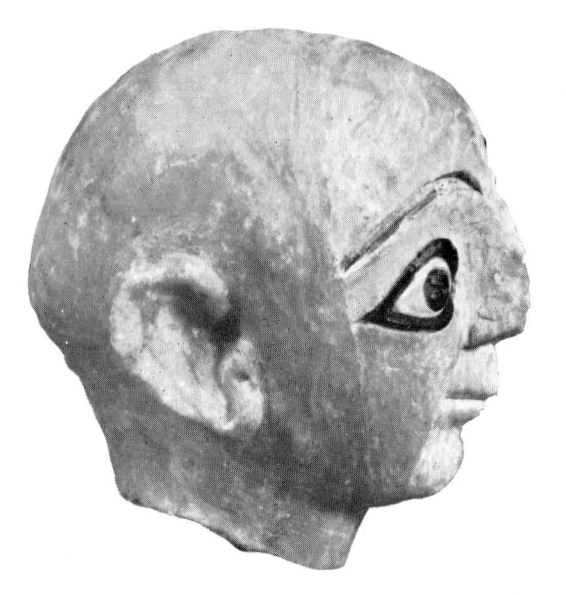

A Sumerian Gypseous Stone Head of a Priest, early Dynastic Period, *circa* 2700–2400 B.C.
London £1,700 ($4,760).
From the collections of the late Adolphe Stoclet and Mr Philippe R. Stoclet.

Above An Islamic Bronze Figure of a Hare, Fatimid, A.D. 967–1171, from Check-Abada.
London £800 ($2,240).

Below A Caucasian Bronze Openwork Square Plaque, early 4th century B.C.
London £850 ($2,380).

From the collections of the late Adolphe Stoclet and Mr Philippe R. Stoclet.

A Benin Ivory Leopard's Mask.
This was brought back from Benin at the time of the Punitive Expedition in 1897.
London £3,500 ($9,800).
From the collection of Mrs E. C. Gaze and R. H. H. Barneby, Esq.

A Benin Bronze Male Head.
This was brought back from Benin at the time of the Punitive Expedition in 1897.
London £4,300 ($11,760).
From the collection of Mrs E. C. Gaze and R. H. H. Barneby, Esq.

A Balega Carved Ivory Double Statuette, in the form of two human figures, from west of Lake Kivu, North-West Congo.
London £1,100 ($3,080).
From the collections of the late Adolphe Stoclet and Mr Philippe R. Stoclet.

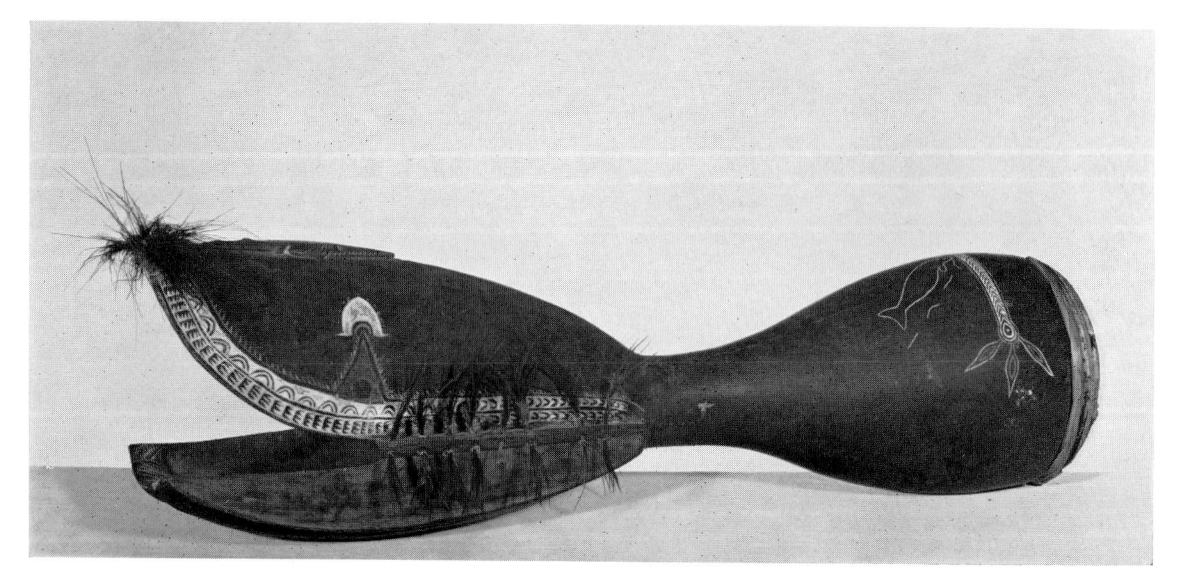

A 'Fish-Mouth' Drum or Warup, from the Torres Straits, New Guinea.
New York $2,100 (£750).

A Balega Carved Ivory Janus Statuette, from west of Lake Kivu, North-West Congo.
London £900 ($2,520).
From the collections of the late Adolphe Stoclet and Mr Philippe R. Stoclet

A Quimbaya Hollow Cast Gold Seated Female Figure, *circa* A.D. 1000–1500. From the Central Cauca River Valley, South-Western Colombia.
London £1,500 ($4,200).

An early 17th-century Japanese Lacquer Box with a European Subject on the lid.
London £620 ($1,736).
From the collections of the late Adolphe Stoclet and Mr Philippe R. Stoclet.

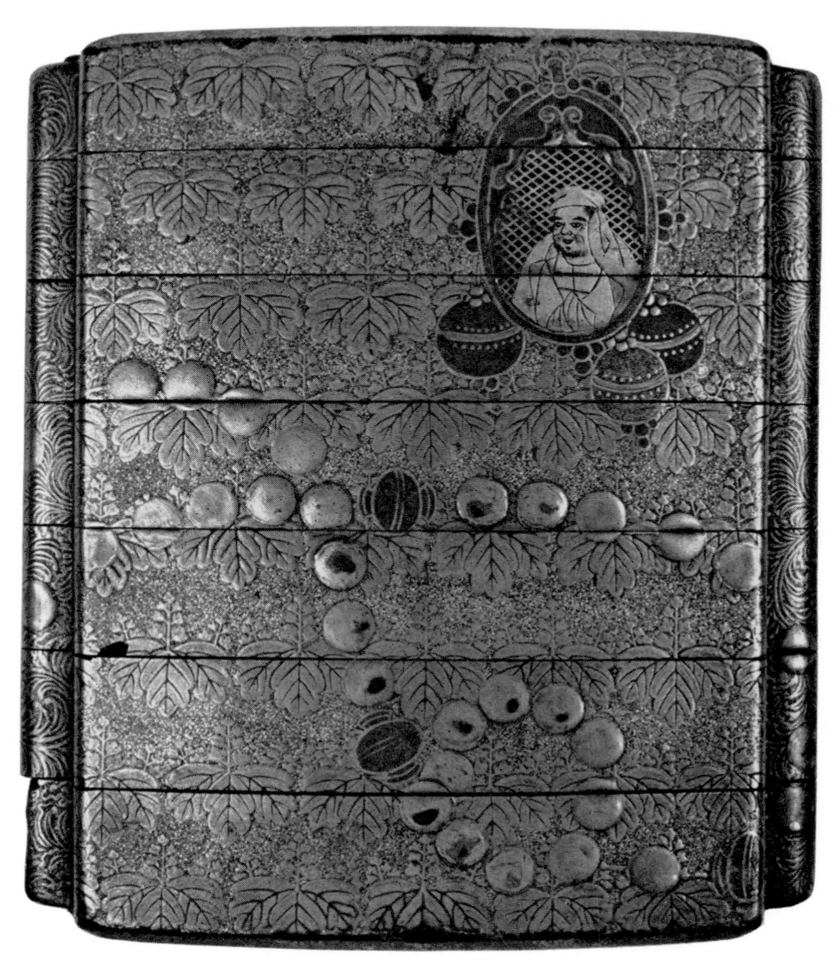

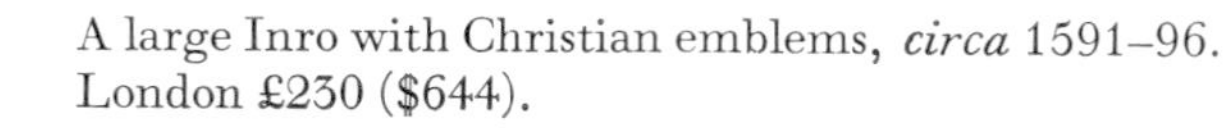

A large Inro with Christian emblems, *circa* 1591–96.
London £230 ($644).

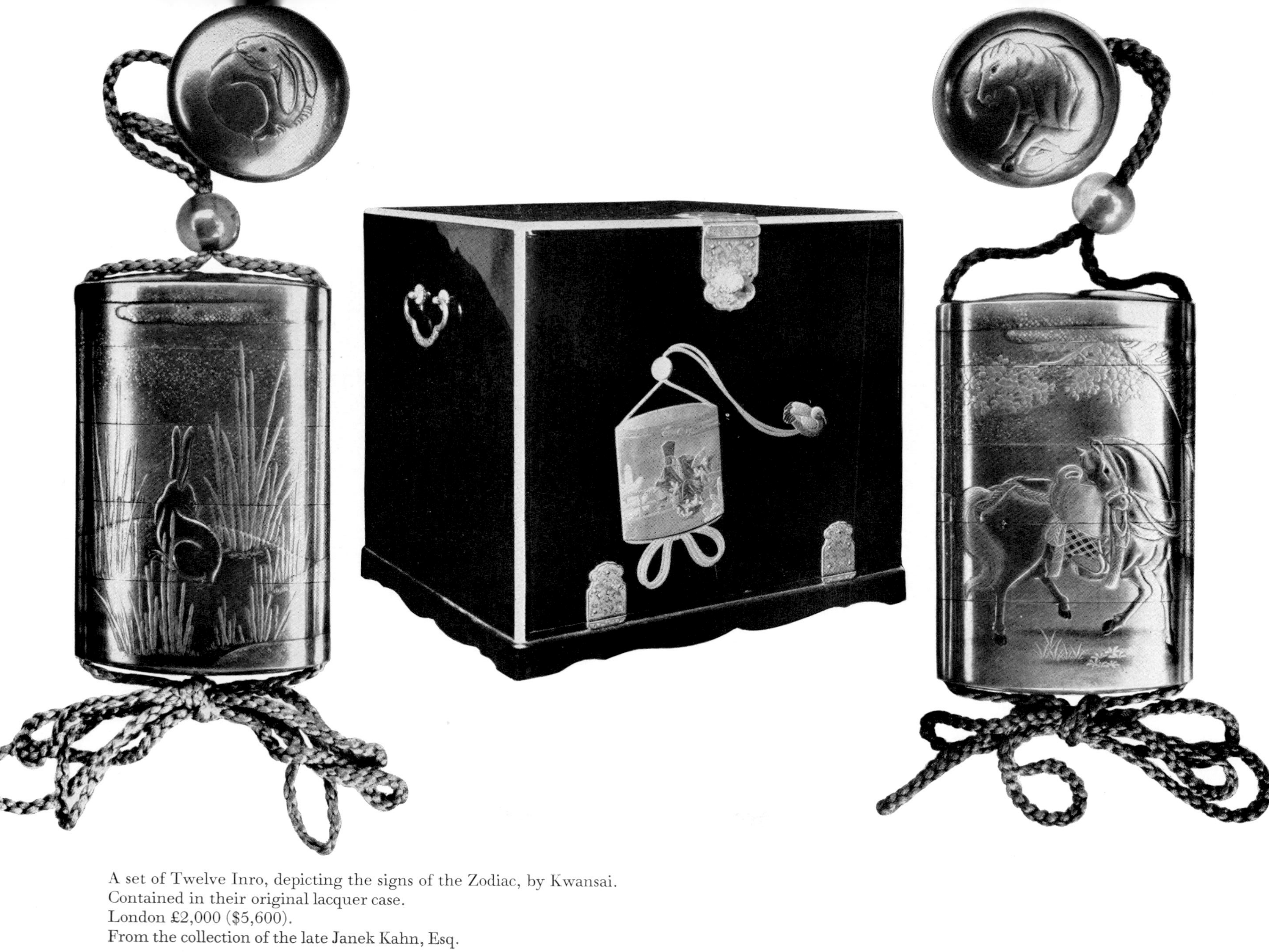

A set of Twelve Inro, depicting the signs of the Zodiac, by Kwansai.
Contained in their original lacquer case.
London £2,000 ($5,600).
From the collection of the late Janek Kahn, Esq.

A Lacquer Inro, modelled on an old cake of Chinese ink, by Ritsuo.
London £290 ($812).
From the collection of the late Janek Kahn, Esq.

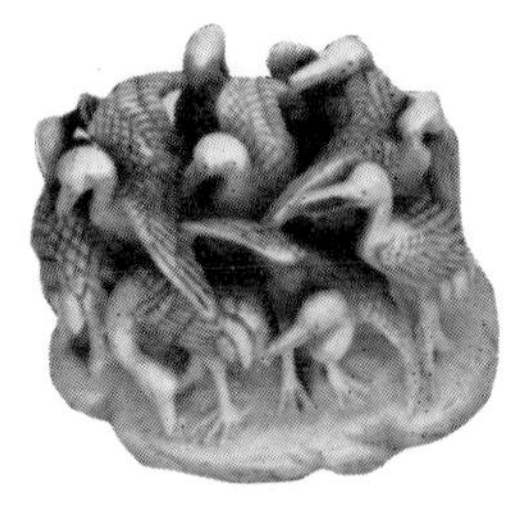

Ivory Netsuke. *A Group of eleven Cranes*, by Kagetoshi.
London £390 ($1,092).

Ivory Netsuke. *A Boar*, by Ikkwan.
London £400 ($1,120).

Wood Netsuke. *A Horse*, by Tomokazu.
London £210 ($588).

SUGIMURA JIHEI
Two Lovers.
London £1,300 ($3,640).
From the collections of the late Adolphe Stoclet and Mr Philippe R. Stoclet.

KIYOMASU
The Poet Teika Travelling.
London £2,000 ($5,600).
From the collections of the late Adolphe Stoclet and Mr Philippe R.Stoclet.

HOKUSAI
The Poet Li Po extolling the waterfall of Lo-Shan.
One of a complete set of the ten prints, 'Poems of China and Japan mirrored to the life'.
London £2,300 ($6,440).
Formerly in the Happer Collection, sold at Sotheby's in 1909 for £340 ($952).

SHARAKU
Sakata Hangoro III.
Woodcut on a mica ground.
London £1,100 ($3,080).

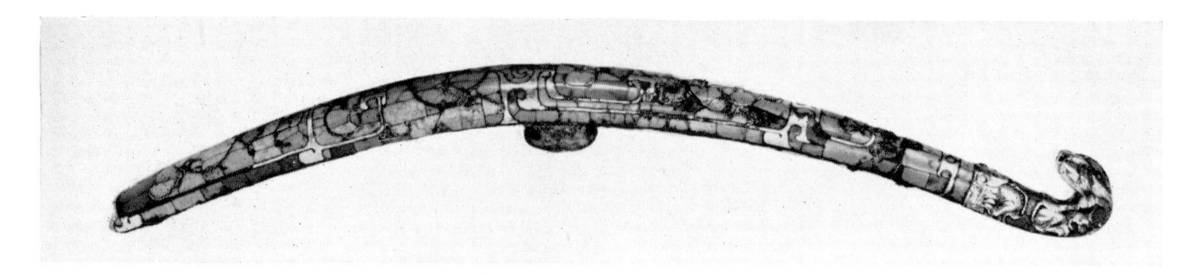

A Warring States Gilt-Bronze and Turquoise Belt Hook.
London £2,200 ($6,160).

Above A Chou Bronze Mirror.
London £1,900 ($5,320).

Right A Chou Bronze Ritual Axe-Head.
London £2,800 ($7,840).

From the collections of the late Adolphe Stoclet and
Mr Philippe R. Stoclet.

A late Chou Bronze Bell or Chung, from the Wei Hui Chime, of which four other bells are recorded, two in the Fogg Museum of Art, one in the Asiatic Museum, Amsterdam, and a fourth which was formerly in the Berlin State Museum.
London £28,000 ($78,400).
From the collections of the late Adolphe Stoclet and Mr Philippe R. Stoclet.
Now in The British Museum.

A Han Animal Style Gilt-Bronze Applique of Sarmatian type.
London £1,350 ($3,780).

Left A Han Gilt-Bronze Figure of a Bear.
London £950 ($2,660).
Right A Shang Bronze Plaque, inlaid with turquoise.
London £1,600 ($4,480).

From the collections of the late Adolphe Stoclet and Mr Philippe R. Stoclet.

A T'ang Gilt-Bronze Engraved Wine Cup, from a miniature set of tomb vessels.
London £1,350 ($3,780).
Formerly in the Joseph Homberg Collection, sold at Sotheby's in July 1949, for £85 ($238).

Left A Shang Spear Head.
London £180 ($504).
Centre A Shang Archaic Ivory Carving of a Bird, from An-yang.
London £1,600 ($4,480).
Right A Northern Wei Gilt-Bronze Stele of Avalokitesvara. Dated 516 or 517.
London £5,200 ($14,560).

From the collections of the late Adolphe Stoclet and Mr Philippe R. Stoclet.

A Yüan Painting of a Mongol horseman in ink and colours on silk, in the manner of Chao Mêng-fu.
$38\frac{3}{4}$ in. by 32 in.
London £2,800 ($7,840).
From the collections of the late Adolphe Stoclet and Mr. Philippe R. Stoclet.

A T'ang Pottery Figure of a Polo Player.
London £3,500 ($9,800).
From the collection of Lady Mitchell.

Above A 14th-century Yüan Copper-Red Dish.
London £1,700 ($4,760).
From the collection of Max Robertson, Esq.

Below A 15th-century Ming Blue and White Saucer Dish.
London £1,900 ($5,320).
From the collection of His Excellency Hugo Wistrand.

Above A mid-15th-century Ming Blue and White Potiche.
London £3,400 ($9,520).

Below A Sung Moulded Ting-Yao Saucer Dish.
London £1,900 ($5,320).
Formerly in the Steiner Collection, sold at Sotheby's in May 1948, for £225 ($620).

A late 17th-century Kakiemon Jar.
London £850 ($2,380).
From the collection of Mrs E. Gandon.

A Ch'ien Lung Export Ware Plate (one of a pair), painted *en grisaille* with the gateway of the Botanical Gardens at Oxford.
London £360 ($1,008).
From the collection of J. H. S. Lucas-Scudamore, Esq.

A pair of Ch'ien Lung 'Famille-Rose' Clogs. London £580 ($1,624).

A Chia Ch'ing Cow Tureen and Cover. London £410 ($1,148).

Left A Lac Burgaute Snuffbottle.
London £180 ($504).
Centre A Lapis Lazuli Snuffbottle.
London £170 ($476).
Right An 18th-century Moon-Shaped Coral Snuffbottle.
London £190 ($532).

From the collection of the late Janek Kahn, Esq.

A Chi'en Lung Cloisonné Enamel Ram Desk Ornament.
London £700 ($1,960).
From the collection of Colonel J. B. Sherwood.

A Ch'ien Lung Jade Covered Bowl.
London £1,700 ($4,760).
From the collection of Mrs G. D. Gibson.

A K'ang Hsi Spinach Green Jade
Brush Holder.
London £4,000 ($11,200).
From the collection of Mrs
R. Gladstone.

An Ormolu-Mounted Meissen Figure of a Jay,
by J. J. Kaendler (one of a pair).
London £5,000 ($14,000).

A Louis XV Ormolu-Mounted Meissen Swan Candlestick (one of a pair),
by J. J. Kaendler.
London £1,600 ($4,480).
From the collection of Commander P. C. O. Langley, R.N.

A pair of Meissen Quail Tureens, by J. J. Kaendler.
London £850 ($2,380).
From the collection of H.R.H. the Princess Dimitri of Russia.

A Meissen 'Gold Chinese' Tankard with Silver-Gilt Mounts.
London £1,700 ($4,760).
From the collection of H.R.H. Princess Olga of Greece.

An early Meissen Silver-Mounted 'Hausmalerei' Tankard, by H. G. von Bressler, dated 1727.
London £700 ($1,960).

A Meissen 'Hausmalerei' Tureen and Cover, in the manner of Mayer of Pressnitz, *circa* 1755.
London £800 ($2,240).
From the collection of H.R.H. Princess Olga of Greece.

Above An early Meissen Sucrier and Cover, painted in the manner of J. G. Herold.
London £440 ($1,232).
From the collection of Mrs Emma de Groote.

A Meissen 'Hausmalerei' Sucrier and Cover, *circa* 1740.
London £360 ($1,008).
From the collection of Mrs Emma de Groote.

An early Ormolu-Mounted Meissen Group of a Chinaman and a Bird,
by Georg Fritzsche.
London £2,200 ($6,160).

A Meissen Powdered-Puce Ground Tea and Coffee Service (consisting of forty-seven pieces).
Probably decorated by C. F. Herold.
London £5,000 ($14,000).
From the collection of Ernest Wolf, Esq.

A Meissen Figure of Pantaloon,
by J. J. Kaendler.
London £1,500 ($4,200).

A Meissen Figure of Harlequin with a Dog,
by J. J. Kaendler.
London £2,300 ($6,440)

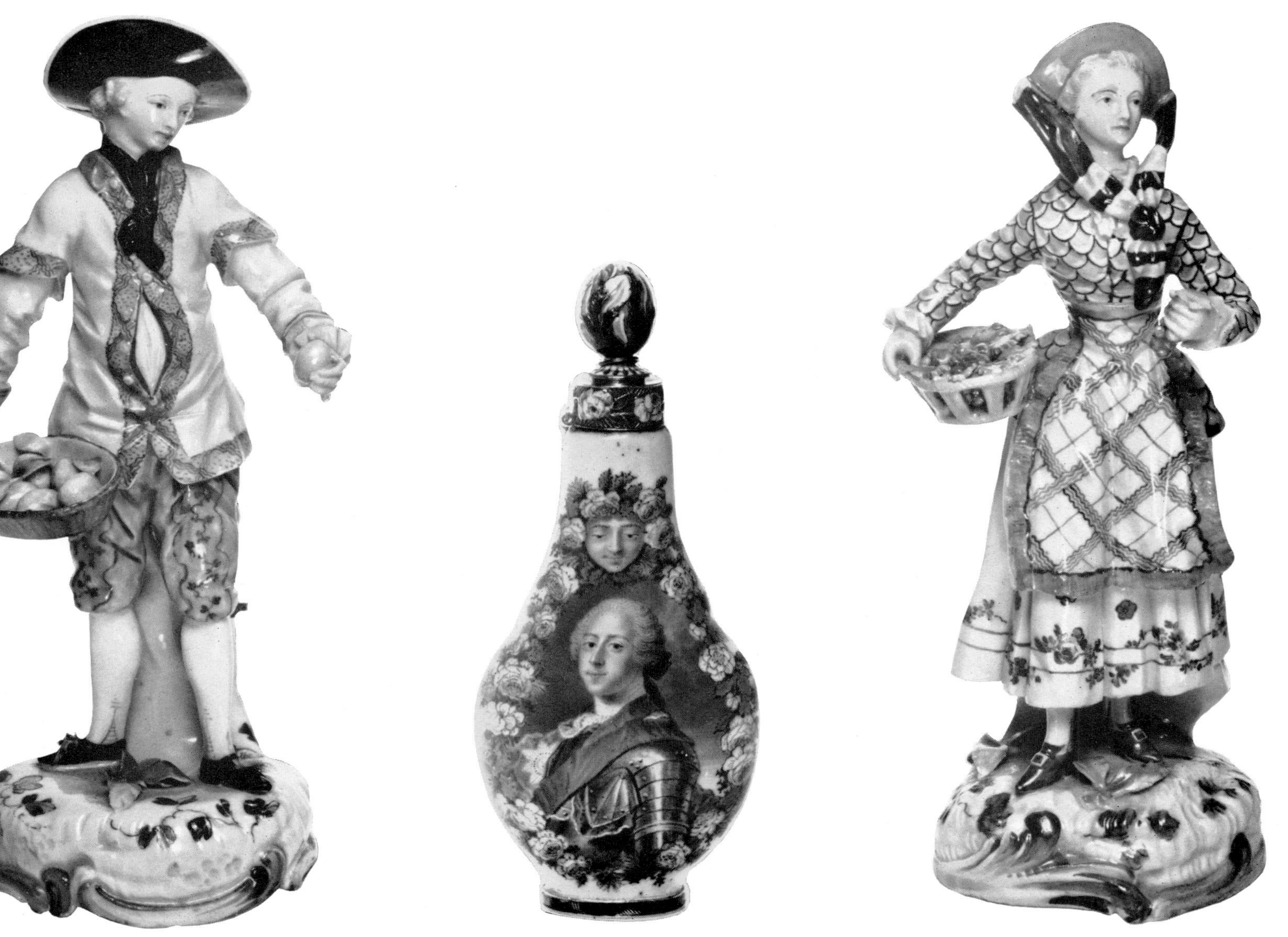

Left and Right A pair of Fulda Figures of Fruit Sellers.
London £950 ($2,660).
From the collection of the late Janek Kahn, Esq.

A Capodimonte 'Jacobite' Scent Bottle, painted with the portrait of The Young Pretender, Prince Charles Edward.
London £750 ($2,100).

The centre-piece of a Vincennes Gros-Bleu 'Garniture-de-Cheminée' of three *Vases Hollandais*, dated 1756.
London £2,300 ($6,440).
From the collection of Mrs Derek Fitzgerald.

A Sèvres Gros-Bleu and Apple-Green Cabaret Set, painted in the manner of Boucher, by Vieillard, 1758.
London £1,200 ($3,360).

An Imperial St Petersburg Empire Vase (one of a pair), decorated by Simon Golov, 1836.
Presented by the Emperor of Russia to the Earl of Durham in April 1836.
London £2,600 ($7,280).

a b c d

(a) A Chelsea 'Girl in a Swing' Scent Bottle.

(b) A Chelsea Triple Scent Bottle.

(c) A Chelsea 'Fish in a Net' Scent Bottle.

(d) A Chelsea Cat Scent Bottle (previously unrecorded).

a b c d

(a) A Chelsea Fable Scent Bottle.

(b) A Chelsea 'Girl in a Swing' Double Scent Bottle.

(c) A Chelsea Swan Scent Bottle.

(d) A Chelsea Peacock Scent Bottle.

The eight scent bottles were sold in London for a total of £5,450 ($15,260)
From the collections of the late Mrs Meyer Sassoon and Mrs Derek Fitzgerald.

A Worcester Pink-Scale Cup and Saucer.
London £620 ($1,736).

An early Chelsea Fluted Beaker.
London £300 ($840).

A set of Bristol Figures of *The Elements*, by Pierre Stefan.
London £950 ($2,660).

A pair of early Chelsea White Figures of Owls.
London £2,500 ($7,000).

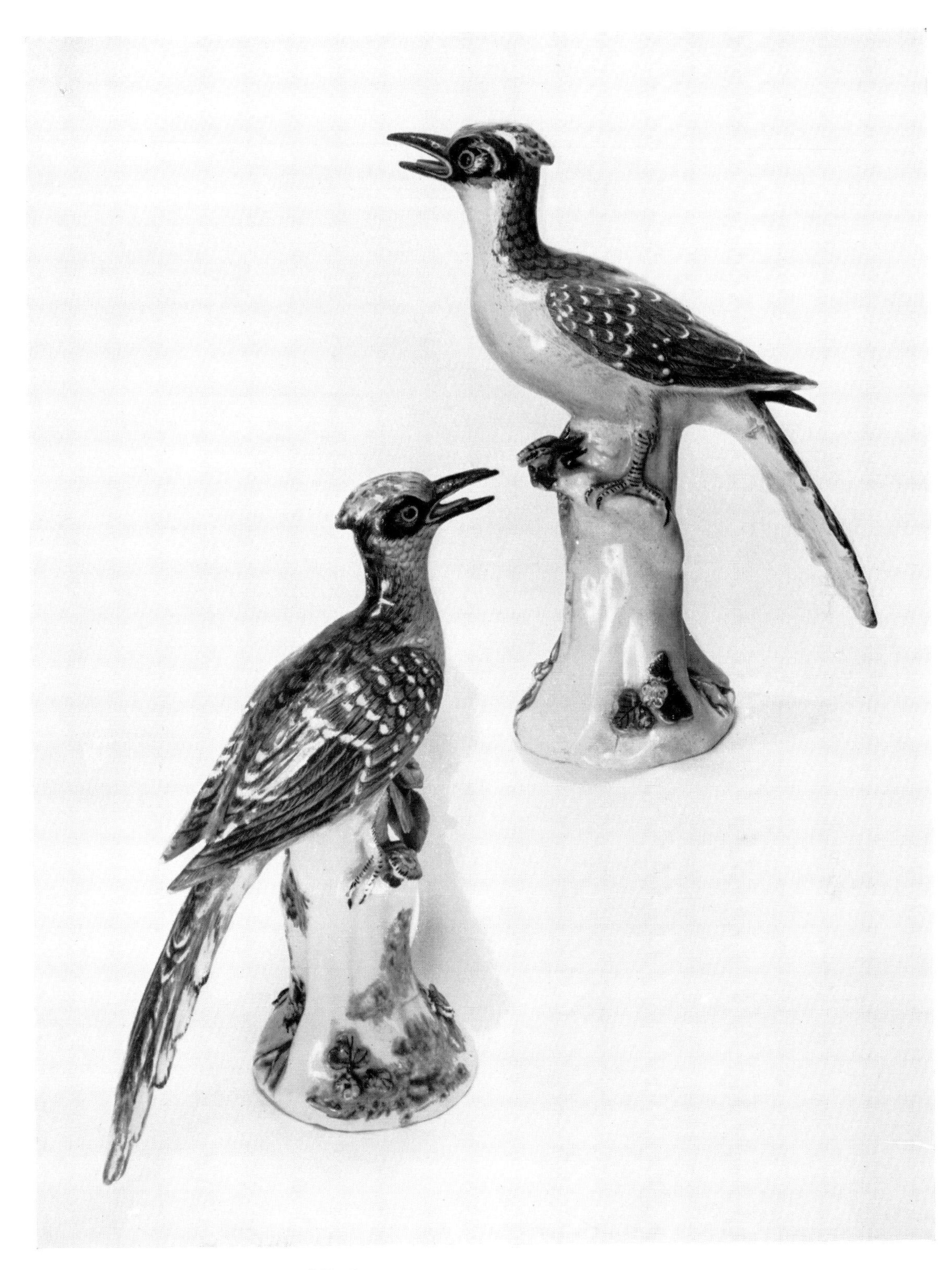

A pair of early Chelsea Figures of Cuckoos.
London £1,250 ($3,550)
From the collection of Mrs W. P. Thursby.

A Chelsea Blue and White Cream Jug.
Chelsea porcelain with underglaze-blue decoration is extremely rare in any form, and up to now unrecorded on a jug.
London £1,400 ($3,920).
From the collection of J. C. C. F. Rowley, Esq.

Right An early Chelsea 'Tea Plant' Coffee Pot and Cover.
London £1,450 ($4,060)
From the collection of Lt-Col. M. H. S. Last.

An early Chelsea Fable dish, painted with the fable of 'The Tygre and Fox'.
London £1,050 ($2,940).

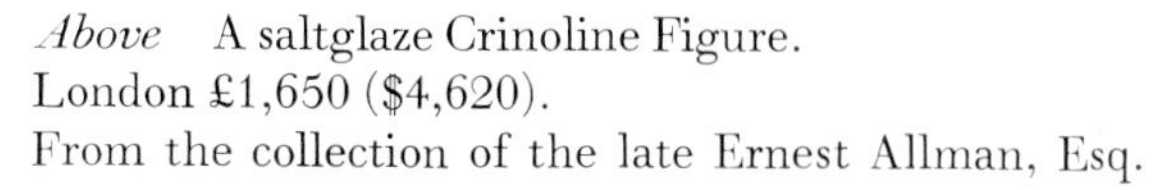

Above A saltglaze Crinoline Figure.
London £1,650 ($4,620).
From the collection of the late Ernest Allman, Esq.

Below A Lambeth Barber's Bowl, dated 1706.
London £680 ($1,904).
From the collection of the late Professor F. H. Garner

Above right A Worcester Transfer-Printed cylindrical Mug, of General Wolfe.
London £280 ($784). From the collection of G. W. Capell, Esq.

Centre A Dwight Fulham Silver-Mounted Stoneware Cup, *circa* 1690.
London £400 ($1,120). From the collection of the late Professor F. H. Garner.

Below A 17th-century Fuddling Cup.
London £85 ($238). From the collection of the late Professor F. H. Garner.

A Pâte-sur-Pâte Amphora, by L. Solon. Signed and dated 1903.
London £2,250 ($6,300).
From the collection of the late Dr Alfred Murgatroyd.

Left A Battersea Transfer-Printed and Painted Plaque, by Robert Hancock (one of a pair). London £1,250 ($2,500).

Right A Battersea Transfer-Printed Plaque, after Simon Francois Ravenet. London £200 ($560).

Left A Staffordshire Landscape Plaque, after Claude Lorraine. London £720 ($2,016).

Right A Battersea Portrait Plaque of Maria Gunning (one of a pair, of the Gunning Sisters). London £850 ($2,380).

From the collection of the late The Hon. Mrs Nellie Ionides.

An early enamel Staffordshire Knife Case.
London £2,500 ($7,000).
From the collection of the late The Hon. Mrs Nellie Ionides.

Right JOHN SMART
A Miniature of a Child.
Signed and dated 1809.
London £500 ($1,400).
From the collection of S. H. V. Hickson, Esq.

Above left SAMUEL COOPER
A Miniature of Lodowicke Muggleton.
London £470 ($1,316).
From the collections of J. Pierpont Morgan and S. H. V. Hickson, Esq.

Centre JEAN PETITOT, JUNIOR
A Miniature of Louis XIV.
Signed and dated 1699.
London £300 ($840).

Right SIR JAMES PALMER
A Miniature of George Villiers, Duke of Buckingham.
Signed and dated 1627.
London £270 ($756).
From the collection of Mrs D. Guthrie.

HENRI TOUTIN (?)
A Miniature of a Lady.
London £420 ($1,176).
From the collection of S. H. V. Hickson, Esq.

Hilliard, Heretics and Humphry

BY EDWINA CLIFFORD-SMITH

The art of miniature painting is 'a thing apart from all other painting or drawing.' This was how Nicholas Hilliard (1547–1619) described the art which he himself practised, in *A Treatise Concerning the Arte of Limning*, which he wrote in 1600.

Basing his methods on those of Holbein, of whom he wrote: 'I neuer heard of any better than hee . . . Holbeans maner of limning I haue euer imitated and howld it for the best . . .', Hilliard was the first great exponent of limning, or the painting of portraits in miniature. This was an art which was carried on successfully by the British until it was superseded by photography in the middle of the 19th century. Although there were many fine Continental exponents of the art, this was a form of painting at which the British excelled and its school of miniature painters is the finest in the world.

Portrait miniatures have never really found the popularity accorded to other works of art and it is regrettable that such little attention has been paid to them. Many students of miniature painting were fine artists and the portrait miniatures they painted provide us with a precise documentation of the styles, costumes and personalities of the nation, spanning a period of three and a half centuries.

In March of this year miniatures from the collection of Mr S. H. V. Hickson were sold and some fine and rare examples of work by both English and Continental artists came on to the market. The outstanding piece in the collection was undoubtedly the superb miniature of a lady by Nicholas Hilliard (see page 199 centre right). Brilliantly painted and in excellent condition, it had been locked away for many years and was thus unrecorded. It may now be counted amongst the finest examples of this artist's work.

Like the majority of Hilliard's miniatures it is unsigned, but it bears the date 1602 and the motto 'Videtur et Vere est.' It has not been established to whom this motto belonged, but it has been suggested that it may be a punning motto of the de Vere family. If this is the case, the most likely person to be represented in the miniature is Elizabeth Trentham, second wife of Edward de Vere, seventeenth Earl of Oxford, whom she married in 1591. The date of her birth is not known and before her marriage she was a maid-of-honour to Queen Elizabeth. A son and heir was born to the Earl of Oxford in 1593 and it would seem fairly reasonable to suppose that his wife was not more than about twenty years old when he married her, approximately the same age as his eldest daughter, by his first marriage to Anne Cecil.

If indeed the inscription on the miniature does relate to the de Veres, then the portrait could not represent either of Edward's two older daughters, Elizabeth and Bridget, who were both married before 1602 and would no longer use their father's motto. Equally well the sitter could not be his youngest daughter, Susan, who was only fifteen at the time and unmarried, while the person represented is wearing what would appear to be a wedding ring on a ribbon attached to the bodice of her dress.

Whoever the sitter was she was certainly someone of importance, for great trouble was taken in the painting of the miniature. She was not a particularly attractive woman, but the artist has captured her charming expression and the whole is made beautiful by the delicacy of the painting and the jewellery and tiny flowers which adorn the dress. These accessories are a hall-mark of Hilliard's work. He was a goldsmith as well as a limner and delighted in making the most of the jewellery worn by his sitters. The delicate touch of flowers, placed in the dress and hair, is typical of the romanticism and poetry of the Elizabethan age to which he belonged.

This miniature had a companion in another, of similar date, by a follower of Hilliard, probably Edward Norgate (1581–1660). Norgate took up limning and heraldry and although principally an illuminator, he painted miniatures, purchased pictures for Henrietta Maria and wrote a treatise called *Miniatura or the Art of Limning*. Although this miniature lacks the romantic appeal, simple lines and superb draughtsmanship of Hilliard, it is, nevertheless, a fine example of the work of a courtier painter of the early 17th century (see page 199 centre left).

A miniature by another gentleman at the court of Charles I was sold a month before the Hickson collection. It is a portrait of George Villiers, Duke of Buckingham, by Sir James Palmer (d. 1657) who was a friend of the king and advised him on the formation of the Royal picture collection. It is only within the last fifteen years or so that Mr Graham Reynolds, of the Victoria and Albert Museum, has discovered a series of miniatures by this artist and this was the second example of Palmer's work to come under the hammer (see page 198 centre right).

One of the most interesting miniatures from the Hickson collection is that of an unknown lady by Nathaniel Thach (b. 1616?) (see page 198 above). Little is known about this artist and there are only two documented miniatures by him, this and another, also in a private collection. Signed and dated 1651, this miniature shows Thach to have been an artist of some considerable talent and it is surprising that more miniatures by him have not come to light.

Samuel Cooper (1609–72), considered by many to be the greatest of all English miniaturists, was represented in the Hickson collection by a portrait of a gentleman named Lodowicke Muggleton (see page 198 centre left). Mr Muggleton was a heretic and the founder of a society bearing his name. In 1653 he was imprisoned for blasphemy, a year after the publication of a 'commission book', which he wrote in conjunction with his cousin, William Reeve, entitled *Transcendent Spirituall Treatise*. At heart Muggleton was a puritan, but he dispised the religious movements of the time, withdrew from all worship and adopted an agnostic position as regards theology. He was, in fact, gaoled several times and wrote a great many published works on the Muggletonian doctrine, before he eventually died in 1698, at the age of 89.

Samuel Cooper was something of an extrovert and whatever loyalties he may have had during the Civil War they did not affect his work as an artist. He was well-liked and respected as a painter and worked both for Cromwell and Charles II and his court. Writing in his *Diary*, on 10 July 1668, Samuel Pepys spoke of Cooper's 'great skill in musick, his playing and setting to the French lute most excellently; and speaks French, and indeed is a most excellent man.' Whereas Hilliard chose to paint with pure lines, devoid of shadow, Cooper worked with quite a different technique, as is seen in this reference made by John Evelyn in his *Diary*, on 10 January 1662: 'Being called into his Majesty's closet when Mr Cooper, the rare limner, was crayoning of the King's face and head, to take the stamps for the new milled money now contriving, I had the honour to hold the candle whilst it was doing, he choosing the night and candle-light for the better finding out the shadows.' This difference in style between these two great masters can be seen to advantage in Hilliard's miniature of a lady and the miniature of Lodowicke Muggleton by Cooper.

Two enamel miniatures of note came into the saleroom in October last year. The first was a small but important miniature by Jean Petitot Junior (b. 1653), fully signed, and dated 1699, representing Louis XIV (see page 198 centre).

Like most sons following in the footsteps of a famous father, Jean Petitot II never reached the heights achieved by his illustrious parent. Nevertheless, he was no mean enamellist, although this would appear to be the only medium in which he worked. He was sent by his father to England to study limning under Samuel Cooper, but this manner of painting apparently did not suit him, for George Vertue wrote: 'After his return to France (Petitot Senior) sent over his son, to have some instructions from Cooper to learn limning – which the Junior Petito not much liking or the method of his instructions, returned to France without much improvement.'

Interest in the second enamel miniature lies in the sitter rather than in the artist (see page 199 below). It is a copy by Henry Spicer (1743?–1804), after Romney, of a portrait of Ozias Humphry. Humphry (1742–1810) was himself a miniaturist who in turn, as well as painting miniatures *ad vivum*, made a great many copies of oil portraits, especially those at Knole. The original portrait of Humphry by Romney is at Knole Park, where the two artists stayed in 1773, on their way to Italy.

Humphry stayed in Italy for about four years, studying and copying the works of the old masters. This, however, did not appear to influence the style of his painting and his works in miniature resemble more the quality of the oil paintings of Sir Joshua Reynolds, who did a great deal towards establishing Humphry in his career as an artist.

Henry Spicer, who painted the miniature copy in enamel of the Romney portrait of Humphry, also copied the work of Humphry himself. He was a friend of Humphry's and it was at lodgings kept by Spicer's widow that Humphry died in 1810.

These are just a few of the more interesting miniatures sold during the past season, which has seen a considerable improvement, over recent years, in the quality of miniatures offered for sale. At the same time it is encouraging to see that new collectors are becoming interested in these small portraits. Over the years numerous books have been written on the subject of portrait miniatures, but, as in all fields of art, there is a great deal more to be learned about the artists who painted them. It is only through wider public interest that our knowledge of this subject can be increased.

NATHANIEL THACH
A Miniature of a Lady.
Signed and dated 1651.
This miniature has so far been unrecorded.
London £320 ($896).
From the collection of S. H. V. Hickson, Esq.

Left SCHOOL OF HILLIARD
A Miniature of a Gentleman, circa 1605.
Hitherto unrecorded, it may possibly be by the rare artist Edward Norgate.
London £1,000 ($2,800).

Right NICHOLAS HILLIARD
A Miniature of a Lady
This miniature, dated 1602, apppears to be unrecorded.
London £5,000 ($14,000)

From the collection of S. H. V. Hickson, Esq.

Below HENRY SPICER
A Miniature of Ozias Humphry.
Signed and dated 1782.
Ozias Humphry was himself a miniaturist.
London £160 ($448).

Above ETIENNE-CHARLES LE GUAY
A Miniature of Pauline Bonaparte.
On a Sèvres porcelain plaque.
London £300 ($840).

Below PIERRE ADOLPH HALL
A Miniature of a Lady.
Signed and dated 1786.
London £400 ($1,120).
From the collection of S. H. V. Hickson, Esq.

A Charles II Pewter Candlestick.
London £360 ($1,008).
From the collection of the late A. V. Sutherland-Graeme, Esq.

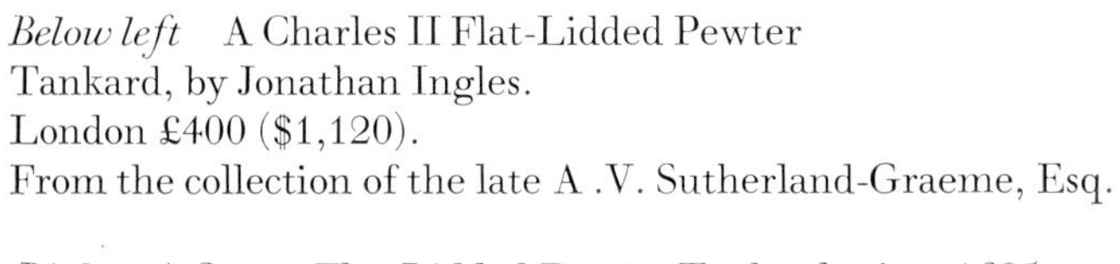

Below left A Charles II Flat-Lidded Pewter Tankard, by Jonathan Ingles.
London £400 ($1,120).
From the collection of the late A .V. Sutherland-Graeme, Esq.

Right A Stuart Flat-Lidded Pewter Tankard, *circa* 1685.
London £320 ($896).
From the collection of the late A. V. Sutherland-Graeme, Esq.

A 17th-century German Nef, by Samuel Lormann Torgau, *circa* 1610.
London £3,900 ($10,920).
From the collection of J. M. H. Janssen, Esq.

A mid-16th-century Spanish Parcel-Gilt Holy Water Bucket.
London £580 ($1,624).

A late 17th-century Belgian Wine Cistern, Brussels, *circa* 1690.
London £15,000 ($42,000).
From the collections of Lord Middleton and Monsieur J. G. de Thouars.

A late 17th-century Incense Burner, *circa* 1680.
London £800 ($2,240).

A Scottish Quaich, possibly by John Falconer, Glasgow, *circa* 1707–8.
London £1,450 ($4,060).
From the collection of Mrs A. Burns.

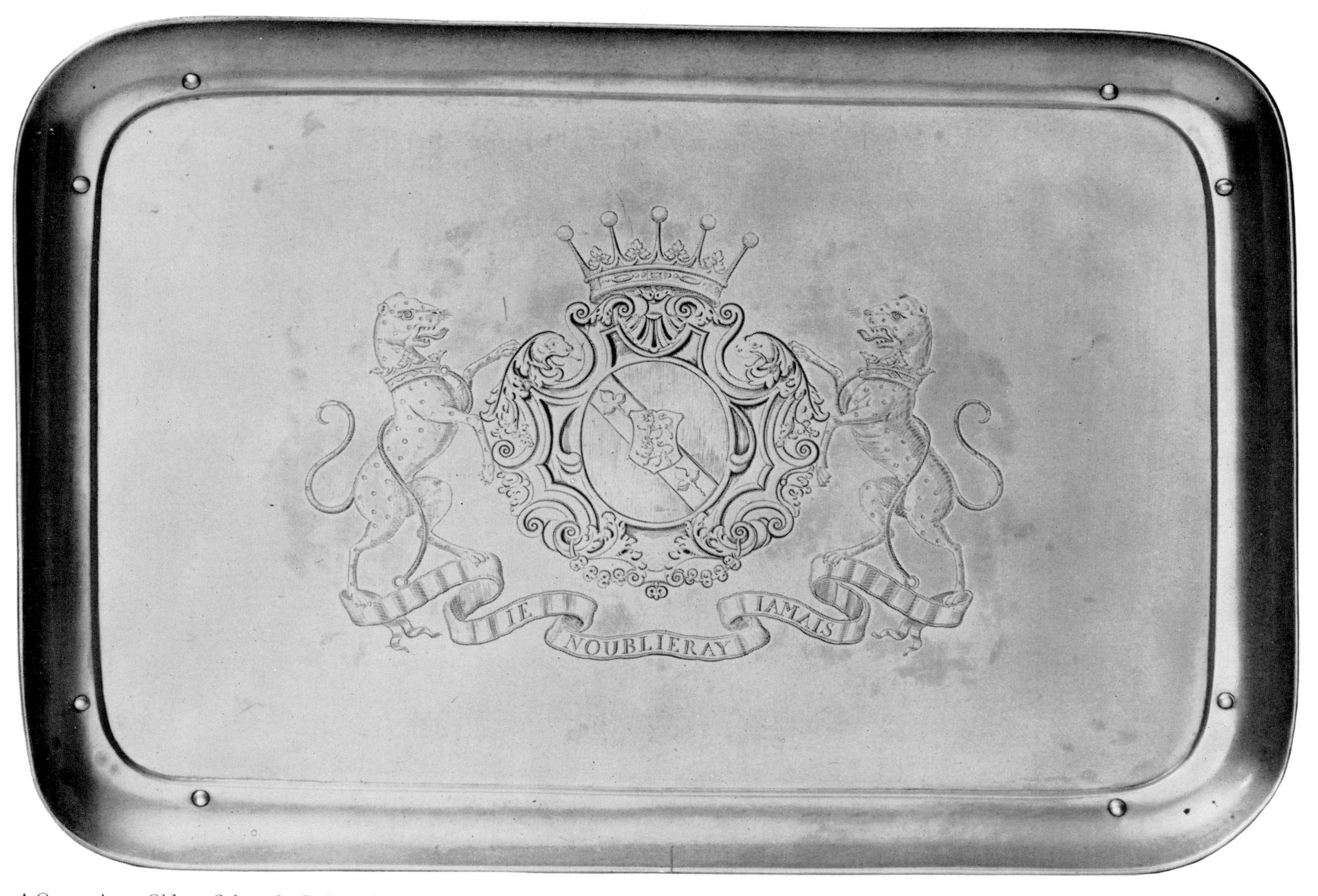

A Queen Anne Oblong Salver, by Robert Cooper, 1712.
London £3,300 ($9,240).
From the collection of The Rt Hon. Lord Cottesloe, C.B.E.

An 18th-century Canadian Ecuelle, by Pierre Huguet Latour, Montreal, *circa* 1775, London £780 ($2,184).

A pair of George II Beakers (from a set of four), by Aymé Videau, 1743.
London £3,800 ($10,640).
From the collection of A. V. Alexander, Esq.

A set of George I Communion Plate, by Anthony Nelme, 1717.
London £2,900 ($8,120).
From the collection of The Rt Hon the Earl of Devon.

A Queen Anne Chocolate Pot, by Isaac Dighton, 1704.
New York $5,000 (£1,785).
From the collection of Mrs A. Hamilton Rice.

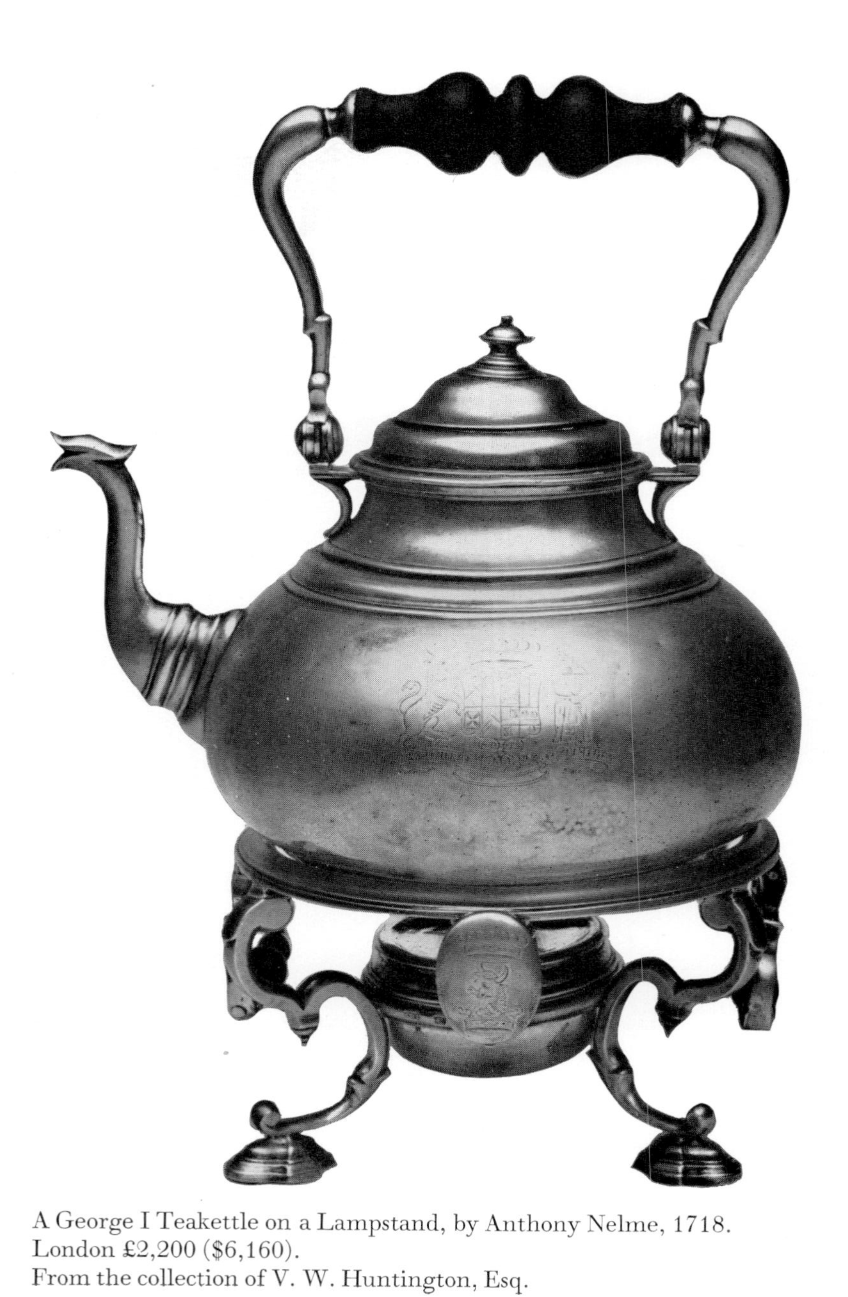

A George I Teakettle on a Lampstand, by Anthony Nelme, 1718.
London £2,200 ($6,160).
From the collection of V. W. Huntington, Esq.

A George I Silver-Gilt Table Candlestick (one of a pair).
by Pierre Platel, 1717.
London £3,000 ($8,400).

A Queen Anne Octagonal Candlestick, 1707 (one of a set of four).
New York $16,500 (£5,890).
From the collection of Mrs A. Hamilton Rice.

A George II Salver, by Edward Vincent, 1728 (one of a pair).
London £6,500 ($18, 200).
From the collection of John Eyre Matcham, Esq.

Detail of the coat-of-arms

A George II Two-Handled Cup and Cover, by John Le Sage, 1734.
London £2,800 ($7,840).
From the collection of The Rt Hon. the Earl of Devon.

A German Silver-Gilt Covered Bowl and Stand,
by Johann Erhard Heuglin II, Augsburg, *circa* 1725.
London £1,350 ($3,780).
From the collection of Prince Herman of Saxe-Weimar.

Above left A George III Three-Light Candelabra (one of a pair), by John Schofield, 1795.
New York $8,000 (£2,855).
From the collection of Mrs A. Hamilton Rice.

Above right A George III Table Candlestick in the French taste (from a set of four), by Thomas Heming, 1770.
London £1,500 ($4,200).

Below A Louis XVI Oval Dish (one of a set of four), by Jean Baptiste François Cheret, Paris, 1787.
London £2,200 ($6,160).

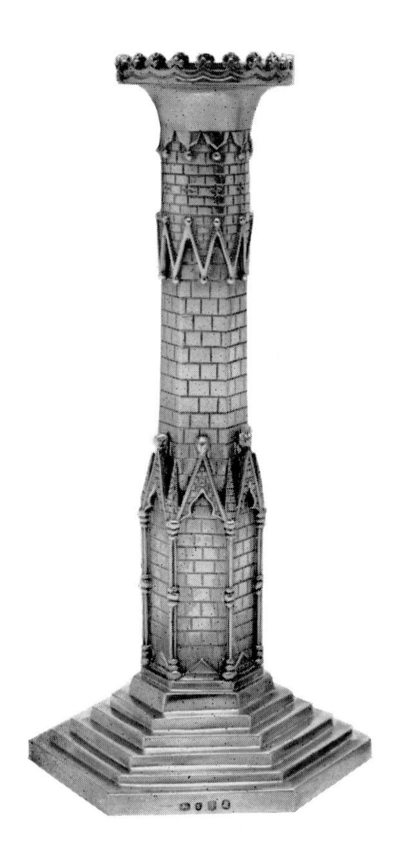

Above left A George III Candlestick in the "Gothick" style (from a set of four), by William Elliott, 1814. London £600 ($1,680).

Above right A Silver-Gilt George III Candelabra (from a set of six), by John Schofield, 1798. London £3,200 ($8,960).

Below An Austrian Spirit Wagon, Vienna, 1828. Length 12¼ in.
The Arms are those of Baron Nathan de Rothschild, of Frankfurt and London (1777–1836).
London £920 ($2,576).
From the collection of S. R. Houfe, Esq.

A Step-Cut Diamond (weighing 30.58 carats).
London £70,000 ($196,000).

A Step-Cut Emerald (weighing approximately 142 carats).
London £52,000 ($145,600).

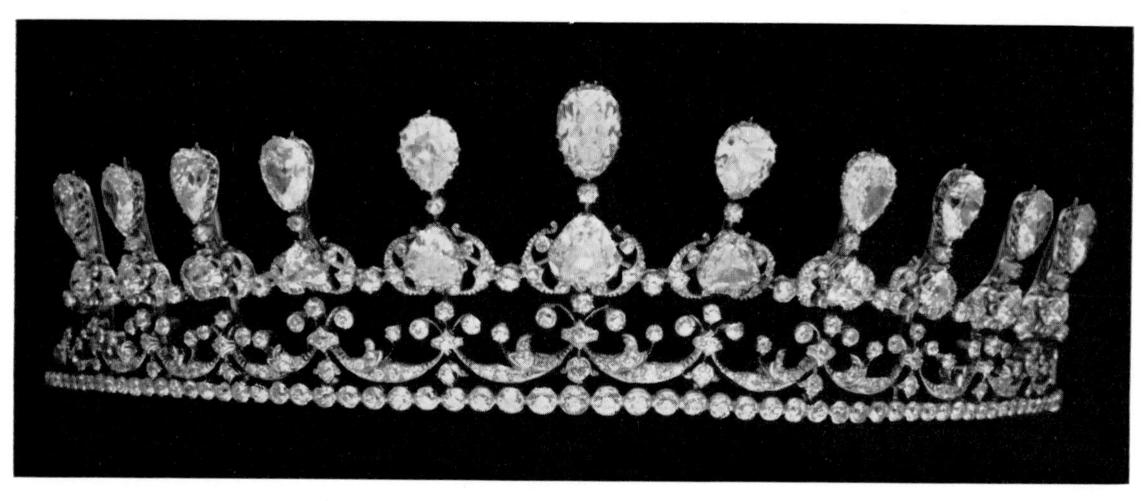

A Diamond Tiara.
A chain of circular-cut diamonds with a cluster snap enabled part of this Tiara to be worn as a necklace.
London £6,200 ($17,360).

Right A Step-Cut Diamond (weighing 5.63 carats).
London £4,400 ($12,320).

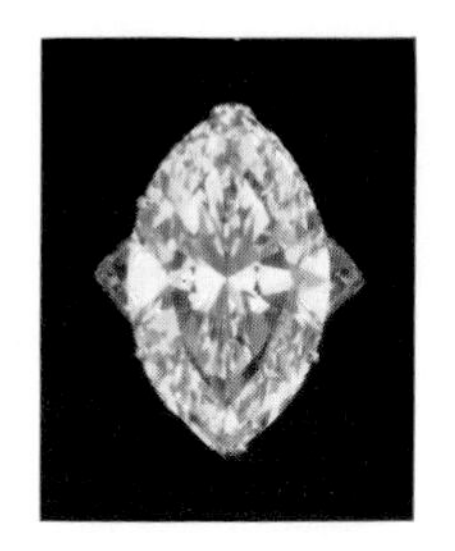

Above left A Square-Cut Diamond (weighing 23.05 carats), mounted as a ring.
London £44,000 ($123,200).

Right A Marquise-Shaped Diamond (weighing 15.45 carats) mounted as a ring,
London £17,000 ($47,600).

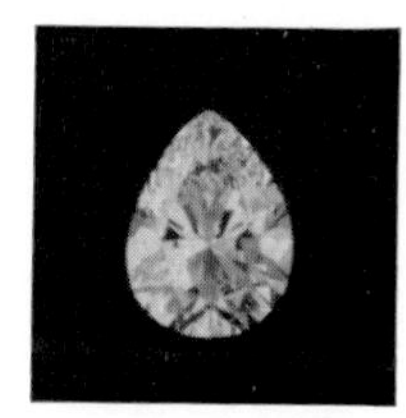

Right A Diamond Brooch Pendant by Cartier
London £4,300 ($10,040).

Left A Pear-Shaped Diamond (weighing 6.72 carats).
London £8,400 ($23,520).

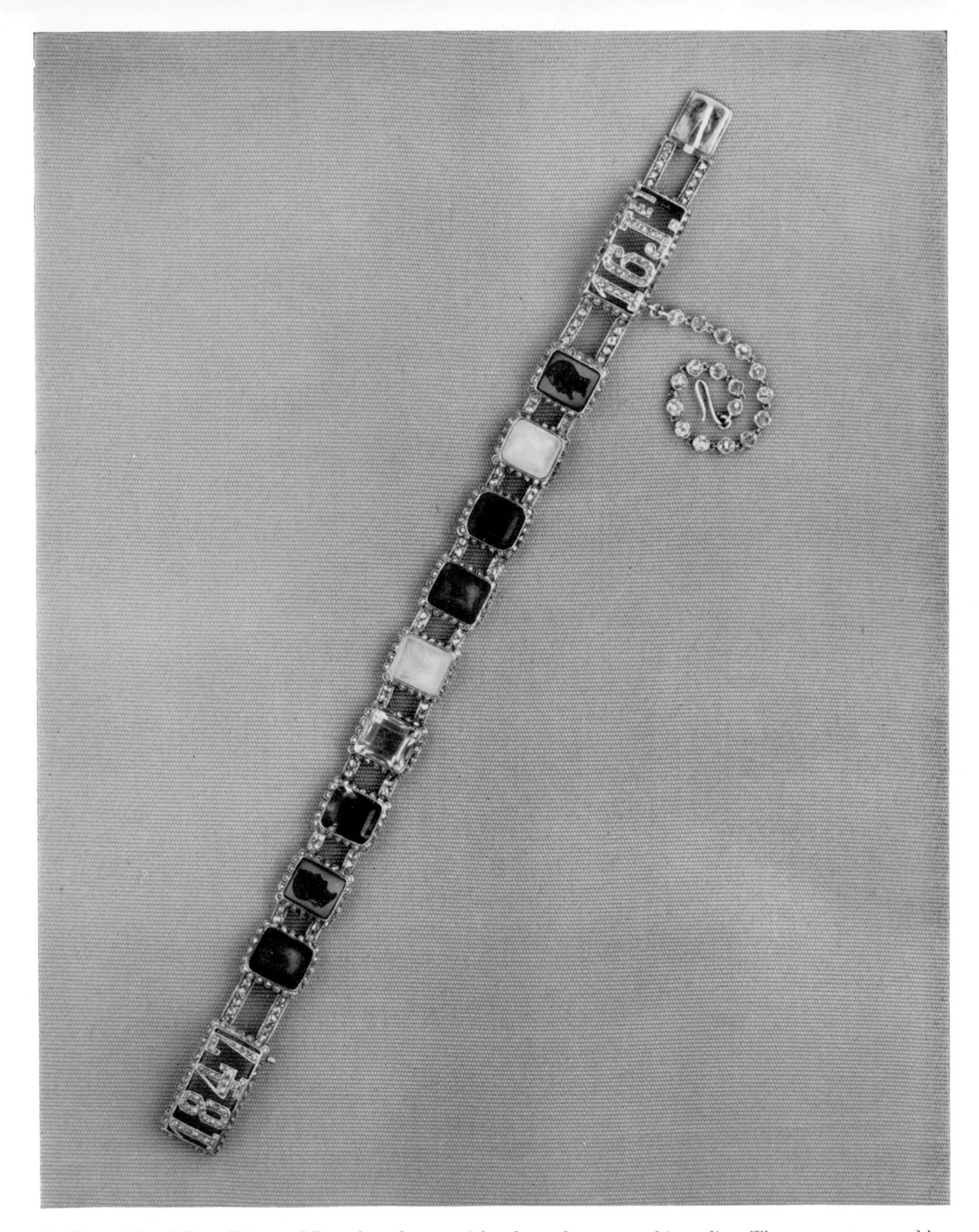

An Emerald and Rose Diamond Bracelet, also set with coloured stones and intaglios. The step-cut emerald is mounted with lapis-lazuli, amethyst, peridot and opals arranged so that the first letters of each spell L NAPOLEON, the letters N represented by Nicolos of the two Emperors.

The documents which accompanied this bracelet suggested that it was a gift from the Emperor Napoleon III to Harriet Howard, the self-styled Countess Beauregard, who was born Elizabeth Anne Haryett. At the age of sixteen she ran away from home to become an actress and appeared at the Haymarket Theatre in 1840. At this time she was living with Jem Mason, a horsecoper's son and famous steeplechase rider. Leaving Mason in 1841 she formed a liaison with Francis Mountjoy Martin, a Major in The Life Guards, whose son she bore, and whose generosity left her a millionairess. A superb horsewoman and of rare beauty, she attracted the attentions of Prince Louis Napoleon, at that time seeking asylum in London, after his escape from life imprisonment in the castle of Ham, and it was her fortune which financed his rise to power. After his marriage to Eugenie Montijo she herself married Clarence Trelawny, an Englishman holding a commission in an Austrian huzzar regiment, and retired to the Château de Beauregard where she died in 1865.

London £2,400 ($6,720). From the collection of Mrs P. M. Alexander.

An Oriental Pearl Necklace, by Cartier.
New York $60,000 (£21,425).
From the collection of Mrs A. Hamilton Rice.

The Collection of Precious Stone Jewellery formed by Mrs A. Hamilton Rice was sold in May 1965 for $1,341,560 (£479,065).

A Fabergé Hardstone Figure of a Captain of the 4th Harkovski Lancers Regiment.
Dated 1914–15, workmaster Henrik Wigstrom. Height $5\frac{1}{4}$ in.
London £6,950 ($19,460).

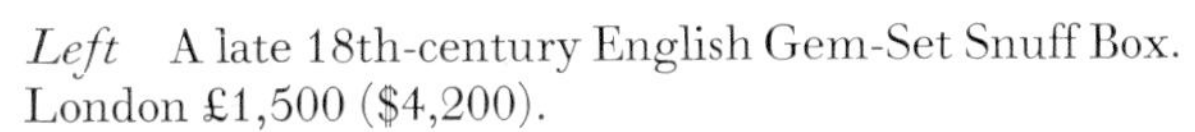

Left A late 18th-century English Gem-Set Snuff Box.
London £1,500 ($4,200).

Right A late 18th-century German Horse's Head Bonbonniere.
London £1,100 ($3,080).

A Fabergé Gold and Enamel Strut Clock, workmaster Michael Perchin.
London £900 ($2,520).

A Diamond Necklace, by Cartier.
The round diamonds are from a rivière given to Princess Irina of Russia
by her Uncle, Czar Nicholas II, on the occasion of her marriage to Prince Youssoupoff.
New York $105,000 (£37,495).
From the collection of the late Helen W. Rivas.

Above A Sapphire Ring.
New York $64,000 (£22,875).
From the collection of Mrs A. Hamilton Rice.

Above A pair of Emerald and Diamond Clips,
by Cartier.
New York $26,000 (£9,285).
From the collection of Mrs A. Hamilton Rice.

Below A pair of Sapphire and Diamond Ear Clips,
by Cartier.
New York $16,000 (£5,715).
From the collection of Mrs A. Hamilton Rice.

Below An Opal and Diamond Clip,
by Cartier.
London £1,500 ($4,200).
From the collection of the late Contessa di Sant'Elia.

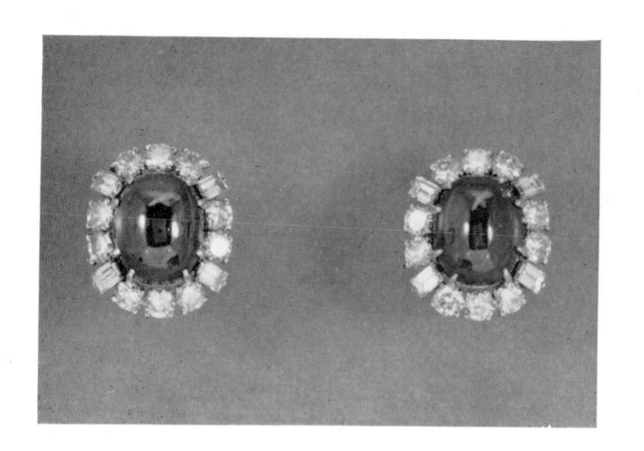

An Antique Sapphire and Diamond Necklace and a pair of pendant ear-rings
London £14,500 ($40,600).

An Antique Diamond Corsage Ornament, in the form of a bouquet of fuchsias and lilies of the valley.
London £3,600 ($10,080).

A Gold-Mounted Hardstone Covered Tazza, by Charles Duron, Paris 1857.
London £1,400 ($3,920).
From the collection of Mrs M. Joyce.

A Fabergé Miniature Frame, in the Louis XVI style.
London £700 ($1,960).

A Fabergé Nephrite Garniture de Bureau.
Workmaster Karl Gustav Hjalmar Armfelt, Julius Alexandeovitch Rappoport *et al*
London £3,000 ($8,400).
From the collection of C. E. Sutton, Esq.

Right A Miniature Fabergé Vitrine.
London £1,050 ($2,940).

A Ruby and Baguette-Diamond Bracelet, by Cartier.
London £25,000 ($70,000).

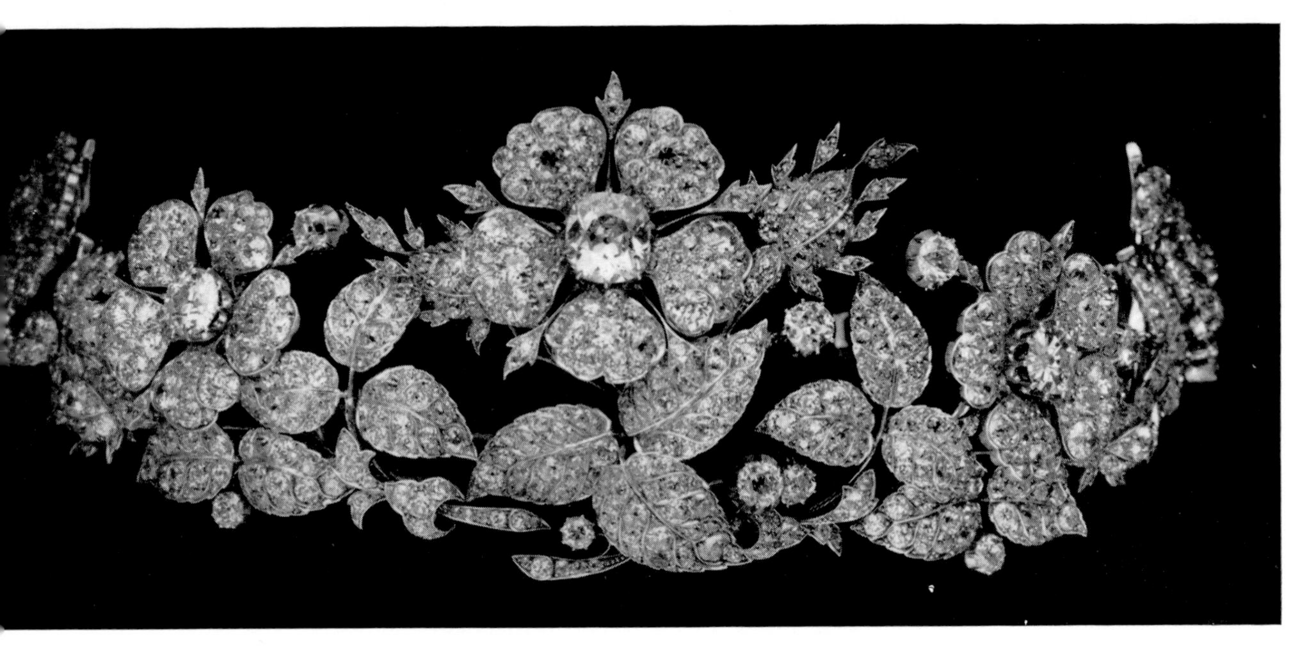

A Diamond Tiara, consisting of five sprays, all of which may be detached and worn as brooches.
London £11,000 ($30,800).
From the collection of Lt-Colonel G. A. M. Vandeleur, D.S.O.

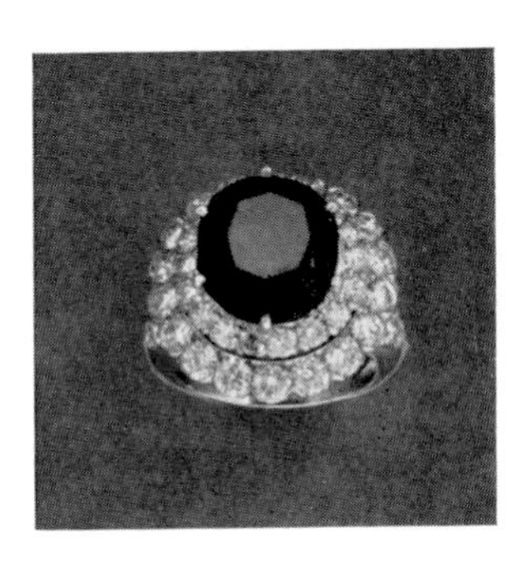

A Ruby Ring, by Van Cleef and Arpels.
New York $85,000 (£30,350).
From the collection of Mrs A. Hamilton Rice

An Art Nouveau Brooch, by René Lalique.
London £300 ($840).
From the collection of C. Handley-Read, Esq.

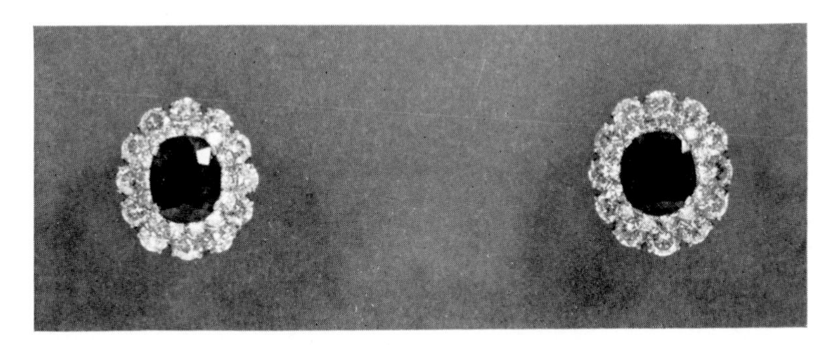

A pair of Ruby and Diamond Ear Clips, by Van Cleef and Arpels.
New York $65,000 (£23,210).
From the collection of Mrs A. Hamilton Rice.

A Fabergé Clock in the form of an egg in gold, enriched with rose and white enamel. Dated 1902. Workmaster Michael Perchin. Height 9 in. New York $50,000 (£17,855).

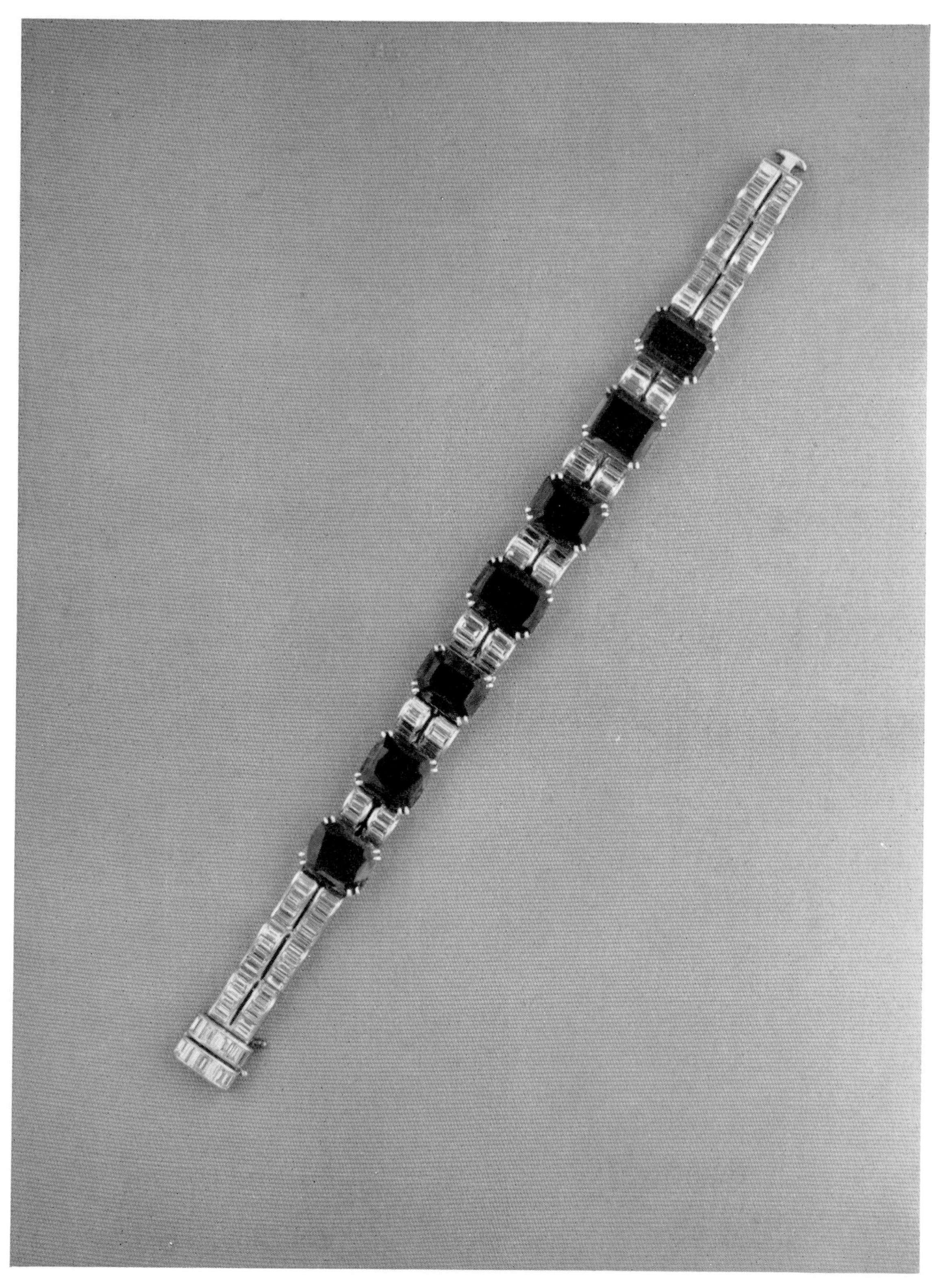

An Emerald and Diamond Bracelet, by Boucheron.
London £12,000 ($33,600).

A Silesian "Hochschnitt" Covered Goblet, from the Schaffgotsch glassworks, *circa* 1700.
£2,600 ($7,280).
From the Beck collection.

The Beck collection of Continental Glass was sold in November 1964 for £26,889 ($75,282).

Above left A German Portrait Goblet of Prince Eugene of Savoy, by S. Schwartz, dated Nuremberg, 1719.
London £1,900 ($5,320).

Above right A Portrait Roundel, engraved by Dominik Bimann, *circa* 1835.
London £1,650 ($4,620).

An 'In Memoriam' Beaker, by G. S. Mohn, Vienna *circa* 1817.
London £420 ($1,176).

From the Beck collection.

Above left A Viennese Floral 'Ranftbecher', by Anton Kothgasser, *circa* 1825.
London £550 ($1,540).

Above centre A Musical Score Tumbler, by G. S. Mohn, with a musical setting of Schiller's poem, *An die Freude*.
Signed and dated 1811.
London £520 ($1,456).

Above right A Commemorative Ballooning Beaker and Cover, depicting Vincent Lunardi in his balloon ascending over the harbour at Naples.
Circa 1791.
London £1,450 ($4,060).

Right A late 17th-century Ruby Glass Beaker.
London £1,300 ($3,640).
Formerly in the collection of Oscar Dusendschon, sold at Sotheby's in December 1960 for £380 ($1,064.)

From the Beck Collection.

Left A St Louis Encased Pink Overlay Weight. London £3,300 ($9,240).

Right A Baccarat Triple Weight.
Weights of each section are well recorded but a combination of all three into a triple weight of gourd form is completely unrecorded.
London £2,100 ($5,880).

An Inscribed Bowl, enamelled by the Beilby's of Newcastle, dated 1764.
London £460 ($1,288).

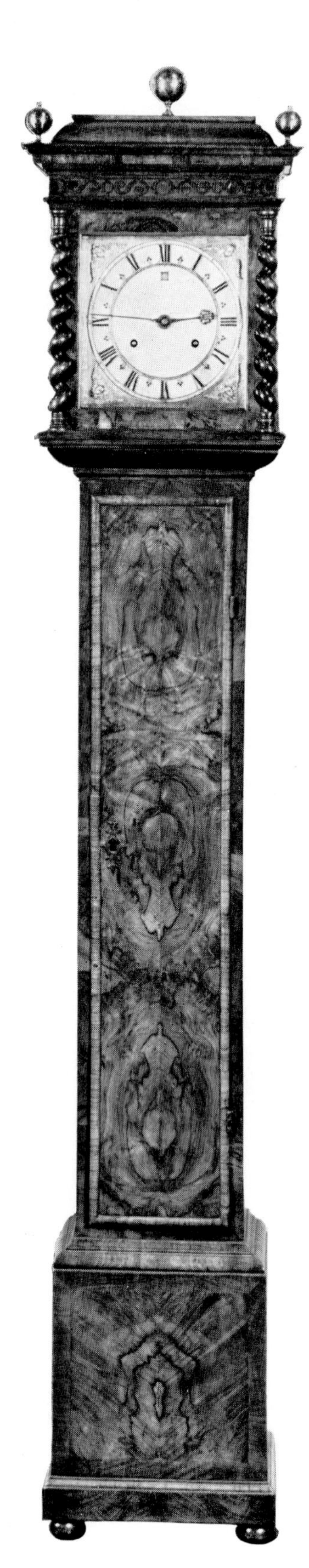

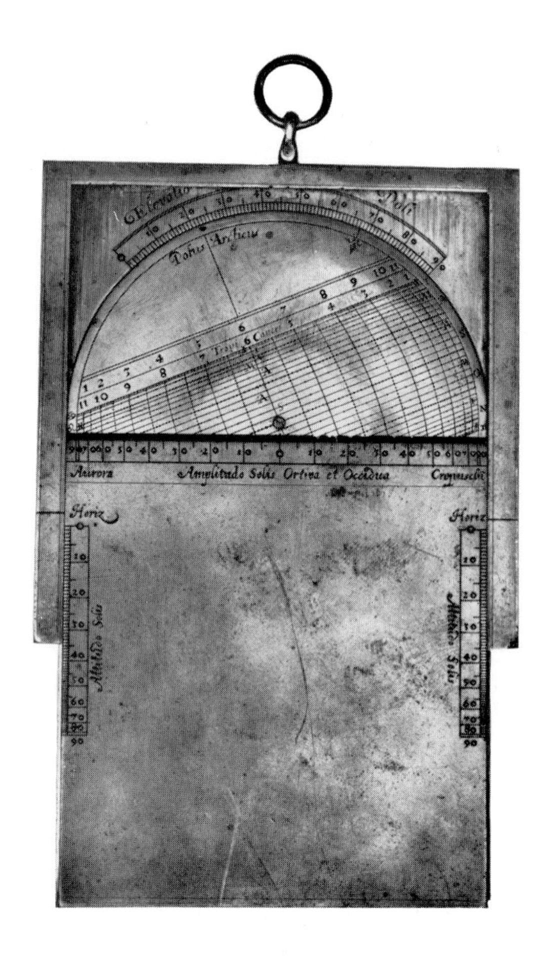

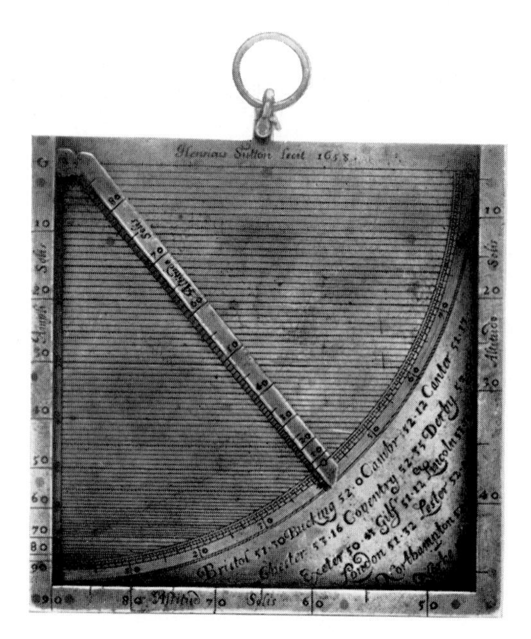

Above A Walnut Month Longcase Clock, by Joseph Knibb.
London £2,600 ($7,280).
From the collection of the late Walter J. Iden and Dr L. Phillips

Above and below right A 17th-century Scientific Instrument in brass, by Henry Sutton, 1658
London £420 ($1,176).

An early 16th-century Automaton Table Clock, possibly Dresden.
London £5,800 ($16,240).
From the collection of the late Dr Axel Wenner-Gren.

A Louis XV Parquetry Longcase Clock, by Julien Le Roy.
London £2,300 ($6,440).
From the collection of the Rt Hon. the Countess of Craven.

A Gold and Enamel Watch-Case with a later verge movement.
London £560 ($1,568).

Left and right A 17th-century Enamel Watch, by Henry Grendon of London.
London £900 ($2,520).

Below left A 17th-century Gold Repoussé Watch-Case.
London £340 ($952).

Below right A Gold and Enamel-Cased Verge Watch, signed Martineau, London, *circa* 1690.
London £610 ($1,708).

A 17th-century Square Gold and Enamel Watch, by Paul Bizot, St Germain.
London £1,850 ($5,180).

Right An early Marquetry Longcase Clock, by Thomas Tompion.
London £4,800 ($13,400).
From the collection of the late Walter J. Iden and Dr L. Phillips

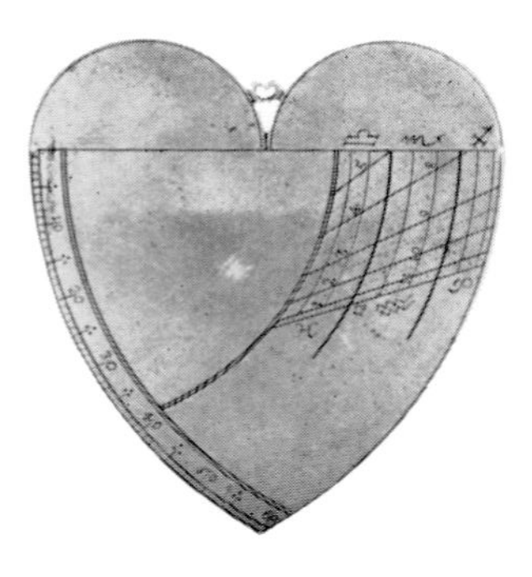

An 18th-century Turkish Astrolabic Watch.
Probably made at Galata, *circa* 1740.
London £1,100 ($3,080).

Above right A 17th-century Heart-Shaped Altitude Dial.
London £60 ($168).

Below right A Gold-Cased Chronoscope, by William Knottesford of London.
London £900 ($2,520).

A small Ebonized Bracket Clock, by John Knibb, *circa* 1685.
London £1,400 ($3,920).
From the collection of the late M. F. G. Ash, Esq.

An Augsburg Monstrance Clock, *circa* 1580.
London £1,300 ($3,640).

A Small Naval Gold Medal, awarded to Admiral Sir Edward Hamilton, when Captain of H.M.S. *The Surprise*, on the 25th October, 1799.
Sir Edward Hamilton was knighted and obtained the gold medal for his gallantry in cutting out His Majesty's late ship *Hermione* from under the batteries of Porto Cavallo in South America.
London £1,900 ($5,320).
From the collection of C. J. Hamilton, Esq.

A Victoria Devoted Service Medal, one of three separate medals awarded to John Brown.
London £550 ($1,540).

THE MEDALS AWARDED TO JOHN BROWN, ESQ.

(*Queen Victoria's Personal Attendant*)

Of the many incidents experienced by Queen Victoria, the one for which she inaugurated a medal and awarded it to John Brown is for most people a piece of forgotten, or never learnt, history; but at the time it had seemed that the Queen was about to die from an assassin's bullet.

On 29th February, 1872, Queen Victoria had been for her afternoon carriage ride, and returned to Buckingham Palace through the garden entrance. As the carriage came to a standstill, the Queen saw a pistol aimed at her through the open window. She and the other passenger, Jane Churchill, were both helpless. The pistol was held by a seventeen-year-old youth named Arthur O'Connor, who had seized this moment to try to force the Queen to sign a long and detailed document of his own composition, that would have secured the freedom of all prisoners held for Irish Fenian activities.

John Brown, on the rumble of the carriage, saw the Queen only seconds away from assassination. He leapt at O'Connor, knocking the pistol away, and after a short struggle, held him to the ground. The pistol was then found to be of great age and damaged beyond repair. However O'Connor was arrested and appeared before Bow Street Magistrates' Court, where he pleaded guilty to the charge and was duly sentenced to one year's hard labour, and twenty strokes of the lash.

For John Brown the reward was the *Victoria Devoted Service Medal* (see page 240 *below*), a unique decoration struck in gold from the same dies as the *Victoria Faithful Service Medal*. The obverse, by J. S. Wyon, shows the Queen, whilst on the reverse is the inscription, 'To John Brown, Esq., in recognition of his presence of mind and devotion at Buckingham Palace, February 29th, 1872.' It is worn from a gold suspender, with a V.R. monogram, over a ribbon of Royal Stewart tartan. The medal held an annuity of £25. The other two medals in the group were his *Victoria Faithful Service Medal*, in silver, with a ten-year bar, and a silver medal 'For Service' of Ludwig III of Hesse. The three sold for £550.

See: *Queen Victoria's John Brown* by E. E. P. Tisdall – Stanley Paul & Co. Ltd., 1938.

The Royal Family Orders, Badges of Office, Royal Household Medals and Souvenirs, by G. P. L. James – Spring Grange Private Press, 1951, also 'The Supplement' to the above, edited by R. E. Harbord. Spring Grange Private Press, 1954.

DANIEL FEARON

The Small Arms room in the Tower of London *circa* 1850. The pillars constructed out of percussion rifles, the chandelier of bayonets and the ballustrades of flintlock sea-service pistols beneath rows of swords.
by courtesy of H.M. The Tower of London Armouries

A Coastguard's Percussion Cap Pistol, dated 1855
London £25 ($70)

The Tower of London as Host to the Board of Ordnance

BY HOWARD RICKETTS

Harrison Ainsworth's romantic literary sketches written in the 19th century did much to condition the modern image of the Tower of London.

To the spectator today this gaunt fortress leaves a composite impression; the atmosphere generated by two museums – the Crown Jewels and the Armouries – set against a background of vividly descriptive case histories of the important prisoners held there, only to end their lives on the block a stone's throw away from the dungeons. So dramatic were the Middle Ages for the Tower that its history even as comparatively recently as the 18th century is for the most part left untold.

This year the Master of the Queen's Armouries dispatched to Sotheby's for sale some several thousand arms which had been stored away in the Tower since they were taken out of service in the 18th and 19th centuries. They were originally under the control of the Board of Ordnance, a British Governmental department responsible for the arms of the soldier and sailor from the Middle Ages, until as a department it was abolished in 1855. This collection serves as a reminder that the Tower of London during this period was custodian of the National Arsenal, housed technicians capable of investigating and testing new firearms with a view to mass-production, and at the same time looked after the armour now considered to be one of the finest collections in the world, which had simply accumulated there in the sixteenth and seventeenth centuries.

The 'curiosities of ancient armour' were looked after by the Ordnance storekeeper, who happily pocketed the entrance fee, which in the 18th century was fixed at the exorbitant sum of three shillings. This was a haphazard exhibition with the most historic pieces set up on painted dummies of monarchs ranging from Henry VI to James II, in the so-called 'line of Kings and nobles': but in the early 19th century, as interest in armour increased during the gothic revival, mainly stimulated by the Waverley novels, pressure was put on the Duke of Wellington, Master General of the Ordnance, to release the armouries from the Board's control, and in 1827 Sir Samuel Meyrick was invited to undertake their reorganisation. A direct result of this was that the Victorian citizen could view the arms, consult a catalogue and all for the reduced fee of one shilling which contributed towards the acquisition of rare pieces to fill gaps in the collection.

The Georgian visitor, however, would have been infinitely more impressed by the display of Britain's armaments in the Grand Storehouse. This vast building, some three hundred and fifty feet long, was festooned with over two hundred thousand arms, 'forming various fancyful devices, stars, crowns, eagles, hydras, triumphal arches etc.', which were 'all in such state as to be fit for immediate and effective service'.[1] A modern parallel might be drawn from the May Day display of missiles and arms, and the overall effect it makes on the average Muscovite. This was all very splendid as a peacetime arsenal, but during hostilities it proved to be inadequate. It is somewhat strange that similar series of blunders took place in the arms industry during the 18th century as in the aircraft industry today. Both depend on a vote of funds from Parliament, and rather naturally they were generous in allowing a sufficient amount during war time when public opinion confirmed that it was a necessity, than in peace time when it seemed a luxury and could successfully be minimised. This left the Board in somewhat of a predicament, since it had not only to conduct experiments to find the perfect weapon, but also to produce enough of them for the armed forces at the right moment. However, the balance was never right and panic always set in at the beginning of armed aggression, so that to satisfy the demand orders went abroad to the gunsmiths of Liège or Rotterdam, who could produce weapons in enormous quantities but inevitably of poor quality.

Until Marlborough's campaigns at the advent of the 18th century the Board had ordered complete arms from gunsmiths, whose workshops were conveniently close to the Tower in the Minories and East Smithfield. However, for the first time there was a major crisis when not only the troops in Europe were clamouring for arms, but also in the same year of 1705 the Governor of Virginia needed a new issue of arms to replace his burnt-out arsenal; the Governor of the Leeward Islands, several thousand pieces to replace the obsolete matchlock gun which was 'dangerous in marches through a county of sugar cane'; and the authorities of Ireland, twelve thousand pieces for protection against invasion and for other duties. The London gun trade simply could not deal with this bulk order, the reason being that they preferred to supply private buyers rather than a Government office which could offer only a very belated settlement of accounts. So the system of ordering had to be remodelled by the Master General of the Ordnance, who very wisely decided to order the component parts from the various gun centres at Birmingham and London, and subsequently assemble them at the Tower or nearby, and also to guard against the possibility of a future shortage by keeping some back. Soon the Tower took on the appearance of a sprawling factory, with the proof house, which was responsible for testing the strength of barrels, the storerooms on the wharf and the Grand Storehouse just north of the White Tower, together with gunsmiths' workshops and cottages.[2]

The Principal Storekeeper, responsible to the Master General of the Ordnance, was in charge of the 'piecemen' and 'daymen', the latter being the permanent staff of craftsmen. It was excellent practical training for the young apprentices, and amongst the attractions was exemption from the press gang, and the prospect of being offered the job of a ship's armourer or a post in one of the colonial or overseas depots. The London gunmakers often tried to steal these young promising craftsmen as well as older and more experienced men away from the Tower, and it was quite difficult for the Ordnance Storekeeper to prevent this happening as their services were vitally necessary for making up guns from component parts and restoring those damaged in action.

One would have thought from this new system of Government contracting, in which this group of expert gunsmiths played an important part, that the British soldier and sailor would be well supplied with modern up-to-date arms. Undoubtedly the most important inventions of the day were referred to the Board by the private gunsmith since they had the best facilities for examining new devices at the trial grounds at Woolwich, and the possible result of a big order for a new weapon was financially attractive to any gunsmith. Theoretically the system which should have attracted the best inventions should have worked perfectly, but in practice the conservative character of the selective committee seemed to foil progress.

Only national disaster could shake the complacency of the Board. The loss of the American colonies in the War of Independence certainly achieved this if nothing else. Until this time the smooth bore flintlock musket was considered quite adequate for the Army; but when the forces across the Atlantic were cut to pieces by the American snipers using the more accurate rifle, with the absence of comparable weapons in store, the Board realised that the only possible way to avoid certain defeat was to despatch Colonel Faucett to Germany to acquire several thousand rifled pieces. They arrived too late to turn the tables. In retrospect the Colonies might well have been retained had Captain Ferguson invented and developed his quick firing breech loading rifle a decade earlier. It was an excellent arm which the inventor demonstrated could fire seven shots in a minute, although while putting it through its paces at Windsor in front of the Royal Family, he modestly observed to the King that 'he would not undertake in that time to knock down above five of His Majesty's enemies'. The Board hastily made enough of these rifles to equip Ferguson's own riflemen who were sent across the Atlantic and proved the superiority of the gun in the attack on Bradywine Hill in September, 1777. It was a severe test, as they were put in the van of the battle, and rather naturally suffered a great many casualties. Unfortunately the accuracy of this weapon depended mainly on the skill of the soldier behind it, and the common infantryman could not fire it to its full advantage. Tragically Ferguson himself was killed at the Battle of Kings Mountain in 1780, and after this the rifle was shelved by the Board and only reappeared as a sporting gun.

After the humiliating defeat in America, England should have taken more advantage of the period of peace in which to re-arm, but instead long and costly experiments were conducted at the Tower, from which few really practical arms emerged. One particular curiosity which is represented in the collection is a volley gun which fired seven shots simultaneously, and was designed to be fired from the maintops of a ship. Few were made, mainly because Nelson, amongst other Admirals, complained that the discharge might easily have set the sails alight. The recoil from this heavy arm must have been devastating, and it is difficult to imagine how a sailor would have remained upright in the riggings when the piece went off. A myth grew up around the volley gun that it was made as a vendetta after Nelson had been killed by a sniper from the riggings of a French man-o'-war, but in fact it was withdrawn from the Navy well before Trafalgar.

Undoubtedly the most important single discovery in the whole evolution of firearms was the invention of the percussion system which took place in the early 19th century, many of the experiments being conducted at the Tower. The venerated flintlock action which had been universally adopted for over a hundred and fifty years had one chief fault, that it sometimes failed to ignite in damp weather; this very rarely happened to the percussion cap arm. The man responsible for this new invention was the Reverend

Alexander John Forsyth, a Presbyterian minister from Aberdeenshire, who experimented with the highly explosive fulmanate of mercury as a possible form of ignition. His advances in this field were accelerated in 1806 when the Master General of the Ordnance, Lord Moyra, invited him to work at the Tower of London. However, it was a slow process and this rather complicated form of detonation could not be simplified enough to facilitate the full-scale production of the service pattern weapon before the end of the war against Napoleon, and consequently the British Army still had to be issued with flintlock arms. Such Dragoon and Light Infantry pieces form a large group in the collection sent in for sale.

After the war Forsyth continued experimenting and set up shop in Piccadilly. Although his original ideas had been far in advance of any of his contemporaries, the patenting of his 'scent-bottle lock' blocked such men as Joseph Manton and Joshua Shaw from manufacturing their safer and simplified lock mechanisms in London. Shaw took his invention of the percussion cap to America to patent it and it was not until the 1830s that this remarkable miniature cup-shaped piece of copper, filled with fulmanates, which when sharply hit detonated, came into current use in England. This object alone laid the foundations for the invention of the centre fire cartridge, which came into use in the middle of the last century and is still in use today. The percussion era was short but the production was prolific, and the largest group of arms in the collection are pistols issued to the Navy and to coastguards dating from 1847 to 1855. The overlap period between a flintlock and a percussion cap gun was prolonged, and the British Army did not receive its first new percussion rifle until 1836. But more notable than the guns produced during this period are the improvements in methods of manufacturing. The Industrial Revolution changed the nature of arms-making enough for the Board of Ordnance to decide to disperse with the old private-contracting system, and instead inaugurate a national firearms factory at Enfield. And so the Tower was evacuated, and the gunsmith's tools removed, but the piles of arms remained.

These stock piles of out-of-date guns at the Tower had been greatly reduced in the Great Fire of 1841. *The Times* for 1st November gives a vivid account of this spectacular conflagration which, having started in a flue in the inspection room, spread quickly to the great storehouse, so that 'the scene which presented itself was at once terrible and awfully magnificent. The flames, which shot up to a most alarming height, had so reddenned the horizon that it had attracted to the neighbourhood of Tower Hill countless multitudes, and the lurid glare which the devastating element shed upon them, and upon the various craft with which the River Thames was studded, was picturesque and appalling in the extreme'. Over two hundred thousand stands of arms perished and the small arms room and the Crown Jewels were saved only by flooding caused by a very high tide. But even after the Board had left the Tower, guns flooded in from the various theatres of war, and the store rooms were once again filled to bursting point. The rarer pieces were absorbed into the primary firearms collection at the New Armouries, and the last traces of the Board of Ordnance's old stock were sent in for auction, consisting of flint-lock and percussion arms, as well as edged weapons numbering about 4,000 pieces.

[1]J. Hewitt 'Tower Armouries'.
[2]H. Blackmore 'British Military Firearms 1650–1850'.

Detail enlarged

A South German Wheel-Lock Pistol, Augsburg, *circa* 1580.
London £2,300 ($6,440).
From the collection of Dr Dagobert D. Runes.

The collection of Firearms formed by Dr Dagobert D. Runes of New York City was sold in June 1964 and March 1965 for £53,188 ($148,926).

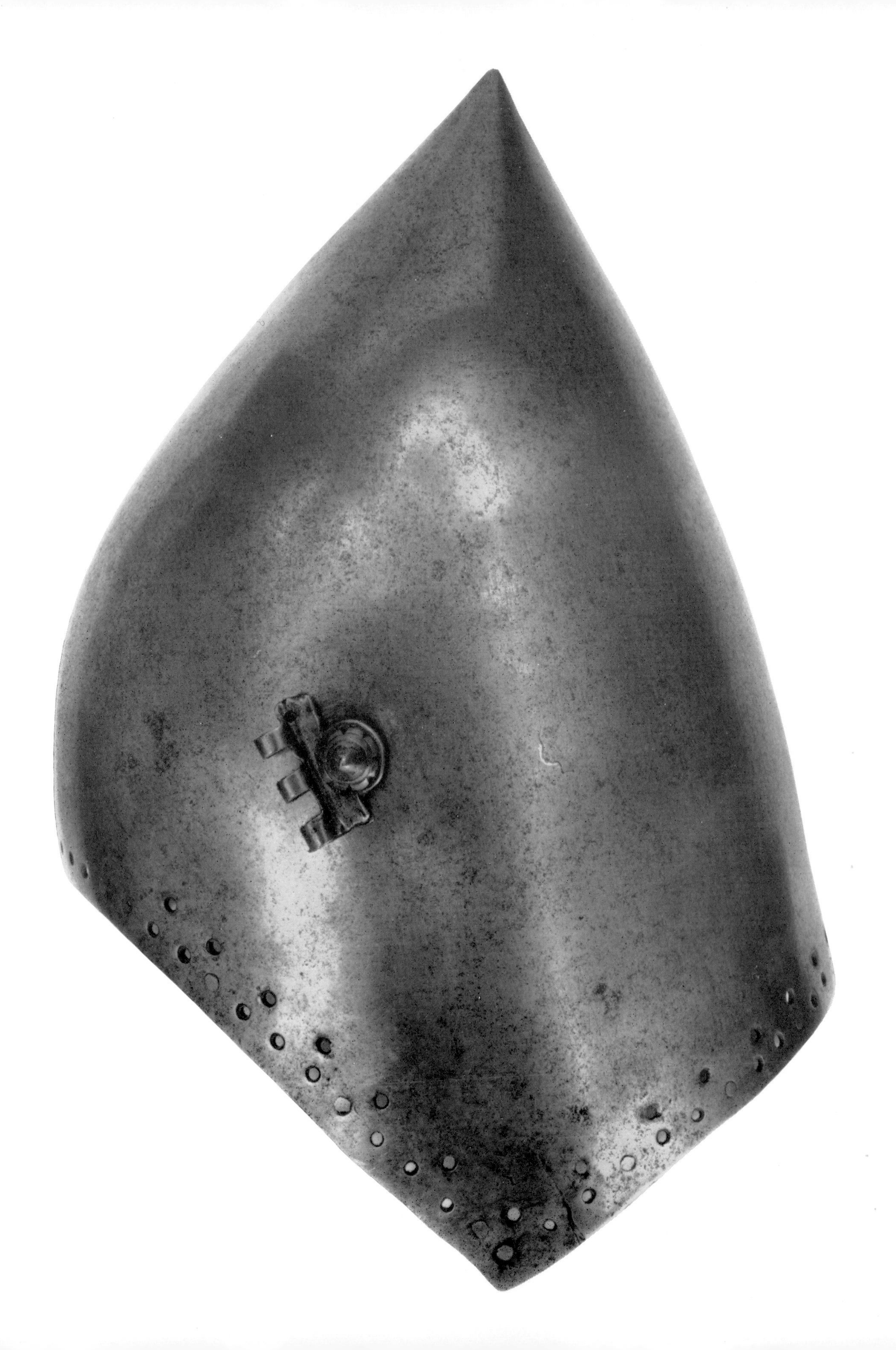

A pair of 15th-century Milanese Gothic Sabatons.
London £3,500 ($9,800).
From the collection of S. H. Barnett, Esq.
Now in the Tower of London Armouries.

The collection of one hundred lots of Arms and Armour formed by the late Sir Edward Barry, mainly during the last decade of the 19th century, was sold by S. H. Barnett, Esq., in July 1965, for £42,446 ($118,848).

Facing page A Western European Bascinet, *circa* 1380.
Said to have come from the Arsenal at Zurich, and looted by one of Napoleon's medical advisers.
London £9,000 ($25,200).
From the collection of S. H. Barnett, Esq.

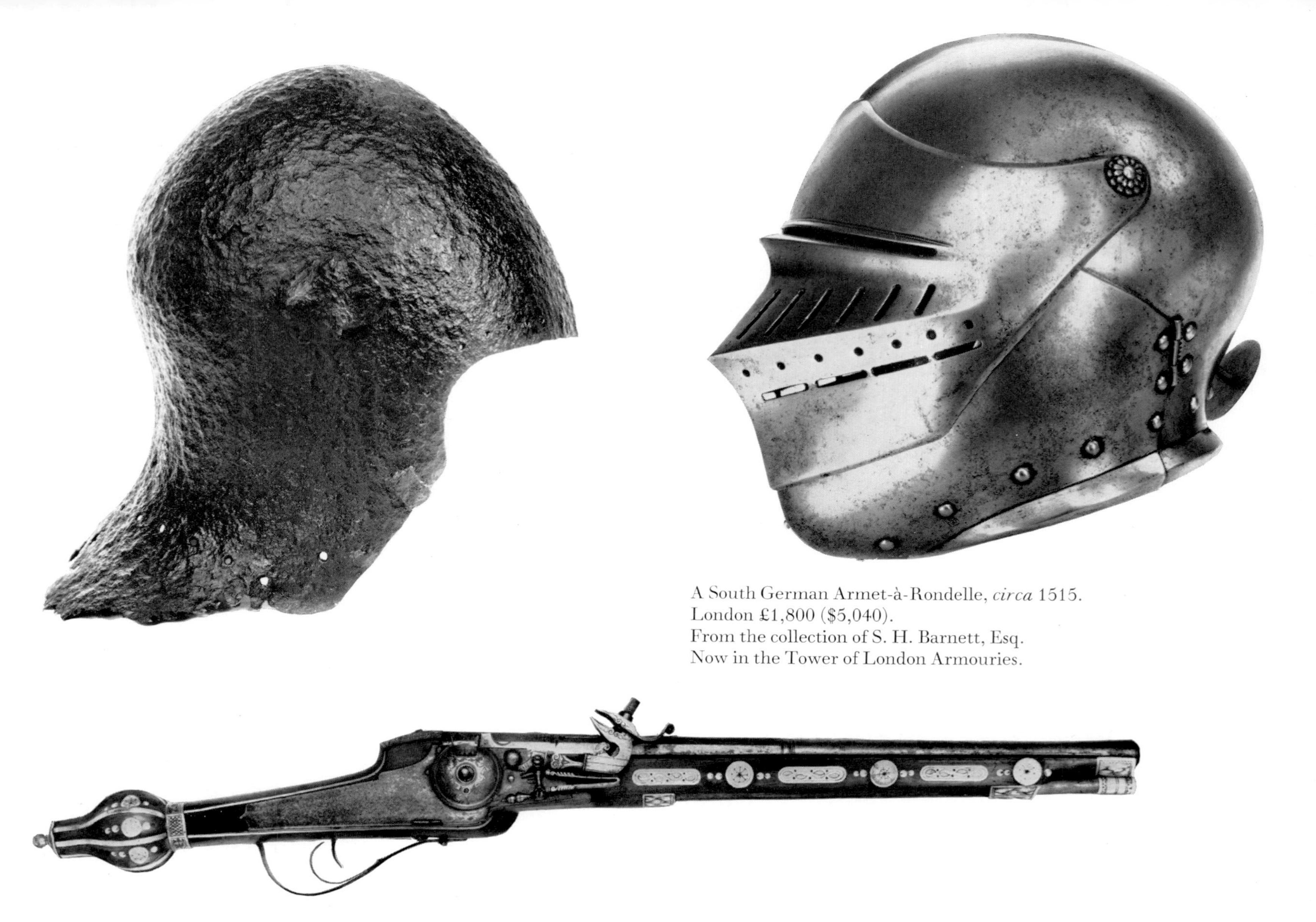

A South German Armet-à-Rondelle, *circa* 1515.
London £1,800 ($5,040).
From the collection of S. H. Barnett, Esq.
Now in the Tower of London Armouries.

Above An early 15th-century Great Bascinet. Excavated in central France.
London £1,150 ($3,220).
From the collection of S. H. Barnett, Esq.
Now in the Tower of London Armouries.

Below A Saxon Wheel-Lock Pistol (one of a pair), by Georg Gessler, dated 1610.
London £1,400 ($3,920).

Above A Double-Barrel Wheel-Lock Pistol, Dresden, *circa* 1610.
London £5,000 ($14,000).
From the Royal Gewehrkammer Johannaeum, Dresden, and the collection of Dr Dagobert D. Runes.

Below A Milanese Visored Sallet, *circa* 1450.
London £4,000 ($11,200).
From the collection of S. H. Barnett, Esq.
Now in the Tower of London Armouries.

An Italian Armet-à-Rondelle, *circa* 1490, probably that of Giovanni di Salimbeni.
London £2,800 ($7,840).
From the collection of S. H. Barnett, Esq.

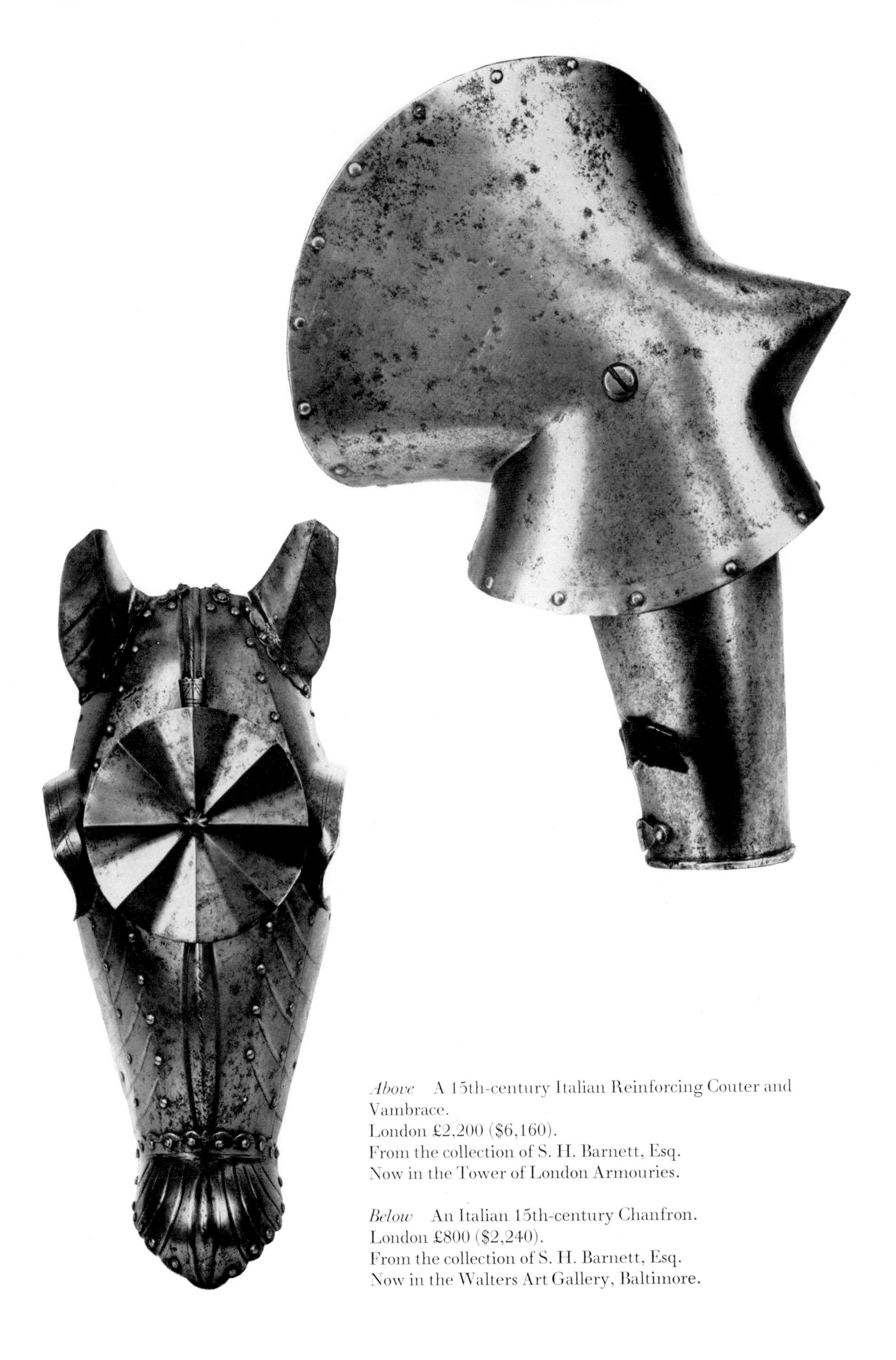

Above A 15th-century Italian Reinforcing Couter and Vambrace.
London £2,200 ($6,160).
From the collection of S. H. Barnett, Esq.
Now in the Tower of London Armouries.

Below An Italian 15th-century Chanfron.
London £800 ($2,240).
From the collection of S. H. Barnett, Esq.
Now in the Walters Art Gallery, Baltimore.

Above A Medieval Sword, *circa* 1350–80, found in Lake Constance.
London £550 ($1,540).
From the collection of S. H. Barnett, Esq.
Now in the Tower of London Armouries.

Below A Reinforcing Breast and Burgonet, by Matthäus Frauenpreiss the Elder of Augsburg, and etched by Jorg Sorg.
This was formerly part of a field armour made for the Emperor Maximilian II in 1550.
London £2,400 ($6,720).
From the collection of the Rt Hon. the Countess of Craven.
Now in the Walters Art Gallery, Baltimore.

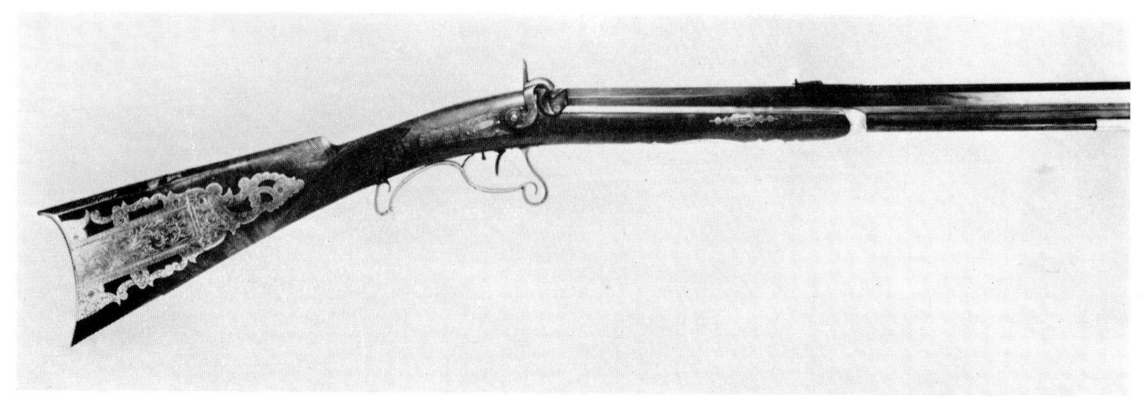

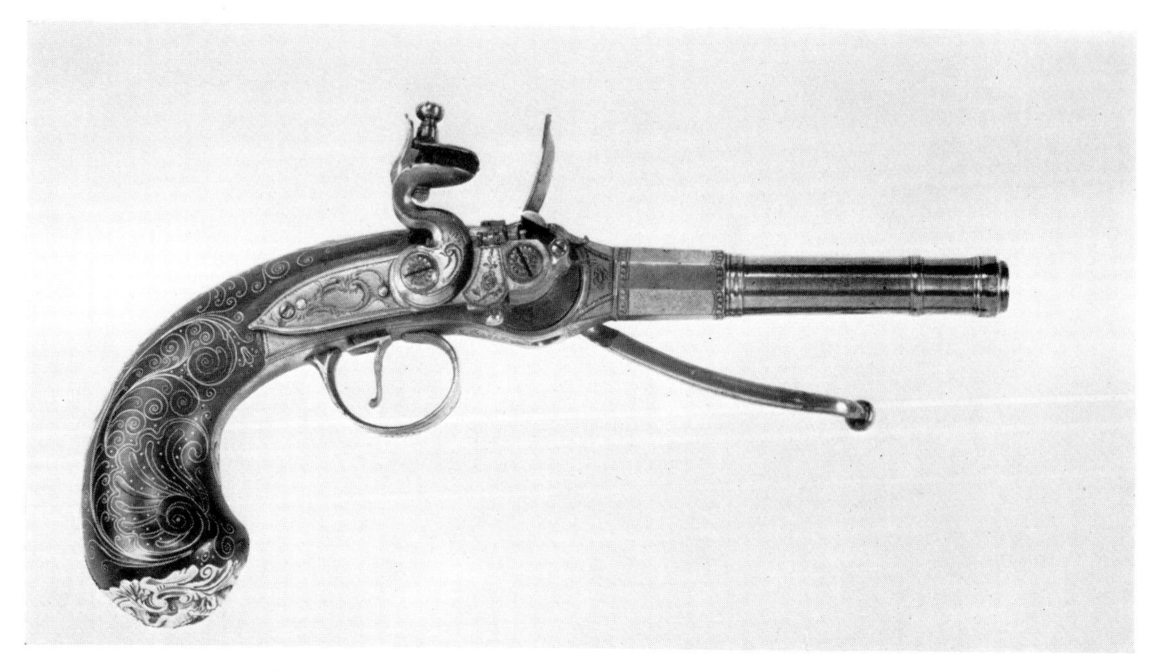

Above An 18th-century Scottish all-steel Flintlock Pistol (one of a pair), signed Alexr. Campbell.
London £1,500 ($4,200).

Centre A 19th-century Pennsylvanian Percussion Cap Rifle, signed Tryon.
London £500 ($1,400).

Below A George III Magazine Repeating Flintlock Pistol, by Charles Freeth, Birmingham, 1785.
London £1,000 ($2,800).

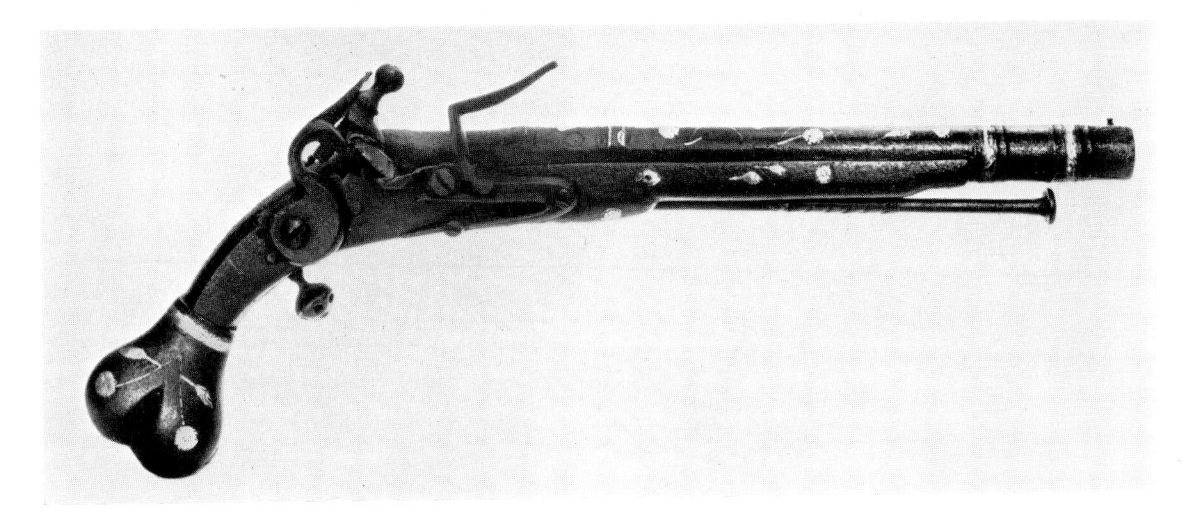

A Scottish all-steel Flintlock Pistol, *circa* 1715.
'A 19th-century notice accompanying this pistol states that it was once the property of Rob Roy MacGregor (*circa* 1660–*circa* 1738). It reads as follows:
Rob Roy received money from the Laird of Gorthie to purchase cattle, failing to fulfil his agreement he was prosecuted in 1716, and judgement given against him, in revenge he waited his opportunity till the Laird was absent from the house of Gorthie, finding it shut up he seized Morris the blacksmith of the estate and ordered him to break open the back door, he himself effected an entrance by the front and ransacked the house, Morris thinking they had forgotten him ran towards the wood at the back, but was fired at in his retreat; but fortunately without injury. When Rob Roy had left Morris found this pistol lying on the kitchen table. It remained in his family till I purchased it in 1868.—G.R.M.'
London £900 ($2,520).

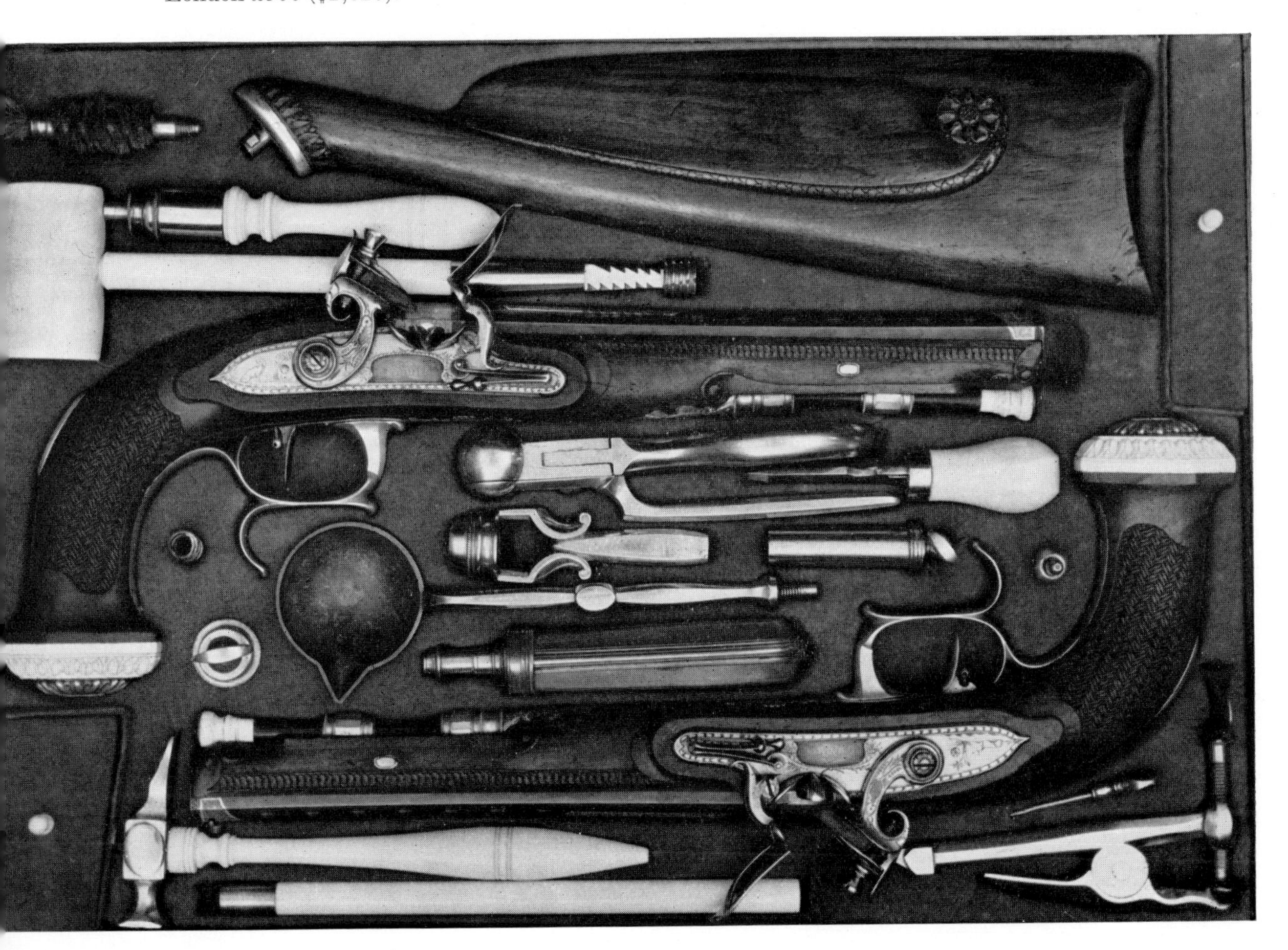

A pair of early 19th-century Flintlock Target Pistols, signed Boutet Manufre àVersailles.
London £1,600 ($4,480).

A late 12th-century Limoges Champlevé Enamel Chasse, with Christ in Majesty.
London £32,000 ($89,600).
From the collections of the late Adolphe Stoclet and Mr Philippe R. Stoclet.

Medieval Champlevé Enamels

BY JOHN HUNT

'It is said that the Barbarians who live near the ocean pour colours upon heated brass, so that these adhere and become like stone',[1] commented Philostratus in the 3rd century. Throughout the Middle Ages the technique of enamelling was amongst the most favoured of adjuncts to the art of the metal worker. Artists have used this medium for the ornamentation of the most important monuments of their time; for the decoration of the most venerated and sacred objects, as well as for the panoply of kings.

The earliest European enamels appeared first in Ireland and the Northern Provinces of the Roman Empire. They are in a Champleve technique, and with few exceptions they take the form of small objects such as brooches for personal adornment or small details and elements for the decoration of larger works. In the flowering medieval world, the coffins of Saints and later the shrines and *chasses* containing their bones and relics, together with the Altar itself and its vessels and ornaments, were obvious subjects for the display of the enameller's skill.

With the close of the Dark Ages, the technique of cloisonné enamelling upon gold had been perfected by Byzantine artists, but, before the fall of Byzantium in 1204, all the finest existing monuments in this style had been produced. Besides the decoration of such large works as the Altar frontal of San Ambrogio at Milan, the Pala d'Oro in St Mark's, the great book covers in Venice and other works, the technique was used in the old traditional way for small brooches and personal jewels. Two such pieces of outstanding quality are the beautiful gold pectoral Cross now in the British Museum, and a clasp from a necklace (see page 253), both from the collection of the late Adolphe Stoclet. They show the metropolitan style of Constantinople at the height of its purity and elegance.

During the Romanesque period, the most important areas of enamel production of the Western world were Germany and France, with the great centres of the Rhine and the Meuse producing the finest work. These brilliant enamels are fired on flat plates of copper with the addition of gilding, and were used to decorate a wide variety of church treasures. The earlier Rhenish and Mosan productions, which included such objects as portable altars, frontals, candlesticks, shrines and reliquaries of various forms, were sometimes most elaborate and were composed of a great number of enamelled scenes interspersed with plaques of filigree and jewels, and panels of 'vernis brun', sometimes combined with figures and scenes in relief. The great Shrine of the Three Kings at Cologne, and of the Emperor Charlemagne at Aachen come from these workshops, and the most important existing example is probably the great altar-piece at Klosterneuburg near Vienna, by Nicholas of Verdun, which has more than fifty large enamelled scenes surrounded by hundreds of smaller decorative enamelled plates forming borders. But the most famous and one of the largest productions of these Mosan ateliers, which has unfortunately disappeared, was the great Cross erected by Abbot Suger in the Abbey Church of Saint Denis in the middle of the 12th century. The crucifix itself, which was of gold, stood on a great four-sided column ornamented with an elaborate sequence of scenes in brilliant enamel work, showing types and anti-types from the Old and New Testament, setting forth the prophecies of the coming of Christ and their fulfilment. This enormous structure was more than twenty feet high, and the history of man's salvation was depicted in the sixty-eight enamel plaques which ornamented the square pillar.

Suger relates that the column occupied sometimes five and at other times seven goldsmiths from Lorraine for the space of two years. One of them was in all probability the great artist Godefroi of Huy. Today, only a few scattered fragments of similar great compositions exist outside the Cathedrals for which they were made, and such enamels are accordingly of the utmost preciousness and rarity. One such enamel is the remarkable champlevé plaque from the Birmingham and Midland Institute (see page 257). It is a work of superb quality and of a similar subject to those which must have ornamented Suger's cross-shaft. Representing Pentecost, the majestic figures of the Apostles in their brilliant robes are arranged, silhouetted, against a gleaming golden background, the Heavenly Jerusalem and descending rays representing the Holy Ghost above their heads. The Stoclet collection was particularly rich in Mosan enamels and another product of this school of similar quality was the plaque showing the Crucifixion, within a circle, flanked by the Blessed Virgin and St John.

In contrast to these German enamels, those attributed to Limoges in general are more of the character of workshop productions, executed less particularly to individual order. The earlier examples of this school, however, those which can be dated to the 12th century, are finer in quality and workmanship than the great mass of 13th-century Limoges work. The artists were more venturesome in their models than those of the Rhineland and besides the plaques and *chasses* which were in the main the usual productions of the Northern ateliers, from the Southern workshops came rounded forms, Saints in relief enriched with enamel, seated Virgins, cruets, Crucifix figures, pyxes and other objects. Besides these productions for the use and decoration of churches and cathedrals, objects of secular use are to be found. Gemellions, or pairs of basins for washing the hands, certainly could be used at the altars during Mass, but many have hunting scenes, gentlemen and ladies with hawks and hounds, coats-of-arms and other devices upon them. Boxes also, such as the Valence casket with the arms of the owner, point to a well-established secular luxury clientèle. Many of these forms, although they were evidently intended for a large entrepôt trade, are of the greatest rarity. Only a handful of cruets, which must have been used in pairs, are recorded. An important example of large size was in the Stoclet collection (see page 251 right). It perhaps formed a pair with the example in the Cluny Museum. Of even greater rarity are the hanging pyxes in the form of a dove. These were intended to hold the Sacrament, and were suspended by a cord, with a counterpoise weight from the tester above the Altar, as may be seen in the Islip Roll at Westminster, or from the roof. The pulleys for its suspension can still be found in many churches. A fine example with brilliantly enamelled wings and tail (to be sold in the autumn) is in the Stoclet collection.

Although these Limoges enamels cannot usually rival the artistry of the Northern Schools, remarkable objects of the highest quality came from these workshops. The various forms in the repertoire of the earlier ateliers, leaving aside the question as to whether these are works emanated from France or from Spain, include some magnificent book covers and reliquaries of the first importance. A splendid example is the superb Chasse from the collection of Adolphe Stocklet, decorated with Christ in Majesty and with figures of Saints in brilliant colours against a gilt background, covered with an intricate vermiculé design (see page 252).

With the 13th century, the workshops and productions followed those of the Rhine and the Meuse into oblivion, only a few late works pointing to the diminishing output and change in taste of the 14th century, but in Spain and Italy workshops continued the tradition of opaque cloisonné technique in minor elements ornamenting larger objects.

Perhaps the increasing wealth of the period, demanding the use of more precious materials, called for changing techniques. The more spectacular art of 'basse taille' enamel, translucent colours on silver and gold, occupied the skill and time of the artists who served the great patrons of the age, and the treasures of Champlevé enamel became a memory resting quietly in the Feretories and Sacristy cupboards of churches and cathedrals.

[1] Philostratus, Icon., lib 1. cap XXVIII

Above A Byzantine Cloisonné Enamel Clasp, Constantinople, 12th century. (actual size)
Said to have been excavated in the Great Palace, Constantinople.
London £6,500 ($18,200).

Below A Byzantine Cloisonné Enamel and Gold Cross, Constantinople, 12th century.
Said to have been excavated in the Great Palace, Constantinople.
London £8,500 ($23,800).

From the collections of the late Adolphe Stoclet and Mr Philippe R. Stoclet.

A Byzantine Mosaic Icon, Constantinople, 14th century. 11 in. by $10\frac{1}{4}$ in.
London £34,000 ($95,200).
From the collections of the late Adolphe Stoclet and Mr Philippe R. Stoclet.

A late 12th-century Limoges Champlevé Crucifix. Height $12\frac{1}{2}$ in.
London £3,600 ($10,080).
From the collections of the late Adolphe Stoclet and Mr Philippe R. Stoclet.

A Mosan Champlevé Enamel Plaque, representing Pentecost, *circa* 1160. (actual size.)
This probably formed part of an altar-piece, possibly with the one depicting the Ascension, preserved in the Goluchow Castle Collection, Poland.
London £35,000 ($98,000).
From the collections of Sir Francis Scott and the Birmingham and Midland Institute.
Now in the Metropolitan Museum, New York.

Facing page A 12th-century Romanesque Gilt-Bronze Figure of Christ.
Height $10\frac{3}{4}$ in.
London £21,000 ($58,600).
From the collections of the late Adolphe Stoclet and Madame Michele Stoclet.
Now in the British Museum.

A pair of early 14th-century Stained Glass Panels representing Henry II and Queen Kunigunde. Henry II (972–1024) was the last Holy Roman Emperor of the House of Saxony and was crowned in Rome by Benedict VIII in 1014. Kunigunde, his wife, having become a nun after her husband's death, was canonized by Innocent III in 1200 and together with the Emperor was adopted by the founder of the church of St Leonhard, Heinrich Croph, as his patron saint. Removed from the Church of St Leonhard in Bad St Leonhard, Austria, in 1935.
London £6,000 ($16,800).
Now in the Metroplitan Museum, New York.

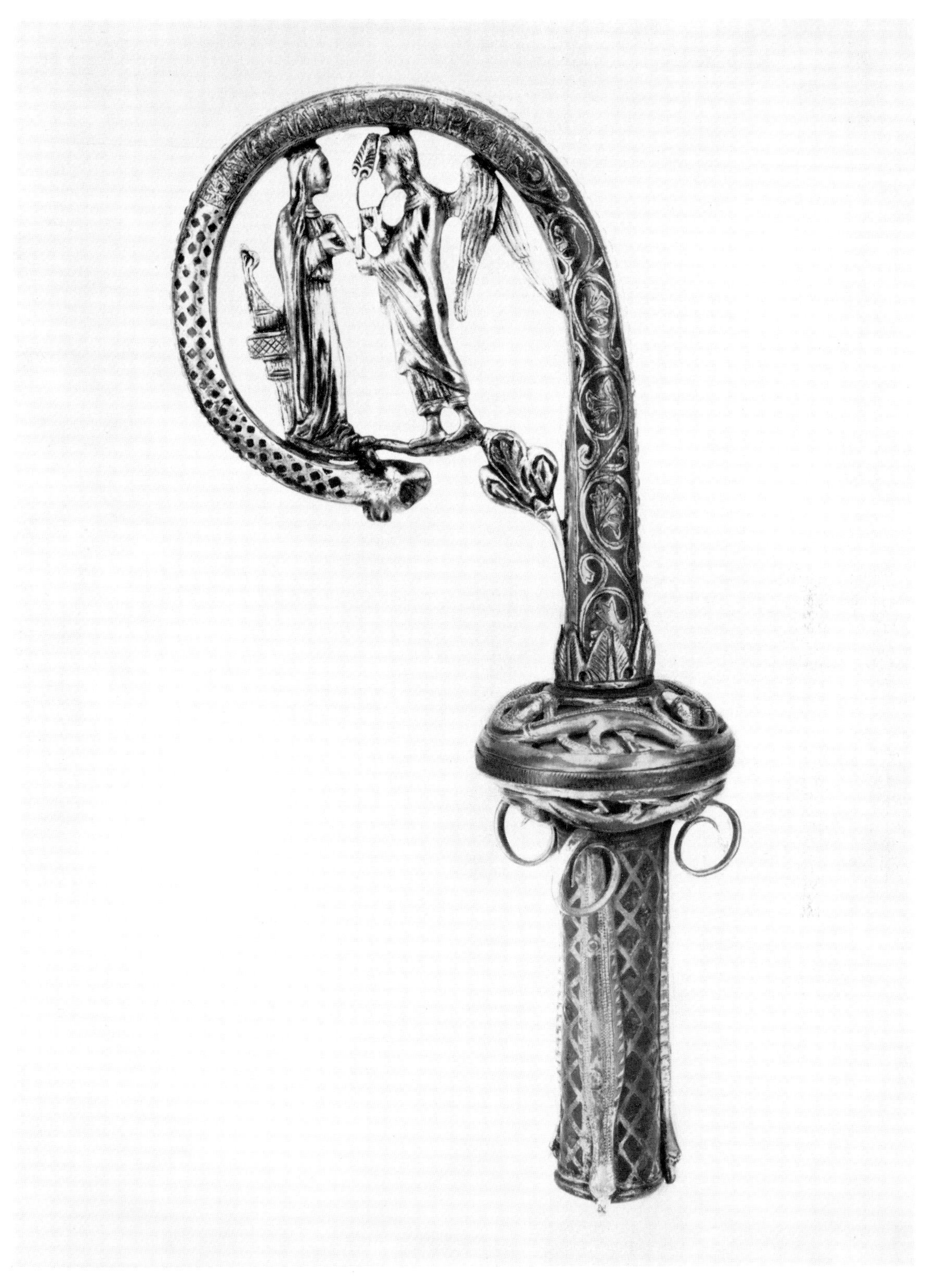

A 13th-century Limoges Champlevé Enamel Crozier.
London £2,200 ($6,160).
From the collection of Mrs L. Pomeroy.

A Romanesque Morse Ivory Chessman, Cologne, end of the 12th century. (enlarged)
Height 3 in.
London £10,000 ($28,000).
From the collections of the late Adolphe Stoclet and Mr Philippe R. Stoclet.

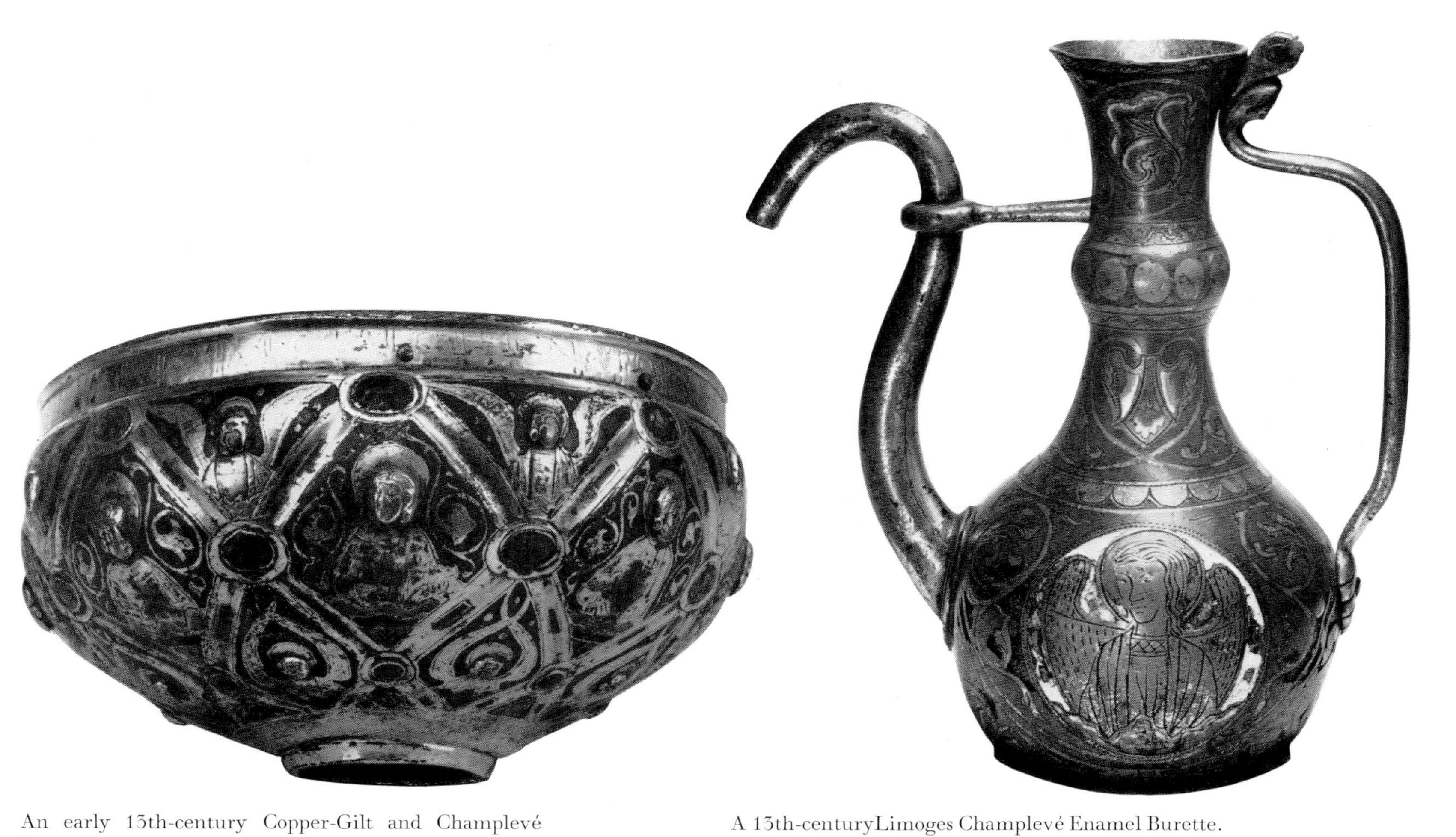

An early 13th-century Copper-Gilt and Champlevé Enamel Limoges Bowl from a Ciborium. Diameter $5\frac{7}{8}$ in.
London £2,600 ($7,280).
From the collection of Mrs M. Craig-de Clèves.

A 13th-century Limoges Champlevé Enamel Burette.
These vessels were presumably made in pairs for the water and wine used during the Mass. Height $5\frac{3}{4}$ in.
London £2,000 ($5,600).
From the collections of the late Adolphe Stoclet and Madame Michele Stoclet.

A 17th-century Italian Bronze Equestrian
Group (one of a pair).
London £1,850 ($5,180).
From the collection of Mrs Mowbray Buller.

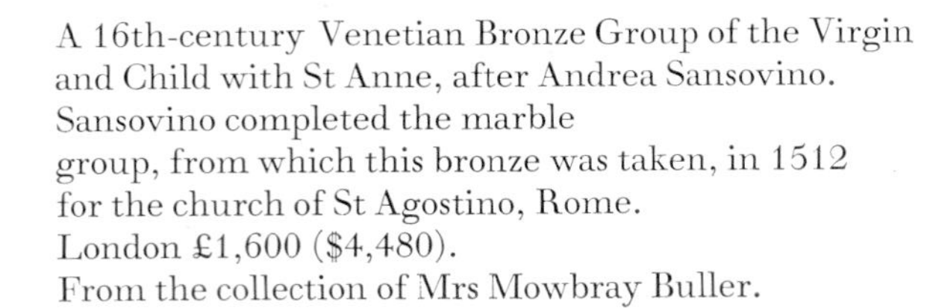

A 16th-century Venetian Bronze Group of the Virgin
and Child with St Anne, after Andrea Sansovino.
Sansovino completed the marble
group, from which this bronze was taken, in 1512
for the church of St Agostino, Rome.
London £1,600 ($4,480).
From the collection of Mrs Mowbray Buller.

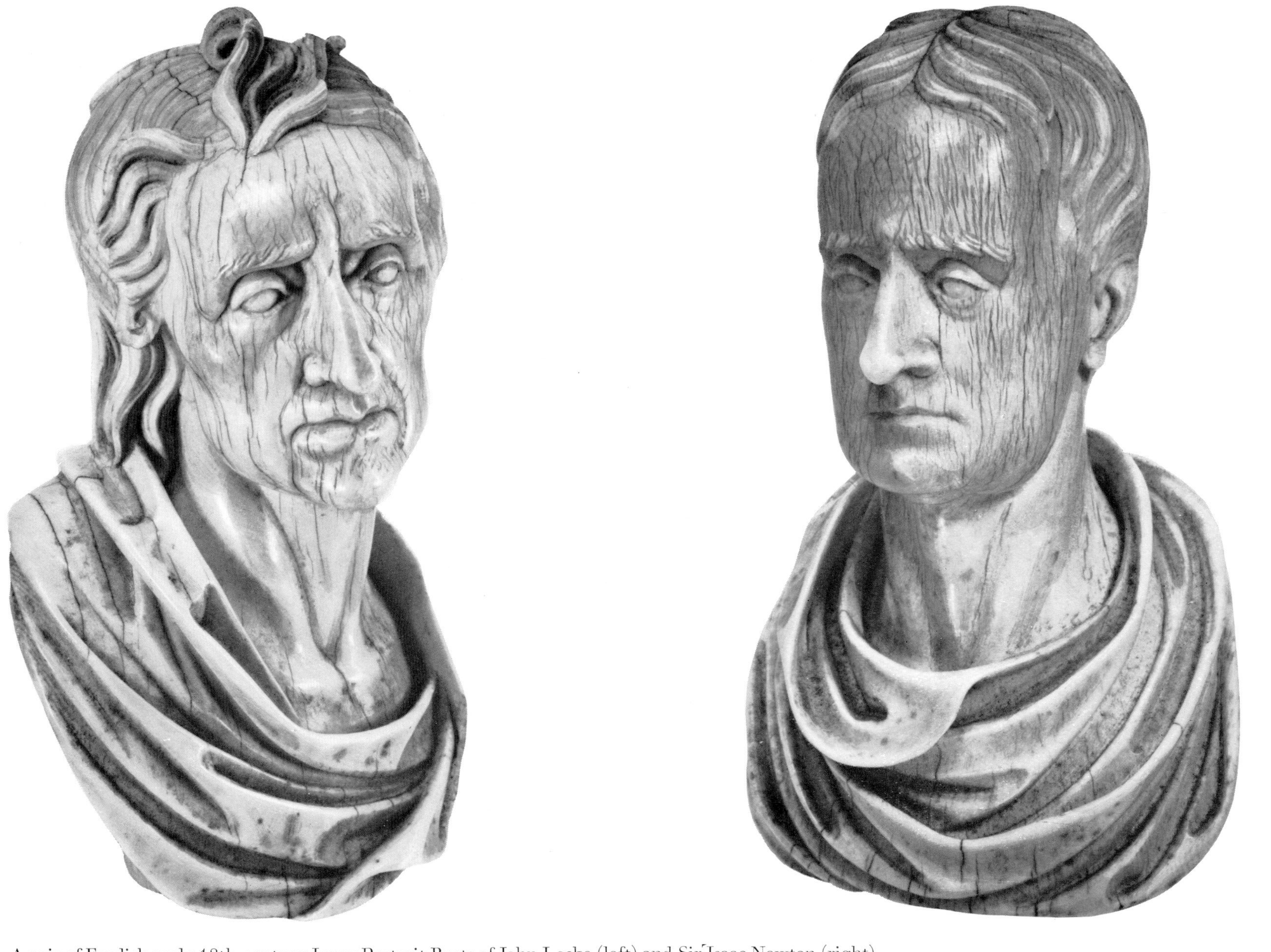

A pair of English early 18th-century Ivory Portrait Busts of John Locke (left) and Sir Isaac Newton (right).
Heights $7\frac{3}{4}$ in. and $7\frac{1}{2}$ in.
London £2,200 ($6,160).
From the collection of Mrs Kavan.

FRENCH ROYAL FURNITURE
A Louis XV Painted Commode by Joubert and the Martin Brothers, made for the Bedroom of Madame Adélaide in the Château de Versailles.
Stamped with the Versailles *marque de feu* and the inventory number 1965. The *Journal du Garde Meuble de la Couronne* records this acquisition, on 11 January 1755, as follows:
'Livré par le Sieur Joubert, ébéniste, pour servir à Madame Adélaide à Versailles; N. 1965. Une commode vernier de Martin, fond blanc à fleurs et filets rougeir et dessus de marbre Seracolin, faite en armoire à bataner fermant à clef, ornée d'une Entrée de Serrure et de chaussons en griffe de Lyon de cuivre cizelé et argenté. Longue de 3 pieds et ½ sur 19 pouces de profondeur et 30 pouces de haut'.
Madame Adélaide (1732–1808) was the eldest daughter of Louis XV.
London £20,000 ($56,000).
From the collection of Herbert L. Bensilum, Esq.
Now in the Château de Versailles.

A Marble Bust of Madame Marie-Adélaide-Clotilde Xavière de France,
by Jean-Antoine Houdon. Signed and dated 1774.
She was the daughter of the Dauphin, son of Louis XV, and thus sister of Louis XVI.
London £8,000 ($22,400).
From the collection of Mrs Madeleine Nurk.

Above A pair of K'ang Hsi and Louis XVI Porcelain and Ormolu Parrot Candelabra.
London £950 ($2,660)
Below A Louis XV Kingwood and Palissandre Serpentine-Front Commode, by François Antoine Mondon.
New York $4,500 (£1,595).

An early Louis XV Beauvais Chinoiserie Tapestry of *Le Prince en Voyage*, originally given by Louis XV to the Emperor of China. The tapestry was presented to the Army and Navy Club in 1864 by Major Geoffrey Rhodes who served as an unattached officer in the China Campaign of 1860. It is supposed to have come from the Emperor's Summer Palace at Pekin and to have been bought by Major Rhodes at the auction of the loot ordered by General Sir Hope Grant for the benefit of the Army. It is therefore probable that this tapestry formed part of the gift sent by Louis XV to the Emperor Ch'ien Lung in 1763.
London £3,900 ($10,920).

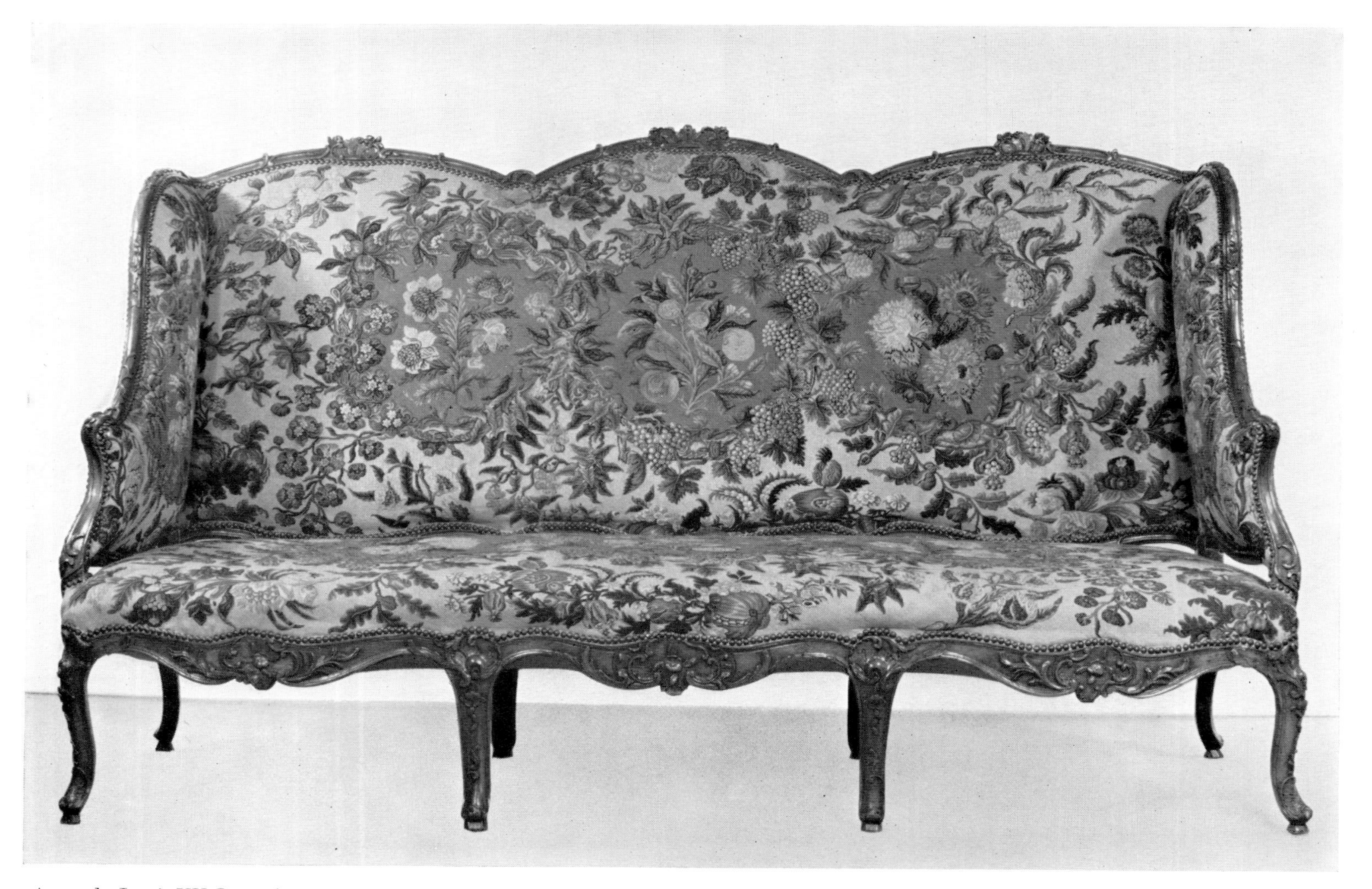

An early Louis XV Canapé.
London £7,000 ($19,600).
From the collection of Mrs Derek Fitzgerald.

A Louis XV Fire Screen painted by Nicolas Lancret depicting
Mezzetin accompagné d'une Femme.
New York $7,250 (£2,587).

A mid-18th-century Venetian Glass Painting of Columbine,
in the style of G-B. Tiepolo (one of a set of four).
London £1,700 ($4,760).

A Louis XVI Ormolu-Mounted Kakiemon Pot-Pourri Vase (one of a pair).
London £3,400 ($9,520).
From the collection of Mrs Derek Fitzgerald.

An early Louis XV Kingwood Bureau Plat.
London £24,000 ($67,200).
From the collection of the Hon. Victor Saumarez.

Facing page above An early Louis XVI ormolu Wall Light (one of a pair).
London £1,400 ($3,920).

Below ROYAL SEAT FURNITURE
A Louis XVI Tapestry-Covered Stool (one of a pair).
These formed part of a set of twenty-four ordered in 1786 for Marie Antoinette's *Salon des Jeux* at Compiègne. The frames by Jean-Baptiste Sené, the carving by Vallois under Hauré's supervision, and the gilding executed by Chatard and Chaudron.
London £3,800 ($10,640).
From the collection of Mrs Derek Fitzgerald.

A Louis XVI Ormolu-Mounted Console Desserte, in the manner of Riesener.
London £10,500 ($29,400).
From the collection of Mrs Derek Fitzgerald.

A Louis XVI Thuyawood Serviteur Muet.
London £3,500 ($9,800).

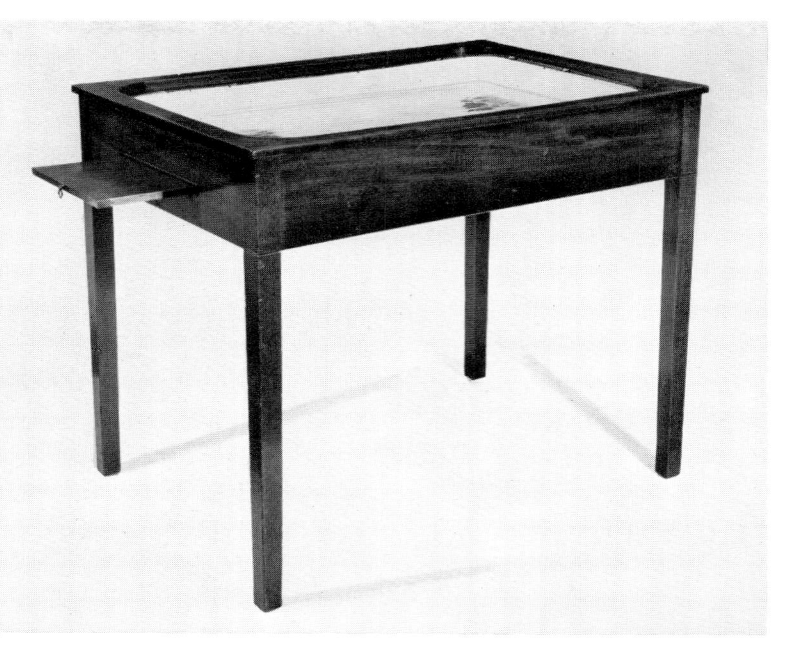

An 18th-century Swedish Smorgasbrod Table,
the tray in Rorstrand faience, painted with a
view of Drottningholm palace in Stockholm, after Elias Martin.
London £720 ($2,016).

The tray of the Smorgasbrod table.

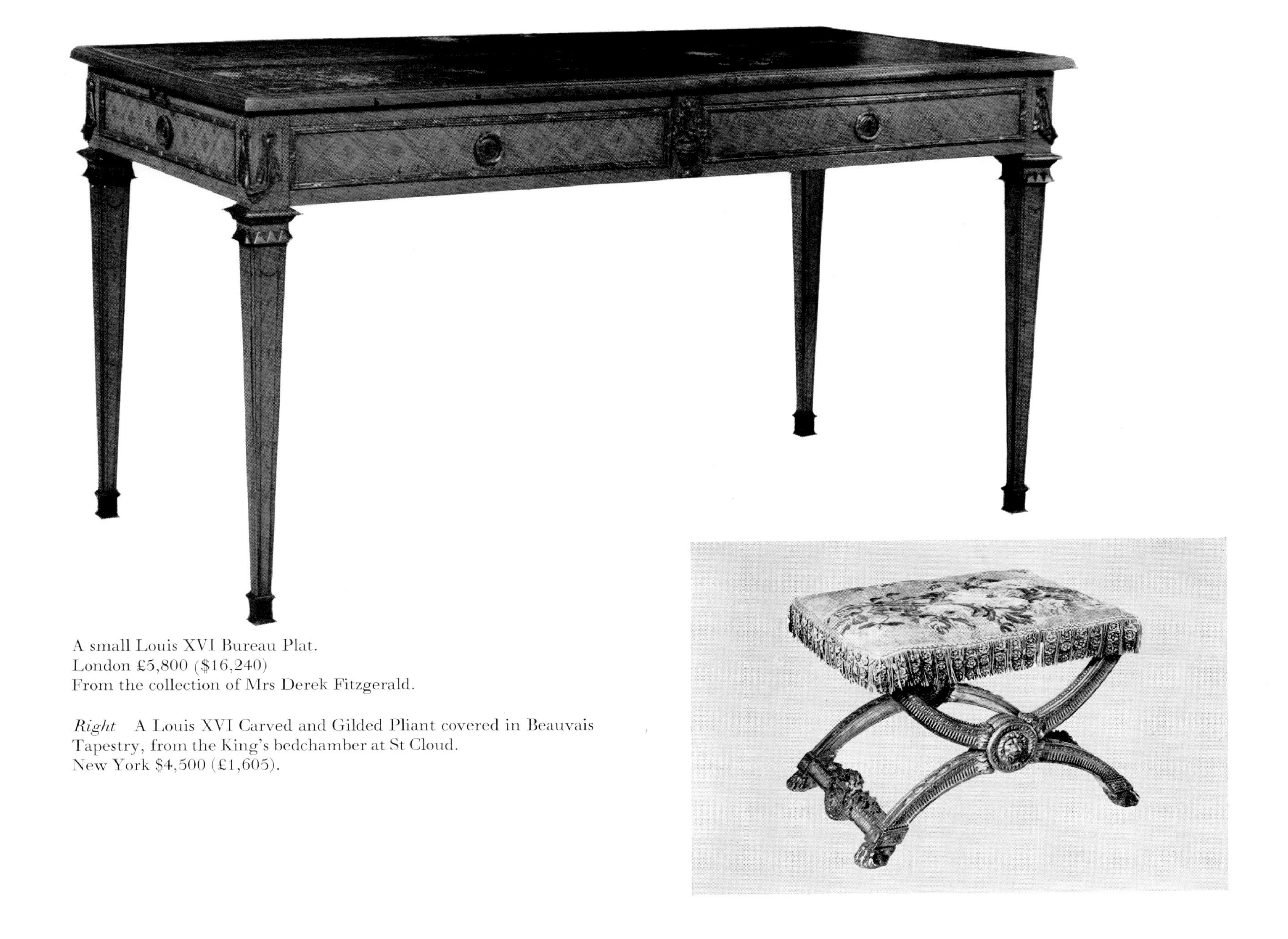

A small Louis XVI Bureau Plat.
London £5,800 ($16,240)
From the collection of Mrs Derek Fitzgerald.

Right A Louis XVI Carved and Gilded Pliant covered in Beauvais Tapestry, from the King's bedchamber at St Cloud.
New York $4,500 (£1,605).

A Queen Anne Walnut Bureau Bookcase.
London £950 ($2,660).

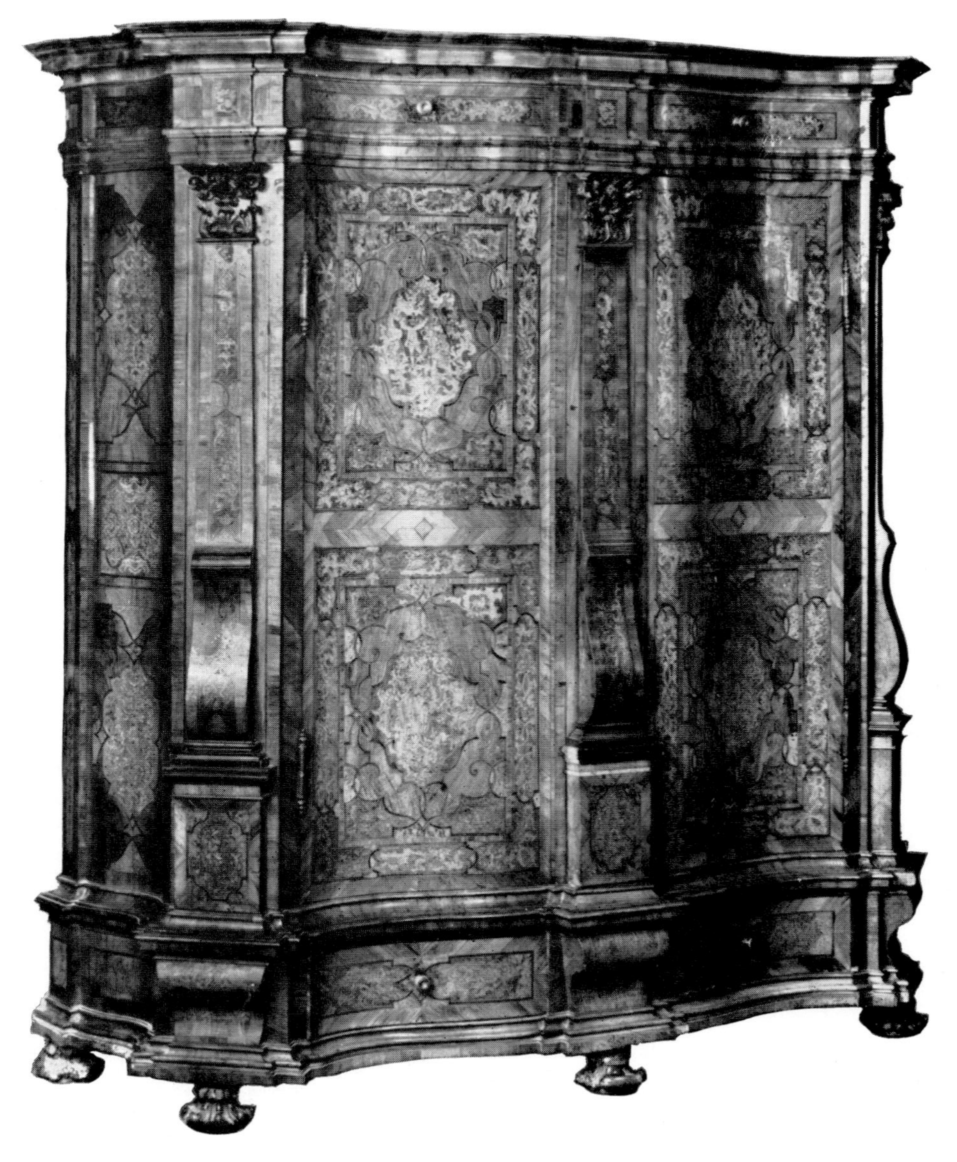

An early 18th-century South German Armoire.
London £1,700 ($4,760).
From the collection of Mrs Anne Beresford.

A George II Mahogany Dining Room Side Table, in the manner of Matthias Lock.
London £2,500 ($7,000).
From the collection of Mrs J. McBarnett.

A Robert Adam Overmantel Mirror (one of a pair).
The original drawing by Robert Adam is dated 1774.
London £1,700 ($4,760).
From the collection of Mrs A. H. Stevens.

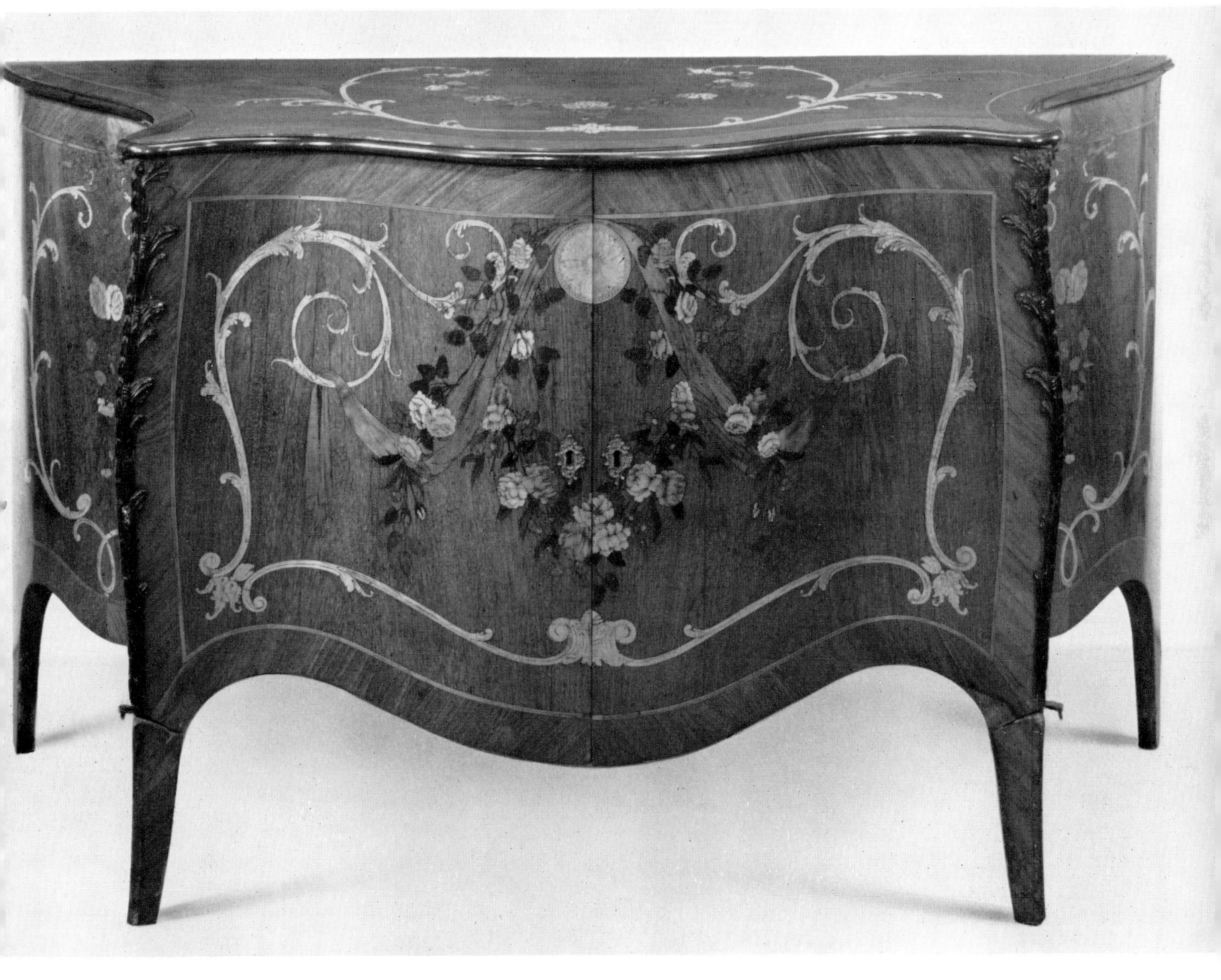

A mid 18th-century Marquetry Serpentine Commode, *circa* 1765.
London £4,200 ($11,760).
From the collection of Mrs C. Reece.

Above A Regency Cut-Glass and Ormulu Table Candelabra (one of a set of six).
London £1,600 ($4,480).
From the collection of Lady Margaret Gower.

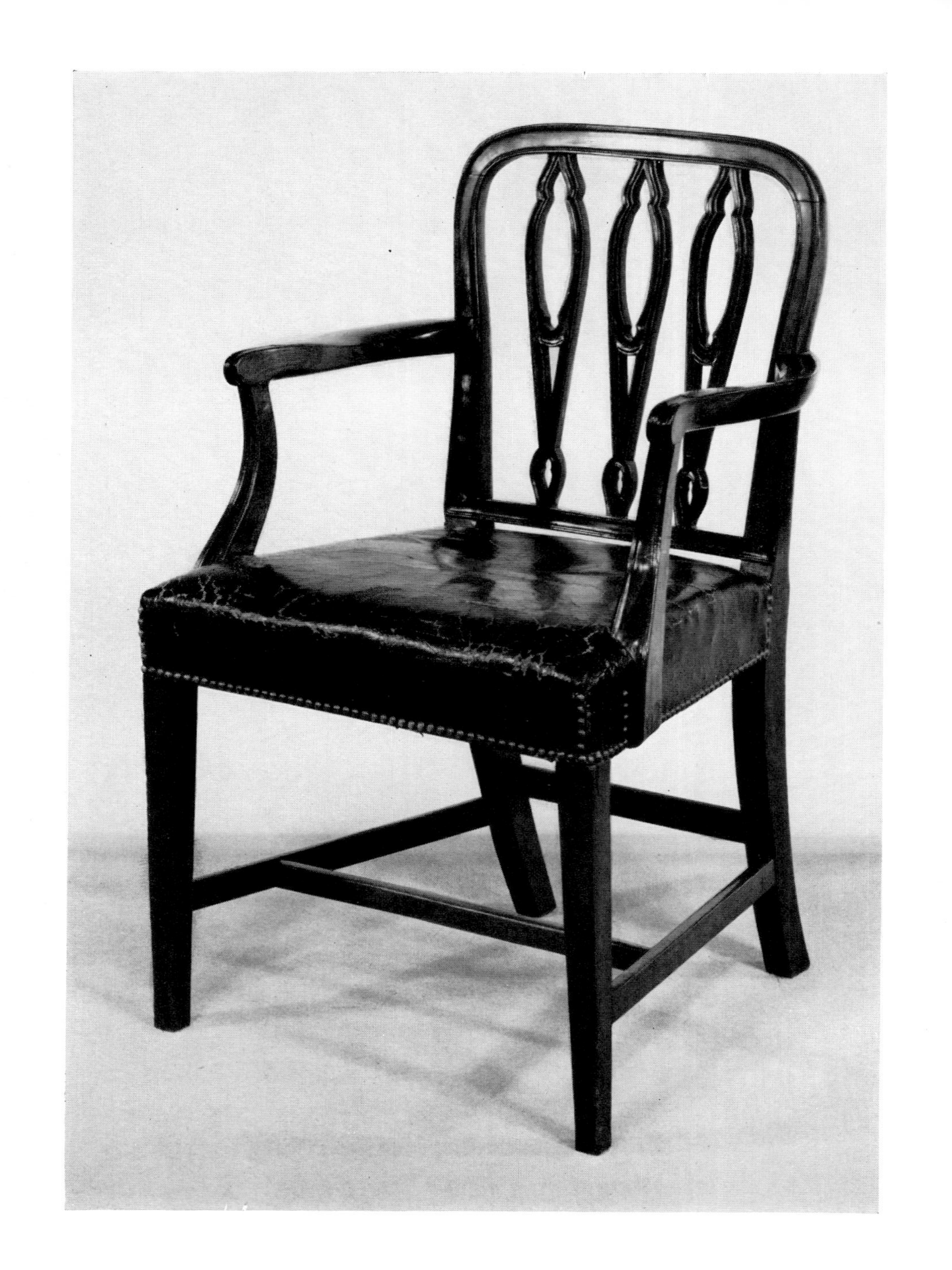

Right A George III Dining Chair, in the manner of Robert Manwaring (one of a set of sixteen).
London £2,600 ($7,280)
From the collection of the late Major F. H. T. Jervoise.

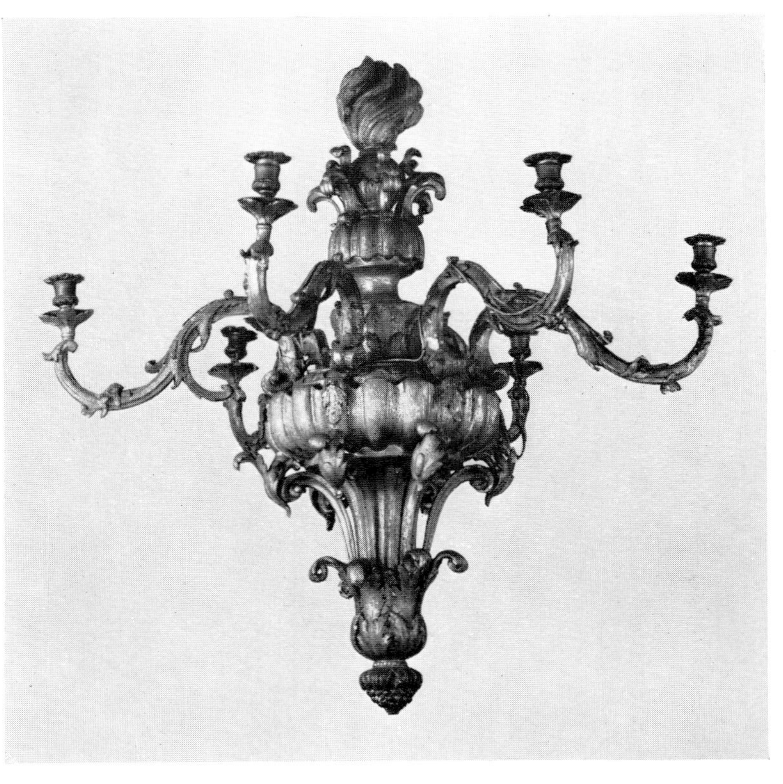

Above A small George II Rococo Chandelier (one of a pair).
London £4,200 ($11,760).
From the collection of Mrs A. H. Stevens.

Left A mid 18th-century Anglo-Indian Gentleman's Wardrobe.
London £560 ($1,568).
From the collection of Mrs Hugh Smith.

CHARLES GRIGNON, *Portrait of John Sotheby*

'Sold to Mr Baker', a portrait of John Sotheby

BY DAVID MITCHELL

While both handwritten and published material on the history of Sotheby's exists, John Sotheby's contribution to the development of the company remains obscure. It could be that he was overshadowed by George Leigh, who had the reputation of being the 'Rafaelle of Auctioneers'. His association has passed almost unrecorded, other than the fact of his inheritance of a partnership in the firm, established in 1744 by his uncle Samuel Baker.

In his will, dated 1774, Samuel Baker left George Leigh twenty pounds and his journeyman, Andrew Edwards, ten pounds. To Thomas Payne, of Castle Street, Westminster, and Lockyer Davis of Holborn he left twenty pounds apiece, to repay their kindness in assisting his nephew, John Sotheby, in dividing his stock in trade with his partner, George Leigh.

'Honest' Tom Payne began his career in much the same manner as Samuel Baker, issuing catalogues with prices affixed, the earliest being dated 29 February 1740/41; he became a bookseller who, according to Nichols, was 'warm in his friendships, a convivial, cheerful companion whose one pursuit in life was fair dealing'. His intimacy with Samuel Baker may account for the preservation, in Sotheby's archives, of a bill of sale relating to books purchased from him by Sir John Evelyn, Bart.

The second executor appointed by Baker was Lockyer Davis, a publisher as well as a bookseller. In business with Charles Reymer, Davis was printer to the House of Commons. When, in 1770, his partnership was dissolved, he too adopted the practice of issuing catalogues.

In his will Samuel Baker called these bookmen his 'two worthy friends', and on his death they carried out his wishes, dividing the property between Leigh and John Sotheby, whose name the firm has borne ever since.

Unfortunately it is not on record that John Sotheby ever conducted an auction. He entered the profession at the age of thirty-eight, and later – in his own will – he styled himself simply *bookseller*. This was probably because the ivory hammer, bequeathed by Abraham Langford (1711–74, the foremost auctioneer of his day) to Samuel Baker, was in 'the courteous hand of Leigh', who was approaching the height of his career.

A good likeness of George Leigh can be seen in the print (see page 283 right) from a drawing by W. Behnes, which shows him at his rostrum holding his pen and his ivory hammer. Baker's portrait is mentioned in Dibden's *Bibliographical Decameron*, of 1817, where, in an interview with Dibden, Samuel Sotheby (John's son and successor) refers to the 'Father of the Tribe', and describes him as being 'as fine a fellow as ever broke a crust of bread; and we have a *portrait* of him, upstairs, taken not long before he died, in his 60th year, and with every tooth in his head as sound as a roach'. Painted by Charles Grignon it has always hung in Sotheby's (see page 283 left).

The existence, however, of a portrait of John Sotheby was not suspected until the autumn of 1964. A picture, sent for sale from Washington, D.C., was being examined, when a note was discovered on the reverse which described it as 'John Sotheby by Charles Grignon (1716–1810). Excellent portrait like that of a fine Stuart. Name of the artist and sitter on original stretcher which was too fragile for relining'. He was dressed in a very formal manner, which in his day would have been considered a trifle old-fashioned, for, in common with a large number of professional people of the time, he was still powdering his hair. His clothes suggest that he sat for the picture between 1780 and 1785 (see page 282. There is a great contrast in the distinct quality of this work and the poorer technique of Grignon's portrayal of Samuel Baker, which, from Samuel Sotheby's assertion, seems to have been painted *circa* 1772–74.

Charles Grignon was related to the clockmaker brothers, Daniel and Thomas Grignon, who lived at the King's Arms and Dial, Great Russell Street, and were finishers to Daniel Quare. Their neighbour and friend was Samuel Baker whose membership they proposed to the Royal Society of Arts. Among the five letters in the archives relating to this period of Samuel Baker's life, there is a domestic one, dated 17 June, 1773, suggesting that as Mr and Mrs Grignon were to dine with them at Woodford, she must 'provide some roast beef', and also 'dress the foregammon instead of pork or Bacon'.

On the face of it there were excellent reasons for believing that the portrait was indisputably that of the first of the three generations of Sotheby's, who between them carried on the business for almost a century. However, the manner by which complete identification was made was unexpected. Shortly before the picture reached London, a letter arrived from Dr Christopher Sotheby Pitcher, a descendant through a female line, who had a genealogical interest in the family. Some months later, and by sheer chance the day before the sale, a conference brought Dr Pitcher to London, who took the opportunity of calling in at 34 New Bond Street. On seeing the portrait he suddenly realised that he owned a replica. It was apt that, at the sale on the 9th of December, 1964, the *nom de vente* 'Samuel Baker' was used when Sotheby's purchased the portrait, especially since a disastrous fire at Wellington Street, off the Strand, in 1865, had destroyed irreplaceable records and documents.

The catalogues of the firm show that soon after John Sotheby became a partner its activities were extended. In 1780, two years after the death of Samuel Baker, a small sale of topographical drawings was held; then, in 1788, came the sale, by the British Museum, of coins and medals along with duplicate books, and when five years later the assistant librarian at the Museum, the Reverend Richard Southgate, died, Leigh and Sotheby were entrusted with the dispersal of his coins, drawings, shells and natural curiosities. It remains, however, to be discovered what part was played by John Sotheby in these the first real steps which ultimately led to the company styling itself 'Fine Art Auctioneers'.

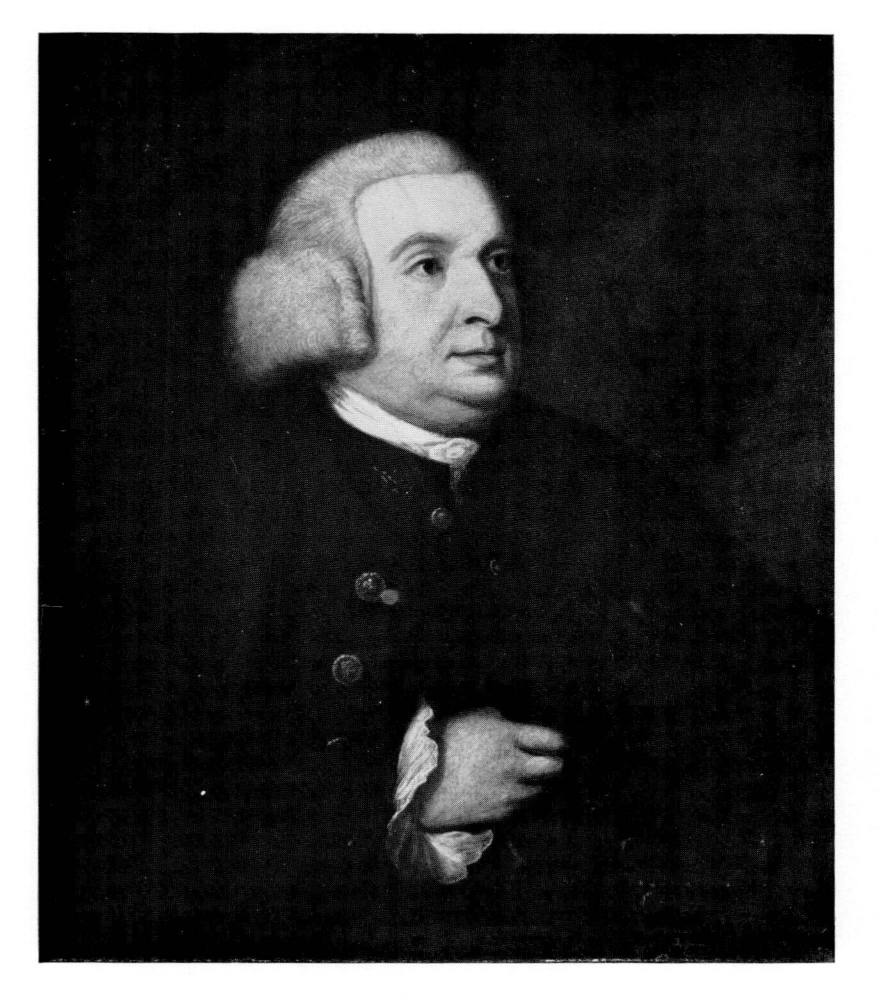

CHARLES GRIGNON, *Portrait of Samuel Baker*

George Leigh, etching, after the drawing by W. Behnes

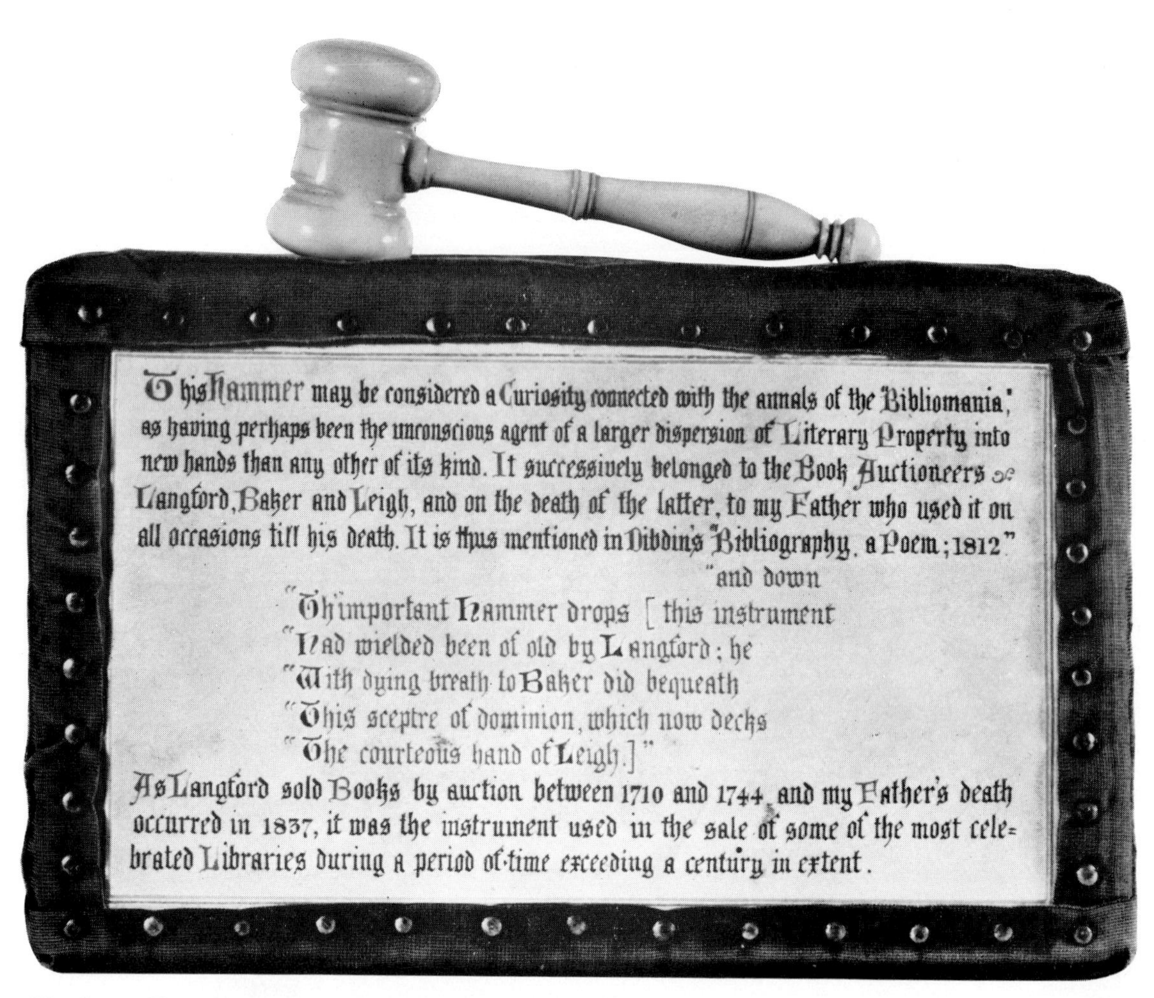

This Hammer may be considered a Curiosity connected with the annals of the Bibliomania,"
as having perhaps been the unconscious agent of a larger dispersion of Literary Property into
new hands than any other of its kind. It successively belonged to the Book Auctioneers
Langford, Baker and Leigh, and on the death of the latter, to my Father who used it on
all occasions till his death. It is thus mentioned in Dibdin's "Bibliography, a Poem; 1812."
"and down
"Th'important Hammer drops [this instrument
"Had wielded been of old by Langford; he
"With dying breath to Baker did bequeath
"This sceptre of dominion, which now decks
"The courteous hand of Leigh.]"
As Langford sold Books by auction between 1710 and 1744, and my Father's death
occurred in 1837, it was the instrument used in the sale of some of the most cele=
brated Libraries during a period of time exceeding a century in extent.

The Ivory Hammer used by Langford, Baker and Leigh.

'This Sceptre of Dominion'

BY M. J. WEBB

Preserved in the General Office at Sotheby's is the hammer used by Langford, Baker and then Leigh, from whom it passed to Benjamin Wheatley, who had once served as clerk to both Leigh and Sotheby and who subsequently set up as a book auctioneer on his own in Piccadilly. He died in 1837, and it had been first used by Langford in 1710 and so for a space of some one hundred and twenty years had been used in the disposal of most of the fine libraries sold in London. It is one of the few hammers which can be fairly accurately dated. It was probably made between 1700 and 1710 and the turning on both the head and handle are similar to other 'bygones' of the same period (see page 284).

A print, also in the General Office, shows this hammer held in the delicately poised right hand of Mr Langford (see page 285 above) in a portrait taken after the sale of Dr Mead's antiquities in 1754, and it is probably also the one in the undated watercolour of a book sale at Sotheby's by Thomas Rowlandson (see page 285 below). In both cases the auctioneer is holding the hammer towards the end of the handle, but on examining the hammer itself, it is obvious that it was principally held by its head. The modern auctioneer invariably unscrews the handle and uses only the head, but not so long ago one of Sotheby's young auctioneers, using a hammer that he had recently been given and from which he had not unscrewed the handle, allowed it to slip from his grasp and fly amongst the would-be purchasers in front of him!

The cover of this book exhibits eight ivory hammers, all made between 1700 and 1850. The early examples are the smaller and particularly those with flattened heads (the two bottom left-hand examples), while the early Victorian hammers are those shown in the centre and the bottom right. These are in fact the most useful to the auctioneer, as their larger size makes them more comfortable to use. The enthusiastic auctioneer banging a small hammer bangs his knuckles too!

While there are few, if any, extant auctioneers' hammers before the late 17th century, the practice of holding auctions is one of remote antiquity. Herodotus, Book I, 196, describes the ancient Babylonian custom in which an annual auction was held when village maidens were disposed of in marriage and, in later times, the Romans were given to disposing of goods by auction on a large scale. After the death of Pertinax, the Pretorian guard even proclaimed the Roman Empire itself for sale by auction. Prisoners and spoils of war were regularly sold by auction, but by far the most famous auction was that held by some "Mr Sotheby" of former years when at Cicero's death his great collection of Greek statuary was dispersed, but it is not known in what manner these auctions were held.

The word auction itself comes from the Latin *auctionem* meaning to increase by amounts or bids, which would at least rule out the Dutch auction, by which the almost reverse method is used.

In England auctions were probably introduced by the Romans and under a charter of Henry VIII, later confirmed by Charles I, special officers were appointed called *outropers* 'all other persons being prohibited by public acclaim or outcry'. Again, it is not known by what method these auctions were held. A popular method was by lighting an inch of candle-wick, the buyer being the last to bid before the wick fell, and by an Act of 1698, all goods imported from the East Indies had to be sold in this fashion. It would be reasonable to suppose that hammers had been used very much earlier than this and even in ancient times, purely in order to make a sharp noise to signify that the bidding was over, though of course the fall of the hammer itself does not seal the transaction and, where justified, bidding can be resumed.

A widely used term for an auctioneer's hammer is 'gavel', but it is not generally known that this term arrived from the United States in about 1860 and refers to a president's hammer. To the auctioneer a hammer is a hammer and dignified in the verse of one Dibden, who, in 1812, in *Bibliography: A Poem*, refers to the hammer mentioned in the beginning of this essay

'and down
Th' important hammer drops [this instrument
Had wielded been of old by Langford; he
With dying breath to Baker did bequeath
This sceptre of dominion, which now decks
The courteous hand of Leigh].'

Mr. Langford

THOMAS ROWLANDSON, *A Book Sale at Sotheby's*

See page 193.
See page 206 below left.

See page 28 above left.

See page 257.

DETAILS FROM ILLUSTRATIONS ON PRECEDING PAGES

See page 16.

See page 215 centre.

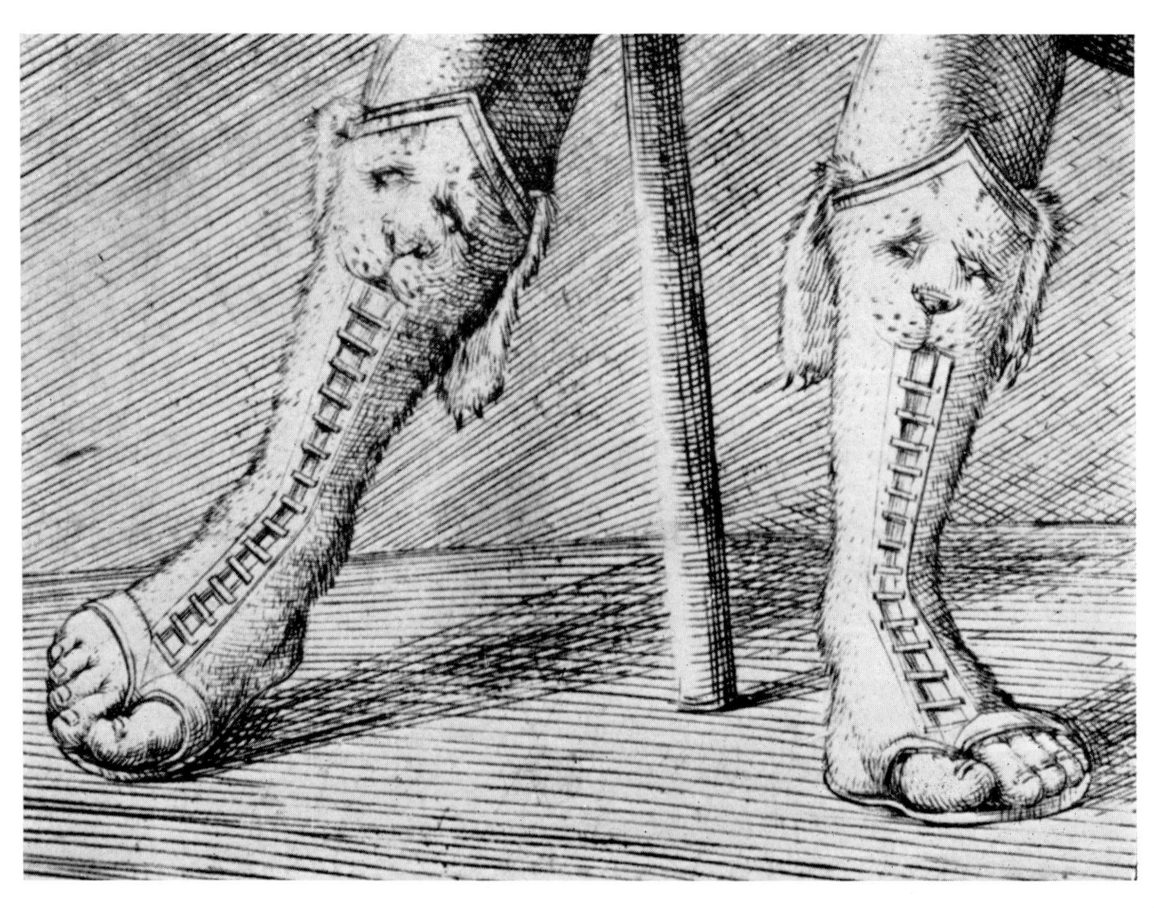

See page 111.

See page 111.

See page 232 above right.

Acknowledgements

Messrs Sotheby are indebted to the following who have allowed their names to be published as the purchasers of works of art illustrated on the preceding pages.
The figures in parentheses refer to the page numbers on which illustrations appear.

Acquavella Galleries. Inc. 119 East 57th Street, New York (23, 68).

Thos Agnew & Sons Ltd (3, 4 right, 5, 6, 10, 16, 17, 18 above, 19 below, 22, 29 above right, 34 above, 35 above and below, 36 above, 37 above, 40, 41 above left, 46 above, 101 below, 116 left, 200 below); Albaco Oil Company (63); Albert Amor Ltd (193); Antique Porcelain Company Ltd (184 left).

Hermann Baer, Esq. (146 below and centre left, 149 left and above right, 231 above right, 260); Czeslaw Bednarczyk (181 left); G. H. Bell (237 right); Berkeley Galleries (166 right); Bluett & Sons (166 left, 167, 172 above and below); C. G. Boerner (112 left); Bragge & Sons (xxii).

Martin Breslauer (128 above right); Arthur Brett & Sons Ltd (276 below); Alfred Brod Gallery (25 below, 28 above left, 29 above left).

Mme G. Chalandon (176 above left); J. Christie, Esq. (211 right); Levi Cohen for Harry Winston (214 below); Levi Cohen (215 below); P. & D. Colnaghi & Co. Ltd (32, 39, 45 below, 60, 73, 86, 100 above and below, 102 above, 104 above, 106 below, 110 below, 112 right, 113 left, 114 above and below); Contemporary Art Establishment (82); Craddock & Barnard (114 below); Crowther of Syon Lodge Ltd (278); Mr Nathan Cummings (98); Camerer Cuss & Co., New Oxford Street, London (238 below right).

E. Davies, Esq. (xiv); Cecil Davis Ltd (231 left, 232 above right); Dawson's of Pall Mall (120, 121 right); Mr Peter Deitsch (118 left); Delomosne & Son Ltd (185 left and right, 280 left); Mr Henry C. Dryon, Belgium (236 below right); Arnold M. Duits (267).

Francis Edwards Limited (120); L. T. Edwards, Esq. (43); House of El Dieff, New York. Lew David Feldman, President (95 above, 138); Ellsworth & Goldie Ltd, New York (117 right); H. Terry-Engell (56 below).

Faerber & Maison Ltd (14); Fine Art Society Ltd (15 below); Fisher Gallery Ltd (232 centre and right); Stanley Fisher, of Bewdley (189 above left); John F. Fleming (137); Ifan Kyrle Fletcher (118 right); H. M. Fletcher (128 below); Robert Fraser Gallery (87); Frost & Reed Ltd (93).

Nicholas Gorevic, Esq. (202 right); James Graham & Sons, Inc. (250 centre); Mrs Gina Gratton-Storey (xxi); Grosvenor Gallery (77 right, 97 right).

The Hallsborough Gallery (18 below, 19 above, 28 below, 102 above); Hammer Galleries, New York (49 right, 52); S. H. Harris & Son (229); Hazlitt Gallery (56 above); W. Heimann, Messrs. Sandbergs Bokhandel (130, 131); K. J. Hewett Ltd (144, 146 centre and above centre, 151, 159 below, 253 below, 255); Bernard Houthakker (105 above and below); How of Edinburgh Ltd (204 right); Cyril Humphris Ltd (262 left).

N. Israel – Rare Books (133 above).

Mr Geoffrey P. Jenkinson, Columbus, Ohio (250 below); W. R. Jeudwine (104 below, 117 left); Oscar & Peter Johnson Ltd, Lowndes Lodge Gallery (36).

Mr Henri A. Kamer, New York (157); Mr Paul Kantor (58); Dr G. Karl, Munich (109 centre); Gerald Kerin Limited (272 above); Herr Rolf Kistner, Nuernberg (132 below); Mr Sol Kittay (80); Leonard Koetser Ltd (27, 29); Kofler-Truniger Collection, Lucerne (252); E. W. Kornfeld, Bern (108); H. P. Kraus (135 right, 136, 139).

August Laube & Sohn (110 above, 111); D. S. Lavender (Antiques) Ltd (224 left); Ronald A. Lee (234 left, 245, 247 right, 248 above, 259, 261 left and right); Leggatt Brothers (15, 28 above right, 30, 31, 33, 34 below); R. O. Lehman, Esq. (148 right); R. M. Light & Co. Inc. (113 right, 115 below); Mr and Mrs Jack Linsky (21); Mr William M. Locke (251); Mr and Mrs Preston H. Long (71); Marcel Lorber, Esq. (162 above left); Thomas Lumley, Esq. (205, 206 below); H. D. Lyon, Esq. (129).

Maggs Bros. Ltd (122, 123, 143); Edgar Mannheimer (235, 238 left and above right, 239 right); S. Marchant & Son (169 right); Marlborough Rare Books Ltd (116 right); Clement Milward, Esq. (160 right); Mr and Mrs Donald S. Morrison (210); Sydney L. Moss Ltd (162 centre left, 176 above centre and right); Mrs Langley Moore (xxi).

Ralph Nash, Esq. (158 above, 159 above); Mr C. B. Nathhorst, Stockholm (72); Newman & Newman (Antiques) Ltd (179 below, 180 right); Mr Ben Nyman (195).

James Oakes (239 left); The Old Clock House, Ascot (269 right); Osborne Gallery, New York (42).

Frank Partridge & Sons Ltd (186, 201 above, 257, 258, 277, 280 right, 281 right); David Peel & Co. Ltd (262 right); Howard Phillips (233 above left and right); S. J. Phillips Ltd (207, 212 below, 213 below, 219 above left, 222, 223).

Bernard Quaritch Ltd (124, 127).

Roland, Browse & Delbanco (77 left); S. & R. Rosenberg Ltd (125, 126); Mr John Vincent Rowan (92).

Dr Alfred Scharf (102 below, 109 right); Monsieur Claude Sere, Paris (106 above); Manfred Seymour Ltd (215 above, 221, 236 above right, 237 below left); John L. E. Smith, Shottesbrooke Park, White Waltham, Berkshire (281 left); John Sparks Limited (169 above left, 171, 173, 174 left); Mr Stephen Spector (44 above); Spink & Son, Ltd (59 below, 145, 176 below, 177 below, 215 centre left, 240 below, 248 below); Sutch and Martin (45 above).

J. T. Tai & Co. Inc. (166 above, 168 below right, 173 below); H. H. Thyssen-Bornemisza, Lugano (211 left); Tilley & Co. (Antiques) Ltd (192 left and right, 194 above left and below right, 233 below); Dr A. Torre (181 below right); Charles W. Traylen (133 below, 134 right, 135 left).

Monsieur Emile Veranneman (168 above and below left).

Wartski, London (219 above right and below, 224 right, 225 left and right); Julius H. Weitzner, Esq. (2); Mr Welbeck (246 below); Wheldon & Wesley Limited (134 left); Winifred Williams (180 left, 181 above right, 189 above right and below, 194 centre right, 196 above left and below right); Walter H. Willson Ltd (213 above right); Charles Woollett & Son (190, 191, 196 below left, 199 above); Douglas J. K. Wright (162 centre right).

The Zwemmer Gallery (81); Zeitlin & Ver Brugge (120).